WILDERNESS BASICS

◆ *SECOND EDITION* ◆

The Complete Handbook for Hikers & Backpackers

WILDERNESS BASICS

◆ *SECOND EDITION* ◆

The Complete Handbook for Hikers & Backpackers

BY THE SAN DIEGO CHAPTER
OF THE SIERRA CLUB

Edited by Jerry Schad and David S. Moser

THE
MOUNTAINEERS

5 4 3
5 4 3

Published by The Mountaineers
1011 SW Klickitat Way, Seattle, Washington 98134

Published simultaneously in Canada by Douglas & McIntyre, Ltd., 1615 Venables Street, Vancouver, B.C. V5L 2H1

Published simultaneously in Great Britain by Cordee, 3a DeMontfort Street, Leicester, England, LE1 7HD

Manufactured in the United States of America

Copyedited by Kris Fulsaas
Illustrations by Robert Frost and Bob Cram
Cover design by Watson Graphics
Book design by Graphics West
Typography by Graphics West

Cover photograph: Backpacking in Washington's North Cascades; photo by Bob and Ira Spring
Frontispiece: Photo by Jerry Schad

Library of Congress Cataloging-in-Publication Data
Wilderness basics : the complete handbook for hikers & backpackers /
    edited by David S. Moser and Jerry Schad. — 2nd ed.
        p.   cm.
    Includes bibliographical references and index.
    ISBN 0-89886-348-1
    1. Outdoor life—West (U.S.)   2. Wilderness survival—West (U.S.)
I. Moser, David S.   II. Schad, Jerry.
GV191.42.W47W55   1992
796.5'0978—dc20   92-23267
                                                                CIP

Contents

Preface

The many volunteers who made this book a reality have perpetuated a tradition stretching back more than three decades. In 1961, the San Diego Chapter of the Sierra Club published the first edition of *Basic Mountaineering*, a handbook for students taking the club-sponsored Basic Mountaineering Course. Perhaps better known as the "Red Book" for the distinctive color of its cover, that book was made possible through contributions of text, artwork, and clerical work by more than two dozen Chapter members, and through the able efforts of Henry I. Mandolf, who served as chief editor.

Mandolf stayed with the project through second (1965) and third (1970) editions, by which time the Red Book's influence was felt among a population far larger than the captive audience of Basic Mountaineering Course students. As a neophyte outdoorsman and newcomer to San Diego in 1972, I learned of the book through a classmate at San Diego State University who helped me discover the joys of peak bagging and snow camping in southern California's mountains.

By the early 1980s, it became necessary for the San Diego Chapter to rework the book in its entirety. The expanded, reorganized, and extensively rewritten book, *Mountaineering Basics*, edited by Lynne Foster and published in 1982, again featured many contributions by Chapter members.

By 1990 it once again became necessary to recast and rewrite the handbook that had long been a standard reference in the field. The interests of Sierra Club members and Basic Mountaineering Course students had shifted and broadened over the years. There were several reasons for this: The faster pace of contemporary urban life left many people with less leisure time, but more of a need than ever to escape to the wild spaces. Day hiking and visits to areas closer to home were becoming more popular. Women and families were taking to the outdoors in greater numbers. Regional parks, open spaces close to metropolitan areas, lesser-known national parks and forests, and formerly ignored expanses of desert became recognized destinations. There was more concern about some of America's remaining wild spaces being supplanted by creeping urban development and others falling victim to air and water pollution. Travelers were becoming more aware of the impacts they impart to the areas they visit.

The broadening of interests and concerns led to an expansion of subject material in both the course and in the accompanying handbook. A new title, "Wilderness Basics," was given to both the course and the book in 1991. The book you now hold in your hands, published by The Mountaineers of Seattle, Washington, represents a refinement of the preliminary edition of *Wilderness Basics*, published by the San Diego Chapter of the Sierra Club in early 1991 and distributed to the Wilderness Basics course students.

The preliminary edition of this book contained a chapter called "Women in the Wilderness," which was based on a lecture given yearly by Carolyn Wood at the San Diego Chapter's Wilderness Basics Course. The chapter was primarily intended for the female novice who might not feel comfortable striking out into the wilderness, and addressed the special concerns of women. However, much of the information is helpful for novices of either sex, and therefore has been incorporated into the appropriate places in various chapters in this edition of *Wilderness Basics*.

Although the content of *Wilderness Basics* overlaps to some degree that of all of its predecessors, almost all of the material is freshly written. New chapters on wilderness ethics, physical conditioning, and traveling with children have been added. The chapters on outdoor equipment and wilderness medicine reflect changes in those fields. The trip planning chapter covers such newer issues as restrictive regulations and trailhead quotas. The chapter on wilderness travel even addresses a new and controversial way of exploring the open spaces—mountain bicycling.

Although this book was originally planned to serve as a reference for students taking a specific course offered in southern California, its geographical scope is not so limited. This latest version has been designed to serve anyone who wants to explore wild places all over North America.

As in previous incarnations of this book, dozens of volunteers contributed text and illustrations, and helped during various phases of editing and review. The key player in this effort was Dave Moser, who as "project manager" solicited and brought together over a period of 18 months the writers, illustrators, and editors who made this book possible. My role as chief editor was to cement together into a coherent whole the diverse contributions of the twenty-one authors and several illustrators. The authors (whose short biographies can be found in the appendix), were encouraged to speak in their own voices, and it is my hope that their individuality still comes through after so many electronic cuts and pastes.

Aside from the authors credited in the individual chapters, Bart Ward made important contributions to Chapter 6, Foods and Cooking, and Nick Soroka's contributions were incorporated into Chapter 12, Mountain Travel. Bill Alley and Dan Anderson contributed material about cross-country skiing to Chapter 14, Winter Mountaineering. Appreciation is due to Chuck Bennett, whose chapter on technical rock climbing and safety in the preliminary edition was deemed beyond the scope of this edition. Other additions and helpful comments (other than authors') were made by those who reviewed the original manuscript, including Joyce Alpert, R. J. Arnold, Ric DeVan, Jo Getchen, Jim Kiefer, Cinde Nowicki, Sandy Sanders, René Schad, and Howard Williams. Comprehensive reviews of the entire original manuscript and much technical editing of some chapters were the work of professional wordsmiths Bev McGahey and Karen O'Connor. Ric DeVan and Pris and Scott Anderson helped prepare the index. Thanks also goes to computer wizard Cal Williams for converting a variety of word processor formats submitted by the various authors into files that could be edited into a coherent whole.

Bob Feuge and Dave Moser coordinated author revisions for this edition of *Wilderness Basics*. The principal illustrator of the current edition, Bob Frost, deserves thanks for his timely work under a tight deadline. Additional illustrations in this edition were contributed by Bob Cram; additional photographs are credited individually.

Final appreciation goes to Margaret Foster, editorial manager at The Mountaineers Books; Kris Fulsaas, copyeditor; and independent reviewers Ann Marshall, Steve Glenn, Bill Fortney, Bill Hucks, Marie Mills, and Lowell Skoog for valuable perspectives on our preliminary edition and final polishing of previous work.

Jerry Schad
May 1992

THE 10 GOLDEN RULES OF
WILDERNESS CAMPING AND TRAVEL

1. Obtain required permits, and abide by local regulations.

2. Use common trail courtesies.

3. Camp in already impacted sites.

4. Bury human waste well away from water and water sources.

5. Use soaps and detergents sparingly or not at all; never allow these or anything else to enter streams or lakes.

6. Change nothing in the natural environment that's not necessary for your health or survival.

7. Avoid costly and intrusive rescues by planning your trip carefully, knowing your limitations, and using the proper equipment during your travels.

8. When appropriate, restore the landscape (pick up litter, break down illegal fire rings, etc.).

9. Pack out what you pack in.

10. Take nothing except pictures and memories.

Hiking beside a canyon river (Photo by Sandra Hinchman)

C H A P T E R   1

The North American Wilderness: An Introduction

OLIVE WENZEL AND JERRY SCHAD

Our earth, the third planet from the sun, is the mildest and softest of the nine. It holds together more than 5 billion people and millions of species of plants, animals, and insects. It drifts through space with all of us on it, like a pale, delicate bubble. It's all we have.

All our lives, and for countless generations before us, humans have been transforming the earth to satisfy our physical needs and our desire for comfort. Today, it's clear that we cannot continue to exploit Earth's resources at current levels without unraveling its life-support systems. We're also becoming increasingly aware of the importance of the dwindling number of places we call wilderness—places largely untouched by direct human intervention.

Almost everyone feels the need sooner or later to cast aside the trappings of civilization and escape to the wilderness—if only for a few hours or a few days. We take to the hills for relaxation, inspiration, education, and excitement. And we bring back memories that enrich our lives forever.

In the wilderness we glimpse the natural world as it once was on a global scale. On mountains, in deserts, and along wild coastlines, our senses drink in simple pleasures: clean air scented with the nectar of a thousand blossoms, muffled silence in the heart of an old-growth forest, the blast of icy air off a glacier, the grace of a bighorn sheep moving on stone, the thunder of breakers felt as well as heard.

In cities we usually live apart from the natural environment; in wilderness we discover that everything is a part of everything else. We learn how plants and animals attain an elegant state of balance independent of most human influences. We become aware of the fragility of each component of the natural world and hence of the ecosystem of the earth itself. We become aware of our responsibility as stewards of our remarkable world.

In most of North America, the contrast between wilderness and the human-altered landscape is more extreme than in most parts of the world. The "New World" of North America is spacious enough with respect to its population that it still contains a large amount of basically natural landscape. Urbanization, agriculture, mining, and timber harvesting have encroached upon many an easily exploited acre. But plenty of less-accessible, less-hospitable, and in many cases stunningly beautiful acres remain relatively untouched, especially in the western United States, much

The desert is an unfamiliar wilderness to many people. (Photo by Jerry Schad)

of Canada and Alaska. These areas can continue to be a source of basic needs such as clean air and water, as well as provide recreational opportunity, as long as we give them the care and the legal protection they deserve.

It's important to note at the outset that for the purposes of this book, our meaning for "wilderness" is intended to be quite broad. Our wilderness includes not only areas specifically earmarked for special protection by government decree, but also

areas that qualify as wilderness by remoteness or pristine character. Whether officially designated as wilderness or not, nearly all such areas are worth preserving to some degree or another. Most are well suited for exploration as well.

It's hard to speak of our native wilderness without rattling off a litany of superlatives. Few coastlines around the world surpass the scenic grandeur of the geologically young Pacific coastline, where mountains sweep dramatically down to the sea. The North American continent contains world-class mountain ranges and peaks in the western half, as well as gentler ranges, such as the Appalachians, which are more remarkable for their flora and fauna than topography. North America lays claim to the world's tallest trees, the world's most massive trees, and the world's oldest trees. It also possesses some of the world's lowest-elevation and hottest deserts, and some of the world's deepest river-cut gorges.

Many of North America's most remarkable landscapes are distinguished by their inclusion in national, state and provincial parks. Aside from that, a staggering amount of land, particularly in the western United States, including Alaska, falls within the public domain. California, even with its exploding population now exceeding 30 million, contains 35 million acres of parks and other lands open to public recreation—about one-third of its total area. States such as Nevada, Utah, Arizona, and Alaska consist overwhelmingly of public lands. Substantial tracts of public land have been set aside in Canada and the eastern half of the United States as well. The national and state parks dotting the Appalachian Mountains from Georgia into Maine would be the envy of most other nations around the world.

Wilderness lovers have worked for decades to improve access to remote areas without damaging them. The 2,000-mile Appalachian Trail offers the dedicated walker a nearly complete perspective of an entire mountain range. Inland from the Pacific coast, the Pacific Crest Trail stretches 2,600 miles along the roof line of California, Oregon, and Washington. Concepts for other continent-spanning trails may be fully implemented by the early twenty-first century.

It is not only the grand and remote landscapes and famous trails that are worth a wilderness traveler's attention. Plenty of wild areas lie just beyond the fringes of some of the biggest cities. Only 20 air miles from downtown Los Angeles—the epitome of the modern, sprawling megalopolis—black bears and bighorn sheep roam the canyons and crags of the Angeles National Forest's San Gabriel Wilderness. A climber living in Denver can take a shot at any of several alpine summits only an hour's drive away. Just over the Golden Gate Bridge from the skyscrapers of San Francisco, serene Muir Redwoods National Monument, a kind of vest-pocket wilderness, beckons those weary of jarring city life. On a clear day in suburban Portland and Seattle, a powerful telescope could reveal the tiny figures of climbers atop the glaciered summits of the Cascade volcanoes.

Even in America's heartland and East Coast, semiwild areas such as the Pine Barrens of New Jersey and the Catskill Mountains of New York lie within a 1- or 2-hour drive of some of the largest cities.

Wherever they lie, the wild, unexploited lands deserve attention and care. This book was written to help you, the outdoors enthusiast, prepare for wilderness outings. We hope you'll enjoy the wilderness, and at the same time protect both yourself and the environment from injury of any kind.

Outdoor experiences lend to the discovery of the inner relationship between ourselves and nature. (Photo by George Ostertag)

C H A P T E R   2
Wilderness Ethics

EUGENE A. TROXELL

Wilderness is where we go to be closer to our roots. As J. T. Whipple wrote in *Study Out the Land*, "All America lies at the end of the wilderness road, and our past is not a dead past but still lives in us . . . Our forebears had civilization inside themselves, the wild outside. We live in the civilization they created, but within us the wilderness still lingers. What they dreamed, we live; and what they lived, we dream."

The Wilderness Act of 1964 was the first major act of the U.S. Congress to reserve large plots of undeveloped land as federally administered wilderness areas. Before that, certain lands were set aside as "primitive areas," but there were no officially designated and protected wilderness areas. The Wilderness Act defines wilderness as "an area where the earth and its community of life are untrammeled by man, where man himself is a visitor who does not remain . . . It is a region which contains no permanent [human] inhabitants, no possibility for motorized travel, and is spacious enough so that a traveler crossing it by foot or horse must have the experience of sleeping out-of-doors." Wilderness, by this definition, included most of the earth's surface as recently as 100 years ago. Today, as the global human population rapidly approaches 6 billion, wilderness is quickly disappearing. Most modern Americans live their entire lives with no real experience of wilderness.

Many of us, however, still dimly recognize the wilderness as home, and we feel comfortable there. After all, the land that "generally appears to have been affected primarily by the forces of nature, with the imprint of man's work substantially unnoticeable," as the Wilderness Act states, is the environment in which all forms of life have evolved over eons. In this chapter we explore some of the reasons why wilderness is important and worth preserving, and discover how our ethical sensibilities—our codes of behavior—are crucial to its preservation.

First, let's identify several "practical" reasons for preserving wilderness areas:

Scientific value. Wilderness areas are invaluable as laboratories for scientific study in many disciplines. From an ecologist's point of view, for instance, a thorough understanding of undisturbed ecosystems is essential in the effort to recognize and hopefully stem the tide of human-induced species extinctions. The wilderness environment provides an absolute standard to which we can compare the health, or deterioration, of the particular environments we live in.

Archaeological value. Humans once occupied some areas that today are uninhabited. Preserving such areas for current or future study keeps open the possibility of understanding cultures that preceded ours.

Wilderness as a storehouse. Wilderness areas are repositories of genes. Genetic diversity keeps ecosystems functioning properly. Plants, in particular, are important sources of raw material for future agricultural and pharmaceutical applications. Human-induced species extinctions are now estimated to be occurring at more than 10,000 times the normal (evolution-driven) rate of extinction. The biggest culprit is the expansion of the human population and the consequent usurpation of habitat.

Wilderness as a playground. Wilderness areas are inherently fun and challenging in their capacity as natural playgrounds or gymnasiums. As an alternative to structured exercise, we can hike a canyon, climb a peak, tour a river by kayak, or explore the woods. The psychological confidence acquired on a wilderness trek often carries over into other areas of life as well.

These practical considerations aren't the only good reasons for wilderness preservation. In a philosophical context, wilderness—and all that is in it—is part of the creative force that has produced everything that exists. Our culture, our thought, and even our technological ability ultimately derive from the creative force that also manifests itself as wilderness. We can call that force "God," "nature," "evolution," "Gaia," or any number of other names. But no matter what we call it, it created us all. We, and all plants, animals, and inanimate matter, are brothers and sisters in the family of creation, connected at junctures in the streams of evolution.

Most of us can best appreciate our connections with nature when we're cut off from the human-altered world. Wilderness is a cathedral, a sacred space—a spiritual state of mind—in which we can acknowledge, appreciate, and thus honor the creative force to which we are intimately bound. We become, in a sense, more complete.

Metaphorically, our individual identities are like discrete droplets in the spray cast off by an ocean wave. Any drop separate from the larger body of water has an individual identity. If it had self-consciousness (which humans have achieved), it might experience fear, hope, suffering, success, defeat, and possibly love while in that state of separation. But the drop soon coalesces with the creative force from which it emerged, becoming again an integral part of the larger whole. This metaphor is adapted from a common Zen concept.

In the cathedral of wilderness, it is not uncommon to reach a clear awareness of what we have recently come from, and of what we will soon return to. As John Muir put it, "I only went out for a walk, and finally concluded to stay out till sundown, for going out, I found, was really going in."

Despite our deep roots within the whole of nature, humans have evolved into something quite distinct from Earth's other inhabitants. Only humans need ethics. This is because we are social animals. Our survival depends on the existence of societies, and societies depend on cooperative behavior. Other social animals behave socially because they have virtually no choice but to do so. Behavior essential to their existence is genetically programmed. This was true for *Homo sapiens'* ancestors as well. But we acquired the ability to choose, which released us from many genetically determined behaviors. As our behavior became increasingly subject to conscious control, rules evolved—particularly for those types of behavior necessary for social living, and thus for survival. Ethics filled the void created by the power of choice. (The term "ethics" has different uses. One use is to refer to an area of study, commonly regarded as an area of philosophy. Thus one might take a college philosophy course dealing with ethics and study the ethical theories of major philosophers. Another use is to designate specific evaluations of types of conduct, as when one speaks of business ethics, or of ethics in government. The term is used in both senses in this chapter.)

Wilderness areas can become natural playgrounds for the whole family. (Photo by Bob and Ira Spring)

Ethical regulation in the past centered on social behaviors necessary for the existence of clans, tribes, and nations, with disregard for the welfare of other societies or other species. That made sense when the only behaviors threatening to the continued existence of the human species were those that endangered the stability of social life.

Today it's not hard to imagine how the inappropriate use of technology could so radically alter the biosphere that Earth could become incapable of supporting future generations of human beings. Of course, most humans have not and are not intentionally trying to damage the biosphere. But it's now clear that the unintended consequences of some applications of technology have been wreaking environmental havoc around the world. There's a new category of human action, different from those threatening our ability to live in societies, that may directly influence our survival.

Previous generations of human beings never realized that unintentional mistreatment of the physical environment could lead to self-extinction.

In *Einstein on Peace*, editors O. Nathan and H. Nordin quote Einstein as saying, "Our world faces a crisis as yet unperceived by those possessing the power to make great decisions for good or evil. The unleashed power of the atom has changed everything save our modes of thinking, and thus we drift towards unparalleled catastrophe . . . A new type of thinking is essential if mankind is to survive."

That new kind of thinking should take into account two salient facts: the first is our exponentially increasing technological power. Even if we don't have an unparalleled catastrophe, misapplied technology today may well affect the environment for generations. The second is our explosive population growth. In a 10-year span, at the current rate, the number of humans in the world increases by a number greater than the total global population at the time of the American Revolution. The increase in human population is squeezing gorillas, cougars, pandas, tigers, eagles, and millions of other organisms out of existence. Our sheer numbers place limits on what used to be ordinary behavior.

Our ethical viewpoint must change to acknowledge these limits. An essential feature of ethical thinking is the realization that what is all right for one person to do must also be all right for other people, unless there is some reason for distinguishing their respective actions. For example, if in the wilderness it is acceptable for you to wash your dishes in a running stream, hide trash at a campsite, or cut corners when hiking a trail, it must also be allowable for other people to do the same things. When we use consequences of actions as a basis for determining the ethics of actions, we cannot just consider the rather negligible consequences of only one person doing the action. What may be negligible consequences arising from an individual action can become immensely harmful when 100 or 1,000 people repeat the action.

A hundred years ago, a camper could cut brush for a campfire, remove tall grasses and saplings to make camp beside a stream, and wash up in the clear, flowing water. The camper would expect that a few others might repeat the same actions in the same area in a year's time, with no appreciable harm done. The natural environment has sufficient regenerative power to heal the wounds inflicted by a few people each year changing things around for the sake of their personal comfort. This does not mean there would be no evidence of people having been there. Desert environments heal even the smallest scars very slowly. But if the number of people likely to camp in the same area each year jumps to a dozen, 100, or 1,000, the cumulative impact may be well beyond the regenerative powers of the natural environment. Even John Muir, a pioneer in the realm of wilderness ethics, would need to alter his wilderness behavior were he to camp today where he camped less than a century ago.

This is why it's so important to observe rules for hiking or camping in park and wilderness areas—even if the rules don't seem to be applicable in individual cases. The seemingly negligible effect of one harmful action introduces a moral dilemma: If it is all right for you to bend the rules, it is also okay for others.

As usage of parks and wilderness areas soars, managers are forced to impose unpopular regulations to minimize the cumulative impact of large numbers of people. We will surely see more of this—permit systems, trailhead quotas, and rules regulating actions as personal as toilet behavior and as sacrosanct as building a campfire. At the time of this writing, the Boy Scouts of America acknowledged population pressures in their announcement that campfires are to be avoided on future Scout outings. The reasons given for this unpopular announcement were similar to the considerations expressed here.

Of course, even if there are no official rules imposed on the area you visit, you should still regulate your own behavior. Be aware of your own impact, and think especially about the consequences of dozens, or hundreds, of people repeating the same acts.

The staggering numbers of human beings, as well as our advanced technology, provide good reasons for rethinking and recasting traditional ethics. We need an ethic based upon an awareness of the interconnections among all things. John Muir put it nicely: "When we try to pick out anything by itself, we find it hitched to everything else in the universe." This ethic should enhance, not destroy, the creative process of evolution by supporting the web of life. If we temper our actions with concern, and tread lightly upon our delicate and beautiful natural world, we can carry that same ethic back into our everyday lives.

We must adopt a conscious effort to leave every site we visit in a more pristine condition than it was when we arrived. We can cultivate an attitude of appreciation and respect for each plant and animal whose home we enter or pass through, taking care to disturb them as little as possible. Our respect can extend not only to the natural surroundings, but also to other people we encounter. Our wilderness experience should not diminish the quality of their experience.

RECOMMENDED READING

Hampton, Bruce and David Cole. *Soft Paths: How to Enjoy the Wilderness Without Harming It.* Stackpole Books, 1988. (An excellent account of specific "do's and don'ts," covering a wide range of outdoor activities.)

Meyer, Kathleen. *How to Shit in the Woods: An Environmentally Sound Approach to a Lost Art.* Ten Speed Press, 1989. (A lighthearted, but serious account of how to take care of toilet needs while enjoying the outdoors.)

A regular fitness program is important preparation for enjoying the outdoors. (Photo by Jerry Schad)

Physical Conditioning

MARY ENGLES AND CAROLYN WOOD

It's a wonderful feeling to be strong and enduring—to trek up a steep ridge or down a boulder-tossed canyon with the greatest of ease. On the other hand, it's not much fun to set out on a hiking or backpack trip, only to realize part of the way through that you're in pain or too fatigued to enjoy the rest of the trip. So, don't use your first backpacking trip to get in shape—be ready before you go!

Conditioning for wilderness travel is no different than conditioning for any other athletic pursuit. The better your physical condition, the more enjoyable the experience. One concern novices frequently express is whether or not they will be strong enough to keep up with the group. Adopting an effective program not only builds the necessary physical strength, it also builds self-confidence.

With today's emphasis on sports and fitness, many people are already pursuing some sort of regular exercise program. Fitness is "priority one" for some; others slack off during busy periods or during the winter months. Regardless of your particular situation, you can only start to improve from where you are right now. In this chapter you'll learn how to gauge your present physical condition, and discover some of the ways to attain or maintain the level of conditioning you desire.

WHAT SHAPE ARE YOU IN?

Wilderness travel involves aerobic exercise. When you exercise aerobically, your heart beats faster and you breathe more rapidly to satisfy the energy demands of your muscles. Aerobic exercise does not consist of short-duration bursts of energy that leave you "out of breath," but rather of longer periods of sustained energy output. You must increase your heart rate and your breathing on a regular basis to improve your aerobic capacity. That means getting your heart pounding and those lungs working several times weekly.

First, let's see what condition your "condition" is in. Good indicators of aerobic fitness are:

- a resting morning heart rate of 60 beats per minute or less
- a stable morning weight
- a stable and repeatable "12-minute test"
- a rapid return to a normal heart rate after exercise

The 12-minute test, originally developed by Dr. Kenneth Cooper in the 1960s (*Aerobics*, Bantam Books, 1968), is one yardstick by which you can measure your aerobic fitness. It refers to how far you can walk, run, or jog in 12 minutes (see fig. 3-1). For example, if you can cover 1.25 to 1.49 miles in 12 minutes, you are considered to be in "fair" condition. At this point, you may need about 10 weeks of regular aerobic exercise to get into "good" condition. "Good" means that you can cover 1.5 to 1.74 miles in 12 minutes. At this point, you're ready for most kinds of vigorous activity, and a maintenance program may be all that you need to stay in that condition.

IF YOU CAN COVER IN 12 MINUTES	YOU ARE IN FITNESS CATEGORY
Less than 1.0 mile	Very Poor
1.0 to 1.24 miles	Poor
1.25 to 1.49 miles	Fair
1.50 to 1.74 miles	Good
1.75 miles or more	Excellent

Fig. 3-1. The 12-minute test

A still-higher level of conditioning may be required if your goal is to tackle the likes of Mount Whitney, Mount Rainier, or Mount Washington. At high altitudes, your lungs and heart are under greater stress due to the reduced oxygen content in the air. And because of the long distances and steep climbing required for such a feat, you'll need more than just the ability to run for 12 minutes. Your training program would in that case include occasional sessions of moderate to vigorous exercise lasting for a number of hours. Long-duration exercise, coupled with frequent, short exercise sessions, will help you attain your highest level of fitness.

GETTING FIT

If you're under 35 and free of significant risk factors such as smoking, high blood pressure, elevated cholesterol, or hereditary heart disease, you can begin an exercise program without medical testing. Even so, you should progress slowly and be alert to the development of unusual signs and symptoms. Beyond age 45, you should have a "maximal exercise" (treadmill) test under professional supervision before embarking on any strenuous exercise program. These are recommendations from the *American College of Sports Medicine: Guidelines for Exercise Testing and Prescription* (3rd edition, Lea & Febiger, 1986).

Contrary to popular belief, you do not have different sets of muscles for different exercise activities. You use the same muscles in different ways and in different amounts. However, exercise does have a very specific effect on those muscles. The best way to improve your ability to hike up hills is to hike up hills on a regular basis. Not all of us live in places where this is possible or convenient, but there are alternatives. Some folks like to jog or take brisk walks regularly. Even donning a full day pack and taking a brisk walk at noon or before or after work can improve your aerobic capacity immensely.

In the broader arena of activities, any rhythmic action maintained for a prolonged period that involves large muscle groups (the legs, for example) is beneficial. Some examples are swimming, skating, bicycling, jogging, rowing, and cross-country skiing. Stop-and-start sports such as tennis, racquetball, and basketball are also effective if maintained for longer periods. The important thing is to do something regularly that increases your heart rate and breathing.

Your regular and frequent exercise sessions (as opposed to the occasional very long sessions that prepare you for major expeditions) should be repeated at least three times per week and last for 20 to 30 minutes. During those sessions, you should aim for a level of activity that is within your personal "training zone." Figure 3-2 will help you determine the "training-sensitive" range of your heart rate for these sessions. Your heart rate can be quickly

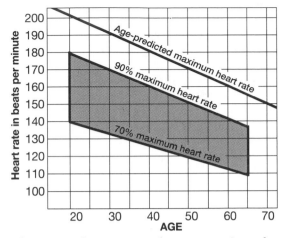

Fig. 3-2. This target heart rate chart assumes that your maximum heart rate is 220 minus your age, and that aerobic exercise (for 20- to 30- minute periods) is most effective in the range of 70 to 90 percent of your maximum heart rate. Your heart rate during aerobic exercise should fall within the shaded area.

determined by feeling your pulse in your wrist and counting the number of beats in 10 seconds as indicated by a digital or sweep-second-hand watch. Multiply the number of beats by six to find the number of beats per minute. For example, if you're 40 years old, you should keep your heart pumping at between 21 and 27 beats every 10 seconds, which corresponds to 126 to 162 beats per minute.

Before you start exercising, you'll need to consider any aches, pains, or other problems you now have. Some of these problems may be helped by exercise and some may be worsened unless remedial measures are taken. Lower back or knee pain, for example, can be eased by the strength and range of motion gained with exercise, or it may be intensified as a result of a particular kind of action (like running on hard surfaces, going downhill, or twisting your body to put on or take off a heavy backpack) that aggravates a preexisting condition such as weak muscles or mild tendonitis. If you know you have a problem, check with an appropriate health professional for some preventative measures before attempting any strenuous workouts. Talk with sports-minded people or with those who have been injured to

find an orthopedist, sports-oriented physician, or physical therapist. Professionals such as these can assist you with a strengthening program that addresses your specific problem.

Regardless of any problem areas, you'll need to strengthen the large muscle groups of the buttocks, thighs, calves, abdomen, and back to be in peak condition for a backpack trip. The abdominals are particularly important, as they help support the lower back. A program can be designed for you to carry out at a local fitness club or at home. You can use weights or exercise machines. You can climb steps or walk inclines at increasing speed to prepare for the elevation gains and losses inherent in mountaineering. Strengthening the shoulder and chest muscles will help you support the dead weight of a full backpack.

STRETCHING

Muscle-strengthening exercise tends to tighten the muscles. The antidote is stretching—both before and after a workout. Stretching improves your leg and back flexibility and reduces your susceptibility to musculoskeletal injury. Good flexibility also maximizes your ability to climb over rocks, hop small streams, and stretch where you need to without fear of injury. When out in the wilderness, don't leave your stretching routines at home. Stretching should be part of your wake-up ritual on trips, especially on those beautiful, cold mornings in the mountains when you emerge from your warm sleeping bag. Browse through the illustrations in this chapter (fig. 3-3), or use Bob Anderson's book *Stretching* (Shulter Publications, 1981) as a guide.

Fig. 3-3. Various stretching exercises

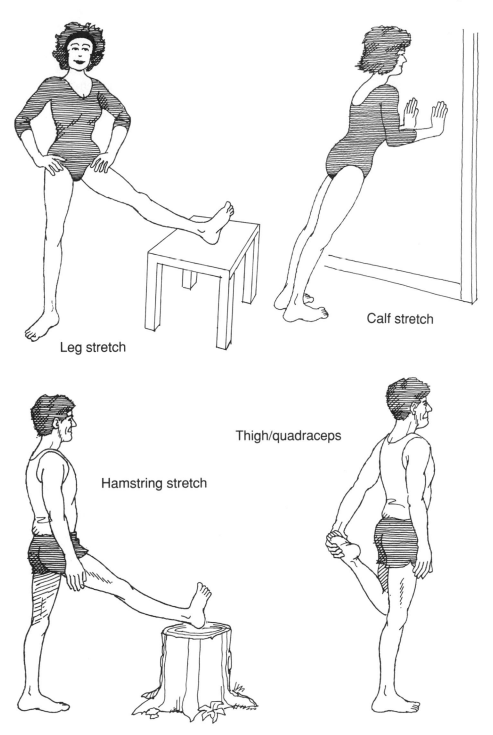

Leg stretch

Calf stretch

Hamstring stretch

Thigh/quadraceps

FEET FIRST

Your feet deserve some special attention before you begin your program and before you encase them in those hiking boots! Lubricate your skin with lanolin (unless you're allergic to it), file calluses with an emery board or pumice stone, and keep your nails clean and trimmed.

When you select a boot, you should know your foot type. Do you have a high arch, or is your foot "flat"? Are your feet flexible or rigid? Also be aware of the kind of terrain you'll be hiking. Not every foot or situation demands a stiff, high-top leather boot.

If your feet are subject to excessive pronation (flattening of the normal arch and inward tipping of the ankle) or other irregularities of motion, you may need an orthotic (shoe-insert) device. A qualified health professional such as a podiatrist or a physical therapist specializing in foot problems can help you solve your problems as well as help with boot selection.

SOME PHYSIOLOGICAL CONSIDERATIONS

SIZE

Your size affects the length of your stride and your pace. In the United States, the average height for women is 5 feet-4 inches and the average height for men is 5 feet-10 inches. If you're shorter than average, your leg length may put you at a slight disadvantage when crossing rough terrain, hopping streams, or scrambling over boulders.

Size and body weight can also affect your muscle mass and carrying capacity when backpacking. For a person in good physical shape, figure a "load-to-body-weight" ratio of one to three (1:3). That means, for instance, that a 180-pound person should carry a maximum load of 60 pounds, and a 120-pound person should carry a maximum load of 40 pounds. This 20-pound difference in pack weight can be significant in planning a trip. If you're a lighter person, you may have to think twice about the personal gear you'll take, and you may not be able to realistically handle the same quantity of community gear that larger or heavier people can carry. Equitable sharing of gear in a group of people of various sizes and abilities doesn't mean that every person must carry the same load.

DIFFERENCES BETWEEN MEN AND WOMEN

Women have a higher proportion of body fat and a lower proportion of muscle mass than men. Women, because they are generally smaller than men, usually have a smaller heart, less blood volume, and less lung capacity. All of this means that the average woman must work a little harder than the average man for most activities involving motion. It's important to note, however, that a woman's response to physical exercise is equal to a man's, and that improvements in training can far outweigh any differences in the average physical abilities of men and women.

In general, women's bodies do not use oxygen as efficiently as men's. Women have fewer red blood cells per unit of blood, according to Dr. Edward L. Fox in *Sports Physiology* (Columbus, Ohio: W. B. Saunders Co., 1979). This is important to consider because red blood cells carry oxygen to the muscles, where the oxygen is used to produce the energy needed for motion. Also, women are more likely to have an undetected iron deficiency, even in the absence of anemia. This can delay the removal of lactic acid from the muscles during exercise, which causes you to tire easily. You may want to have your blood tested for iron deficiency; iron supplements can take care of slight deficiencies.

Since women have wider pelvic struc-

Running on the beach is one way to combine a fitness routine with enjoyment of the outdoors. (Photo by Jerry Schad)

tures and looser knee ligaments, they're more prone to alignment problems of the knee cap. Exercises that strengthen the muscles surrounding the knee are recommended. During the menstrual cycle, certain hormones are released that may cause a general loosening of many of the body's ligaments, resulting in lower back, knee, or arch pain. Since the weight of a pack can aggravate a backache, you may want to use pain reliever, such as aspirin or ibuprofen, to relieve the discomfort.

Many women have the necessary lower-body strength needed to support the weight of a heavy backpack, but they lack the upper-body development that most men have. Upper-body muscles are used particularly when lifting or putting on a pack. Various techniques can overcome any difficulty. For instance, you can use a rock or tree to prop up the pack when putting it on or taking it off. You can also increase the strength of your upper body through weight training. Even a modest program can yield impressive gains in strength.

PREGNANCY

Pregnancy is physiologically normal. But from conception onward, the body undergoes profound adjustments. While pregnancy is no reason to avoid wilderness travel entirely, certain considerations deserve mention. Miscarriages, most common in the early stages of pregnancy, and premature labor, in the later stages, can pose serious complications in isolated areas. Before undertaking any wilderness travel while pregnant, be sure to discuss it with your physician.

In the later months of pregnancy, maintaining balance while walking or scrambling may be a problem. A walking stick may help somewhat. Knee ligaments become looser in late pregnancy, contributing further to instability. Falls, especially on the abdomen, are a serious risk.

Because the pregnant woman provides oxygen to the developing fetus as well as herself, her heart must work harder, even when she's resting. There are more demands on nearly every muscle and organ in the body as well. The pregnant woman must carefully monitor her level of fatigue, and scale back any plans for strenuous travel. During the later months, it may be either uncomfortable or impossible to wear a full-size backpack. In that case, a day pack may have to be substituted.

Studies have shown that pregnant women living for long periods at altitudes of 8,000 feet and up tend to experience increased blood pressure, problems with breathing, water retention, and swelling of the hands and feet. It is not known if such effects are detrimental for short-duration trips. Certainly, any pregnant woman should carefully monitor herself for any adverse symptoms brought on by a high altitude, and be prepared to descend to a safer level if necessary. Certain drugs and chemicals commonly used by mountain travelers, including Flagyl for giardiasis, Diamox for high-altitude symptoms, and iodine for water purification, should not be taken during pregnancy.

CONCLUSION

One final note—an important caveat. Don't pretend you can whip yourself into shape in the last two weeks before a strenuous trip. Last-minute, rigorous exercise will surely deplete your body's energy stores and leave you too exhausted to enjoy the trip. Instead, do as marathoners do: train vigorously for 10 weeks, then ease off on the training for seven to ten days before the big event. A short period of rest on top of a good training base will have you literally exploding from the starting line . . . er, trailhead.

Good luck with your fitness program!

RECOMMENDED READING

Anderson, Bob. *Stretching*. Shulter Publications, 1981. (A well-illustrated reference with stretching exercises for various activities.)

Cooper, Kenneth H. *Aerobics*. Bantam Books, 1968. (A classic work on aerobic testing and conditioning.)

Fixx, James F. *The Complete Book of Running*. Random House, 1976. (Well-researched, practical, and easy-to-read advice on running and sports performance.)

Fox, Edward L. *Sports Physiology*. W. B. Saunders Co., 1979.

Willmore, Jack H. *Training for Sport and Activity: The Physiological Basis of the Conditioning Process*. Allyn & Bacon, 1982.

Trip Preparation

DAVE MOSER

Planning a trip can be almost as much fun as the trip itself. Reading books and spreading maps on the floor gives you a thrill of anticipation. The time and effort you put into your plans will result in greater enjoyment and increased safety.

Although most of this chapter applies to trips of overnight or longer duration, you can benefit by carefully planning even a short day hike. Some of the material below is geared to those in a leadership role. Even if you never take on the responsibility of guiding a large group, you'll profit by a knowledge of the detailed planning incumbent on the leader.

RESEARCHING THE TRIP

To help you plan your trip, rely on four primary resources: friends, guidebooks, maps, and rangers.

The first and most obvious resource is your friends. Wisdom gained by experience is the best kind. Ask them which areas they liked the best. Ask them how difficult each trip was, and whether they would do things differently another time around. If you want to get a second opinion, get the names and phone numbers of others who have visited the same areas.

Of the hundreds of guidebooks published for wilderness areas, there's probably one or more just right for the area or region you'd like to visit. Keep in mind, however, that conditions and trails may have changed since the books were writ-

ten. Note copyright dates and verify information with the local authorities. You may want to follow up on some of the books and articles that are listed in the bibliography or "recommended reading" appendix of some guidebooks.

Obtain detailed maps of the area so that you can meticulously follow any verbal or printed description of a trip you want to take. Road maps, especially county maps, are good for showing the major and minor roads leading to the trailhead. Topographic maps allow you to visualize in great detail the topography and trails of the area you plan to explore. Different maps show different features of the same area, so try to obtain as many as possible. Remember that even the most current maps may not show the newer trails, and that existing trails can become eroded or overgrown so as to be unusable. Outdated maps are not necessarily useless—they may indicate old mines, defunct trails, historic towns, and other features erased from the newer maps that you may want to explore. A complete research effort might involve a trip to a public or university library for a look at old maps in the historical collection.

Rangers are another excellent source of information and are generally helpful. However, you should do some homework before contacting a ranger so you can ask intelligent questions. A "cold" call to a ranger asking for a good place to hike may waste both your time and the ranger's. When calling a ranger, have your maps and guidebooks in front of you. Ask to

Obtain current information about proposed trips from a local ranger. (Photo by James Glenn Pearson)

speak with someone who is familiar with the specific area you plan to visit. The office worker who answers the phone may not have the information you need. You may have to wait for a backcountry ranger to return your call, but the information will be worth the wait. Describe your plans and don't hesitate to ask for any additional information or suggestions. In some instances, the ranger may recommend an alternate trail that would better suit your needs.

If you're the trip leader, it's best to scout the trip in advance. That way you'll get firsthand information on road and trail conditions and the availability of water. Make notes on your maps for further reference. You may discover an interesting side trip, or you might end up deciding the trip is somehow not appropriate for the group you intend to lead.

DESIGNING THE TRIP

Designing a trip itinerary is exciting! Using your topographic map, you can mentally "walk" along and visualize your intended route. Take the time to study and "see" the elevation gains and losses, the distances to be traveled, the meadows, lakes, forests, and other features. Identify the best overlooks and the best spots for lunch or snack breaks. When choosing camp sites, try to visualize where the sun will rise and set. In a similar vein, you may want to plan your trip around a full moon. Or go when the moon is new to enjoy zillions of stars in an inky black sky. Consult an almanac or a calendar to determine the moon's phase and the times it rises and sets.

Rather than having to retrace your steps on the trip, try to design a loop route. Or you can design a point-to-point trip using a car-shuttle or a drop-off-and-pick-up service. Using these strategies, you can enjoy twice as much scenery as you would on an out-and-back trip.

When deciding how many cars it will take to carry people and gear, keep in mind that backpack equipment takes up a lot of space. Most compact cars can carry only two people and two backpacks. If someone in your group has a van or pickup truck, consider using it to haul the bulky gear while the participants ride in passenger cars. If you employ a car shuttle for point-to-point trips, remember that everything and everyone may have to fit into half the vehicles.

For a long drive to a distant trailhead, include time for rest breaks or meal stops at least every couple of hours or so. Plan to arrive early enough so you can get plenty of sleep before hiking in. If caravaning, CB radios can be very helpful. If you don't have a CB, try to borrow one—they can be installed quickly and easily. You can chat on the way, reducing the boredom of a long drive. If one vehicle needs to pull over, other drivers can be easily notified. You can also make decisions about when to stop for lunch, whether to take side trips, and the like. (Note: In Mexico you need a permit to operate a CB. Call your local Mexican Consulate.) Always carry extra water in the car on extended drives.

Anticipate what the weather will be like on the trip. You should know, for example, that snow flurries can occur above timberline in July and August. Or that the desert winds can hit 50 miles per hour or more anytime. Rivers swollen with snowmelt can be a problem in the mountains in spring and early summer. Sudden rains may turn dirt roads into quagmires of mud. Flash floods may lash the desert and canyon country during the thunderstorm season. Discuss any potential hazards with the ranger. A call to knowledgeable folks at the area's local weather bureau can result in a wealth of information. Hope for the best, but plan for any eventuality.

How much water will you have to carry? That depends on where the nearest streams are and whether or not they are flowing. Check this out with the ranger when you call. Decide how you'll treat the water. Some trips may require caches of water (and/or food) placed in advance. These supplies must be well hidden, animal-proofed, and protected from the elements. Leave a note, with the date indicated, stating that you are depending on these supplies for your survival. If your trailhead is remote, you may want to leave some food and water in your vehicle (except in bear country).

When hiking at altitudes over 6,000 feet, most people benefit from an acclimation period just before the trip. A day or two spent at high altitude usually does the trick. Do some walking or easy hiking to adjust your body to the thinner air.

To organize all the details of your trip, develop a complete itinerary, starting with the departure. List times and places, and allow a little slack for unforeseen circumstances. Consider the abilities of the slower participants when estimating times of arrival. Plan to arrive at camp with some daylight left. Much of the pertinent planning data can be summarized on the sample trip planning form (fig. 4-1).

PERMITS AND REGULATIONS

Permits are required for entry—day use and camping—into most of the federally designated wilderness areas (some require permits for overnight camping only). Many nonwilderness national parks and forests require camping permits as well. The permit system serves several purposes. In some cases it is used to limit the number of people using a particular area. That helps lessen the impact of too many people, and guarantees a better wilderness experience for visitors. Also, in going through the permit process, wilderness users are notified of the appropriate regulations. By issuing permits, agencies can collect data needed to carry out effective management of the area in question. Finally, permits allow the authorities to keep tabs on your whereabouts in case of an emergency.

Permit policies vary widely. Whereas in most areas permits are free, some agencies charge a reservation fee. Find out well in advance what the permit policy is for the area you're interested in. Permits are usually obtained by mail or in person. Sometimes permits can be issued as the result of a phone call. Guidebooks usually cover the nuts and bolts of permit application, but make sure the information is current.

Quite often, the key to getting the permit you want is to apply early. Permits for the most popular wilderness and park areas may become available only during a very limited time several months in advance. Some are granted "first come, first served" on a postmark basis; other permits are granted by lottery. Be flexible about your dates of entry, and try to avoid the most popular days—Friday and Saturday. Consider group-size restrictions before you invite too many of your friends or accept too many participants. If all else fails, remember that many areas reserve a portion of their permits for people who seek them on the day of entry. You may have a second chance if you missed the first time around (although a lot of your effort in planning can go down the drain if you fail to get one).

Fire regulations vary widely. In some, campfire permits are required; in others campfires are banned altogether because of wildfire hazards or a scarcity of firewood. Some jurisdictions allow fires as long as you bring in your own wood. Wild areas may have various fire restrictions imposed on them during the hot and dry summer and fall seasons. During extremely hazardous conditions, visitors may be prohibited from using any open-flame device at all, or they may be prohibited outright from entering certain areas. Although

TRIP PLANNING SHEET

AREA _____ DATES _____

Personal Contacts	Phone	Comments

Road Maps _____Trail Maps_____

_____   _____

Guidebooks	Date	Comments

Rangers	Phone	Comments

Permit Requirements _____

Maximum Group Size _____ Fires Allowed? _____

Water Availability _____

Weather Bureau Location _____ Phone _____

		DAY									
		1	2	3	4	5	6	7	8	9	10	Total
Destination												
Elev. Gain/Loss												
Mileage												
Hiking Time												
Sun	Rises											
	Sets											
Moon	Rises											
	Sets											
	Phase											

Fig. 4-1. Maximize the enjoyment of your trip by using a planning sheet.

they're a traditional part of the outdoor experience, campfires are not always needed for comfort, especially in summer. Campfires draw attention inward to a small world only a few feet across, while the lack of a campfire opens up to sight and mind the infinite majesty of the night sky.

LEADERSHIP CONSIDERATIONS

CHOOSING TRIP COMPANIONS

If you're the leader, and you aren't familiar with the prospective participants, it's your responsibility to screen them. Each person should have the proper equipment and skills. Each should be in good physical condition and possess the confidence and attitude necessary to handle the trip without depending unduly on other members of the party. In evaluating a large number of prospective participants, the use of a questionnaire such as the sample participant information form (fig. 4-2) is a good idea. Query them on:

- their regular exercise program
- similar trips they've taken in the past
- equipment owned or available to them
- physical limitations or medical disorders that may affect their performance

You can screen participants initially over the phone. At the planning meeting (see the next section) you can do more screening. Even after someone has been accepted for an outing, something could come up that would change that status. A participant's recent injury or illness might be a reason for you to carefully reconsider his or her participation. It's your duty as leader to continue screening right up to the beginning of the trip. Dropping an obviously unqualified individual is fair both to the group and to the individual who might otherwise end up having a miserable time. If the trip is to be a backpack

over rough terrain, effective screening might include a pre-trip day hike over a similar kind of terrain. Those who seem to be having trouble should be informed gently that the trip is not for them.

PLANNING MEETING

Planning meetings are effective for almost all trips, especially those lasting two or more days. At the very least, the participants get to know one another beforehand. During the meeting, the leader explains the general trip plan and the objectives, including:

- the driving route
- the hiking route
- the number of miles to be hiked each day
- the elevation gains and losses

The following details should also be worked out:

- car pools/drivers
- equipment sharing—tents, stoves, et cetera
- cooking groups or a "central commissary" (wherein all share the same menu and cooking/cleaning responsibilities)
- food purchases and participants' dietary restrictions
- sharing of costs

All participants must understand what the trip entails and acknowledge that it's something they want to do. The leader should encourage questions and discussion. The following checklists and printed information should be passed out:

- trip description or summary
- itinerary
- map of the driving route
- map of the hiking route (USGS topographic and other government maps can be photocopied without violating copyright laws)
- list of the required and/or optional maps (if maps aren't provided)

PARTICIPANT INFORMATION

Name _____

Address _____

Birthdate _____ Phone _____ (home)

_____ (work)

Regular Exercise Program _____

_____

_____

Recent Trip Experience:

Location	Dates	Reference	Phone

Physical Disorders _____

Allergies _____

Medications _____

Physician's Name _____ Phone _____

Health Insurance Company _____

Policy Number _____

In Emergency, Contact:

Name _____

Address _____

Phone _____ Relationship _____

Fig. 4-2. The trip leader should have basic information about each member of the group.

- water requirements
- equipment requirements
- important phone numbers; numbers to call in case of an emergency

The more of this the leader puts on paper, the more prepared the participants will be before the trip.

Leaders should also collect the following information, included on the participant information form (see fig. 4-2) about each participant for use in the event of an emergency:

- name and address of a contact person
- name and phone number of personal physician
- disclosure of medical conditions or allergies that may affect participant's welfare
- current medications
- health insurance company and policy number

At the planning meeting, drivers should be reminded to take along an extra car key. That simple precaution could save the group countless hours of wasted time. The extra key can be hidden outside the car or carried along on the trip in a secure place separate from the driver's key ring. Someone else in the party can be told where the extra key is located so that he or she can drive the car if necessary. Before leaving, all drivers must have their vehicles checked to be sure they are in good working order.

The leader should remind everybody about individual responsibilities. The leader can hand out a list of special equipment needed, but it's up to every participant to develop his or her own personal list. We're all forgetful to some degree, which is why a checklist is a must for every participant.

After every trip taken, add to the list any items you wish you had taken. You'll end up eventually with a very long list—too much for any one trip—but at least you won't overlook anything on future trips. It's also helpful to include the weight of each item on your list. That way you can make intelligent decisions when it comes time for the inevitable task of deleting nonessential items that are too heavy or bulky to carry.

SAFETY

While safety is everyone's business, there are several things the leader can do to assure that trip participants are prepared in the event of an emergency.

Familiarize everyone with the location of the nearest emergency telephones and the appropriate emergency numbers. In addition to 911, this includes the numbers for the nearest sheriff, ranger, and fire department. An awareness of evacuation routes is invaluable in the event of an emergency.

Tell someone where you are going, when you expect to return, and what to do if you don't return on time. This is vitally important if you'll be hiking alone. Be sure that you tell someone you can depend on. While it may be a good idea to give a ranger your itinerary, rangers are accustomed to people who forget to check in when they return. It's best to leave full written details with the folks back home. You should include phone numbers of the local sheriff and appropriate rangers, vehicle descriptions, and vehicle license-plate numbers. Ask them to report you missing if you are not back by a certain time.

LAST-MINUTE DETAILS

Some things can't be done until the final day or hours before the trip starts. Fill up the gas tank. Check under the hood. Check the weather—call a ranger or the weather bureau nearest the area you're going to visit. If the weather's been nasty,

Maps are essential for successful trip planning. (Photo by James Glenn Pearson)

ask the ranger about trail damage and hazardous stream crossings. Check road conditions by calling your auto club or your state's highway patrol.

On some trips, you must sign in and sign out at a ranger station. After the trip, don't forget to sign out! If you don't, you may be responsible for an unnecessary search effort.

Finally, if you notice anything during your trip that the authorities should know about, be sure to report it. Those who follow in your footsteps may have a better wilderness experience because of it.

A well-fitting backpack is one of the basics for creating a pleasant wilderness experience. (Photo by Sandra Hinchman)

Outfitting: The Basic Equipment

JAN CRAVEN, MIKE FRY, CAROLYN WOOD, AND
PRISCILLA AND SCOTT ANDERSON

L ife is basic, simple, and clear in the wilderness. A minimalist existence— making do with the least possible possessions—renews a weary spirit and reveals simple pleasures neglected in our hurried lives.

In the wilderness we can: Gaze at the silent stars. Listen to a bird's solo recital. Watch the pogo-stick ballet of a deer. Marvel at the wondrous forms and colors of the flowers, rocks, meadows, valleys, and forests. Concentrate on a thought without interruption. Dream a dream through to its end. Appreciate the sharing of a simple meal cooked over a tiny stove—a culinary masterpiece even with a few twigs or grains of sand thrown in. Listen for the mouth-watering call that energizes even the weariest of campers, "Hot water!"

Such idyllic experiences amidst nature require either lots of luck or careful preparation. This chapter, like the last one, focuses on preparation, not luck. Good choices of equipment are an integral part of preparation for a trip.

ESSENTIALS

Seasoned wilderness travelers always strive to pack the least and the lightest gear that can ensure their survival and comfort. Many people are familiar with the "Ten Essentials" developed by The Mountaineers. This list of items consists of map, compass, flashlight with extra bulb and batteries, sunglasses, extra clothing, extra food and water, pocket knife, candle or fire starter, first aid kit, and waterproof matches.

An expanded list of essentials includes those items necessary to achieve a reasonable measure of safety and comfort in the event of a delay or an emergency. The particular items considered essential varies depending on where, when, and how long a trip is, but each essential item falls into one of the ten categories listed below (not to be confused with the Ten Essentials). Use the ESSENTIALS mnemonic to help you remember them:

Emergencies
Sustenance
Shelter
Extras
Navigation
Toiletries
Incidentals
Attitude
Light
Something to Carry All of It In

EMERGENCIES

- waterproof matches
- candle or flammable material (to assist in starting a stove or fire under adverse conditions)
- first aid kit (don't forget foot care)
- whistle and/or signal mirror

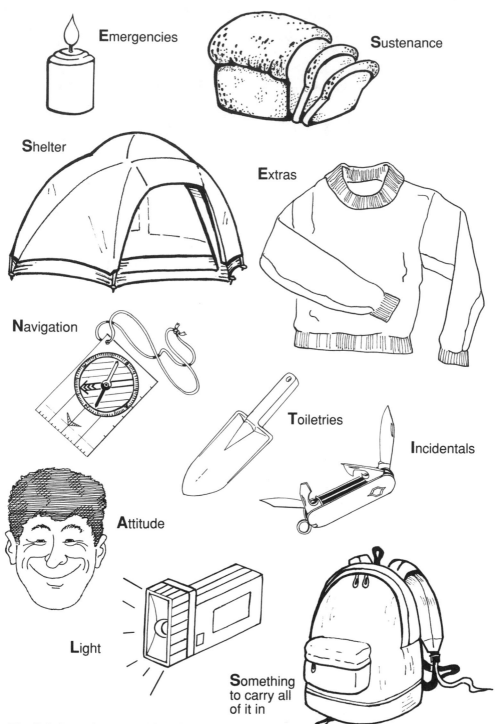

Emergencies

Sustenance

Shelter

Extras

Navigation

Toiletries

Incidentals

Attitude

Light

Something
to carry all
of it in

Fig. 5-1. Items from the ESSENTIALS mnemonic

SUSTENANCE

- food (including cooking gear if appropriate) to meet planned itinerary
- water and/or water-purification device

SHELTER

- sun protection: sunglasses, hat, sunscreen
- rain- and wind-resistant outer clothing
- clothing for expected temperatures
- footwear appropriate for the terrain
- overnight gear (sleeping bag, pad, tent)

EXTRAS

- extra food
- extra water
- extra warm clothing

NAVIGATION

- map(s) of the area
- compass
- pencil and straight-edge
- altimeter (if needed for critical navigation)

TOILETRIES

- toilet paper
- trowel (to bury solid waste)
- sanitation/personal items

INCIDENTALS

- knife
- nylon cord (for securing items or holding a delaminated shoe or boot together)
- needle and thread or dental floss (for mending cloth, eyeglass frames, et cetera)

ATTITUDE

- a positive attitude—the ultimate essential!

LIGHT

- flashlight with fresh batteries
- extra batteries and spare bulb

SOMETHING TO CARRY ALL OF IT IN

- fanny pack, day pack, or backpack
- stuff sacks (for compressing bulky items and organizing gear)

Essential equipment prepares you for the unexpected. If you do encounter adverse conditions on a trip, having the right equipment will keep you comfortable. In the worst of circumstances, the essentials can mean the difference between a safe outcome and a tragic one. Never lighten the load you carry at the expense of essentials, lest you threaten your safety and that of others in your group.

How to fill your list of essentials, as well as nonessentials, for a given trip is up to you. Your personal preferences will change with time as you gain experience.

KEEPING THINGS LIGHT

A loaf of bread and a heavy coat equipped John Muir. He toughed out the elements, lived off the land, trusted the water, and was so at home in the wilderness he couldn't conceive of being lost. Times have changed, and so have our needs and desires.

When camping out of a vehicle, there's almost no limitation on the weight of gear. Just stuff everything in and go. But when your choice of transportation is boots and backpack, every ounce counts. One of the challenges of backpacking and hiking is minimizing the weight you carry. Weight must be considered for every purchase you make. When packing for a trip, you can use a small food scale to weigh and evaluate items (fig. 5-2). Ounces add up fast! Look at everything and think about how you can reduce the amount of weight. Be clever and let one item serve multiple functions. A stuff sack can double as a pillow case, and your extra clothes can be the stuffing. Your rain parka can serve as a wind jacket, your cooking pot can be your bowl, and your bandanna can play the role of towel, napkin, bandage, dust shield, hat, and pillowcase.

Pack only the amount of sunscreen, contact-lens solution, or peanut butter you're likely to use on the trip, using small plastic bottles. Take small sample sizes for personal items such as hand lotion, toothpaste, and deodorant. Eat breakfast out of the plastic bag that holds your cereal. Don't lug the bottle along with the wine! (Wine and alcoholic beverages are heavy, and a little goes a long way.) Leave the radio behind—you can catch up on the latest scores when you get home. Bring only part of your paperback book if you know you won't read the whole thing. Sleep in your clothes for warmth so you can carry a lighter sleeping bag or tent. But don't get carried away on the quest for lightness—you and every other participant on the trip are responsible for carrying the essential items appropriate for that trip (see fig. 5-3).

Here are some other ways to keep your load as light as possible:

- Hike with a partner who carries the lion's share and keeps you warm at night.
- Share tent, stove, cookware, water purifier, et cetera, and divide the common load evenly.
- Travel where there's abundant water and good weather.
- Purchase the lightest equipment available.
- Ask other wilderness travelers how they trim their pack weight.

Finally, weigh your pack! Add the weight for the water you will be carrying (8.3 pounds per gallon). Do not exceed the pack-to-body weight ratio of one to three unless you want to suffer the first day or two, or for some reason have no choice. Recognize that carrying too much

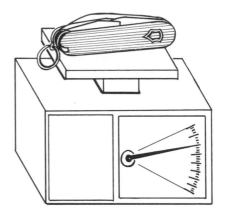

Fig. 5-2. Using a small scale to weigh and evaluate items

weight for your size or level of physical condition will slow down your pace and reduce your enjoyment.

PRODUCTS

Dozens of companies, large and small, manufacture high-quality wilderness gear. Some design for light weight and style as well as function. Check with local stores and read outdoor publications to learn about manufacturers' reputations—the quality of their products, the length of time they've been in business, and their warranty and service capabilities. Check the product labels for specifications, care and cleaning, fit, and guarantees. Ask salespeople if their store offers any guarantees beyond those offered by the manufacturer. After you've made a purchase, follow directions carefully to keep the gear performing as intended.

PRODUCT SOURCES

Where you buy your equipment may be just as important as who manufactures it. Your best bet is to purchase from a source that is reputable, has been in business a

SAMPLE EQUIPMENT LIST

FOR DAY HIKES

Wear or carry in pockets

- ❏ Long pants
- ❏ Polypropylene shirt
- ❏ Long-sleeve, light-colored shirt
- ❏ Wool sweater
- ❏ Hat with brim
- ❏ Bandana or handkerchief
- ❏ Hiking shoes or boots
- ❏ Socks—liners and wool socks
- ❏ Sunscreen
- ❏ Sun-protective lip balm
- ❏ Sunglasses
- ❏ Water bottle (in a belt bag)
- ❏ Hiking stick
- ❏ Swiss army knife with file and scissors
- ❏ Compass
- ❏ Wallet or plastic bag with driver's license, credit card, health insurance info, emergency phone numbers, money, coins for phone

Carry in your daypack

- ❏ Shorts
- ❏ Hooded rain jacket and pants
- ❏ Wool hat and mittens
- ❏ Large trash bag (for emergency shelter)
- ❏ Lunch and snacks (along with extra food for delays or emergencies)
- ❏ Water or electrolyte replacement drink
- ❏ First-aid kit
- ❏ Nylon cord
- ❏ Closed-cell foam sit pad
- ❏ Maps
- ❏ Pencil and paper
- ❏ Flashlight with extra batteries and spare bulb
- ❏ Whistle
- ❏ Lighter or waterproof matches, and candle
- ❏ Toilet bag to carry toilet paper, trowel, plastic bags
- ❏ Ditty bag for personal items (*e.g.,* comb, hand lotion, hair barrette, tweezers, moleskin, pain-relief tablets, towelettes.

FOR BACKPACK TRIPS

Add the following to the day hike list on the left. Select gear and quantities appropriate for your planned trip:

- ❏ Frame backpack (also take along a daypack if you will be day hiking away from camp)
- ❏ Tent
- ❏ Sleeping bag
- ❏ Sleeping pad
- ❏ Ground cloth
- ❏ Stove
- ❏ Cook pots
- ❏ Cup, bowl, utensils
- ❏ Water bottles
- ❏ Water purification (filter, disinfectant tablets, or extra fuel for boiling water)
- ❏ Food and beverage powders
- ❏ Larger first-aid kit
- ❏ Safety gear (rope, ice axe) as needed
- ❏ Long underwear
- ❏ Parka
- ❏ Gaiters
- ❏ Mitten overshells
- ❏ Lightweight shoes or booties (to wear in camp)
- ❏ Toothbrush
- ❏ Biodegradable soap
- ❏ Glacier glasses (for snow)
- ❏ Insect repellent

Note: *Not all of the items listed here are essential for all trips. Some trips require less equipment and some trips require more.*

Fig. 5-3. Use an equipment list to make sure you have everything you may need.

long time, offers a product satisfaction guarantee, has knowledgeable salespeople, and offers rental equipment (this is most helpful for a person evaluating gear).

Fortunately, sports and adventure outfitters tend to attract salespeople who love the outdoors and try out a lot of the equipment they sell. Mail-order outfits may offer considerable savings, but many don't offer personal service. You can also scan outdoor magazines and other newsletters and newspapers for bargains. Even the trendiest outfitters have periodic sales to clear out excess stock or demo and rental equipment. Not all your equipment needs to be brand-new. Swap meets, thrift stores, and surplus outlets are all good hunting grounds.

COST CONSIDERATIONS

When outfitting yourself for the sport of wilderness travel, you may want to prioritize your purchases. The list is short for day hikers—boots (or the appropriate walking shoes), day pack, and miscellaneous essential items. Accumulating backpacking gear, though, involves major purchases. Fortunately, some of the more expensive items needed for backpacking can be easily borrowed or rented. Personal items such as boots and special clothing are probably first priority, then sleeping bag, sleeping pad, and backpack. You may be able to share a stove and cookware for some time before deciding what kinds to buy. A tent is a key purchase—you may want to rent or share one for a while before investing in your own.

Making your own equipment was once an economical way to ensure excellent quality in your gear. It still is—for some— but equipment prices are low compared to the amount of time it takes to create a finished piece of gear. Most people consider it more fun to spend weekends out hiking rather than laboring over a sewing machine. But do keep your needle sharp for repairing or modifying equipment and clothing.

CLOTHING

FOOTWEAR

During a typical hiking day, your feet hit the ground 10,000 to 20,000 times (about 2,000 steps per mile). Your boots must fit well!

Fortunately, running-shoe technology has spread to hiking boots, and many good choices are available. Lightweight boots are relatively inexpensive and comfortable, and provide enough protection for most uses. Choose ankle-high boots with padded ankle collars. Uppers made of nylon or other synthetic material require almost no "break-in," while leather uppers are more rigid. If you're susceptible to ankle twists or if rougher country dictates the need for more protection against rolling rocks, consider the heavier, all-leather models.

Old-fashioned, heavy leather boots are still necessary for most snow travel and for cross-country travel over very rugged terrain. Rigid, plastic boots are appropriate for crampon use when climbing hard snow and ice (see Chapter 14, Winter Mountaineering, *Clothing and Equipment*).

For any use, though, the primary consideration is fit. The latest technology is useless if the boots hurt your feet. Shop very carefully at a store with a knowledgeable staff. Try on several pairs, and accept none if you have any doubts. If you are shopping for other items in addition to boots, go to the footwear department first. When you think you have found the right pair, ask if you can wear the boots in the store while doing your other shopping. The extra time will allow you to better evaluate the fit.

Allow about a half-inch of extra toe room. You'll need that for steep downhill hiking when your foot slips forward inside the boot. The heel cup should slide up and down no more than a quarter-inch with each step. Bring your own thick socks to the fitting (although good stores have extras for your use). If you normally use orthotics or special pads in your shoes, bring them too.

Regarding women's boots, the first thing to know is that the majority of boots manufactured are patterned on men's "lasts," or models of the foot. More and more companies, however, offer boots designed on women's lasts, which are typically narrower, especially in the heel. A snug heel will prevent your foot from sliding around in the boot and causing blisters. When shopping for boots, ask the clerk which brands have women's lasts. Don't let anyone suggest you can adapt your feet to men's boots by lacing the boots tightly or adding extra socks.

No boot can be expected to fit perfectly, so consider these possibilities:

- Will the boot stretch as it "breaks in," or will your foot "break down?" (Note: For leather boots you can wet your socks, wring them out, and then wear them inside your boots as you walk. This may help soften the boot and improve the fit.)
- Can the boot be stretched mechanically in the toe or heel cup areas to improve the fit? (Can you locate a cobbler who will do this?)
- Can the heel cup be padded with glue-in pads to reduce heel slippage?
- Can cushioned insoles be added to the boot to make a thin, hard sole more tolerable? (They may make boots feel narrower, however.)

If nothing works, you can always purchase custom-made boots. Look in outdoor magazines for boot-maker ads.

Ask about resoling before you buy. Even the most durable soles wear out with time, often well before the boot upper is significantly worn. Some boots can live as many as three lives—at a rather modest additional cost—with resoling. Inexpensive boots, however, may be worth less than the cost of a resoling.

Most leather boot uppers deserve a periodic treatment with a beeswax-based boot seal. First, warm the wax and boots to about 120° F. You can do this in a prewarmed (not hot) oven, or outside in the sun on a hot day, or with the use of a hair dryer. Brush on the melted wax until it no longer soaks in. This treatment will keep the leather supple and enhance the boots' ability to repel snow and water. Don't use silicone or petroleum products on your boots. They can dissolve the glue that bonds the sole.

Any pair of boots benefits from an optimum combination of socks. Start with lightweight polypropylene, which keeps moisture away from your feet, and use thick wool as your outer layer. Avoid cotton socks—they trap moisture. In general, two thinner socks used together work better than a single thick one. You may need to add an intermediate layer, or use thicker socks, as your boots stretch with age.

Keeping your feet warm in cold conditions is more a measure of how you enclose them than a measure of your boot's weight. You need full circulation to keep your feet warm, so don't pinch your feet by wearing too many socks or by over-tightening bootlaces. In subfreezing conditions, vapor barriers (moisture-impervious layers) worn close to your feet can be very effective. A vapor barrier, which can be as simple as a plastic bread bag, worn outside a thin polypropylene sock keeps foot perspiration from reaching the outer, insulating wool sock layer. Gaiters, which are designed to keep snow out of boots, also serve to insulate the ankle area. Even when there is no snow, gaiters are useful in keeping sand and dirt out of boots.

APPAREL

Your clothes must shelter your body from sun, wind, rain, and cold—sometimes all in the same day! Each clothing article must continue to function, wet or dry. As you travel, body heat and water vapor (perspiration) must be allowed to escape, while wind and rain are repelled.

Almost every year, clothing and fabric manufacturers introduce new high-tech gear and claim everything else is obsolete. Sales clerks and colorful ads push you to spend a fortune on fabrics that wick, breathe, repel, vent, warm, cool, and, of course, flatter. The sad truth, however, is that even the best garment can perform well only in a limited range of conditions.

The well-equipped wilderness traveler must assemble a lightweight, compact outfit that will do the job, rain or shine. This is done most effectively through the "layering system" (fig. 5-4). That is, each item of clothing should work well with any combination of the others, so that you can quickly adapt to the demands of the environment (or your own heat output) by adding and subtracting layers of clothing. In general, women have a smaller mass and therefore less "heat capacity" (ability to store heat) than men. As a result, some women have difficulty keeping warm in cold weather. This means that careful attention to clothing and dressing in layers is very important. Ideally, you need only adjust the outer layer, but at times even the inner layer must be changed. Using thermal underwear, long pants under regular shorts, and windproof rain pants can keep you as warm as heavier pants. Combining them eliminates the need for carrying another pair of pants. Until you have a system that works for you, be a real busybody and ask experienced hikers for their tips.

Outer layers require different kinds of materials than inner layers, so let's now examine the choices available:

Cotton and silk are great for comfort and fine in warm weather, but are not recommended for most cold-weather conditions. These materials absorb water readily. When wet, cotton is cold and slow to dry. Combine cold with wet conditions, and it is deadly. Blue jeans seem ideal for outdoor use—and so they are for dealing with bucking horses and brambles. But jeans, and other heavy cotton items like sweat shirts, rapidly drain your body heat when the weather turns soggy. On warm, dry days, though, thin, light-colored cotton shorts, shirts, and bandannas can keep you comfortably cool.

Wool, polypropylene, and polyester pile make good insulating garments. They retain much of their insulating ability even when wet. Wool can retain as much as 30 percent of its dry weight and is slow to dry. Oiled wool garments absorb less moisture. Synthetics absorb almost no moisture into the fibers and are easier to wring out in case they do get wet.

Down, typically the inner feathers of geese, is a very effective insulator when dry, but completely useless if wet. It is a poor choice for cold and wet conditions.

Water- and wind-impervious materials, including Gore-Tex, have revolutionized the construction of outerwear. These materials contain a thin membrane perforated with tiny pores. In theory, the pores allow water vapor (from perspiration) to pass but resist the passage of liquid water. Unfortunately, the amount of water vapor these materials can pass is about the same amount as that exuded by a person at rest. With increasing activity or in wet conditions, additional venting is needed. Water-impervious materials cost more, may weigh more, and are bulkier than a cheaper alternative—coated nylon (nylon material coated with a waterproof, nonbreathable plastic). Uncoated nylon is very breathable and blocks the wind, but is not waterproof. Surface treatments improve water repellency but must be renewed.

Vapor-barrier materials (like thin plastic) worn close to the skin in very cold conditions may prevent your skin from perspiring excessively. Human skin exudes water vapor not only to cool but also to maintain a moist layer of air just above the skin. Without the barrier, this water vapor moves outward, where it may condense on the outer layers of your clothing.

With the barrier in place, humid air is kept close to the skin, so the skin no longer needs to keep pumping out moisture (and heat). Vapor barriers that cover a large part of the body are practical only when you're relatively inactive.

When building your layering system for active sports in cold weather, consider the following:

First layer. The purpose of this layer is for comfort and insulation. This layer is normally long underwear, preferably made of polypropylene or polyester. Wool, silk, and cotton are not comfortable and do not insulate when wet. Polypropylene has proven itself very effective over the years, but some prefer polyester. Polyester is more expensive, is less durable, and has the advantage of staying a little fresher (for the nose at least). For most activities, thin underwear is more versatile than medium or expedition weights. If needed for extreme cold, a vapor barrier can be added on top of the long underwear. Adjustable ventilation is extremely important for any vapor barrier used when you are physically active.

Middle layer(s). While the inner layer keeps the skin comfortable, the middle layer provides the bulk insulation needed

Fig. 5-4. The layering system

to protect against the cold. On a trip you may have to adjust the ventilation to this layer a lot as the temperature rises and falls and your activity waxes and wanes. Pile pants and jacket together can offer effective insulation at a weight of only three pounds. For lighter duty, expedition-weight long underwear might suffice (about one pound total). Quilted down or synthetic-fill vests or jackets can be used, but quite often these garments include a heavy shell as well—that cuts down on your versatility. Remember that down fails if it gets wet and is very slow to dry out. Wool sweaters are effective, but they get heavy when wet and are slow to dry out.

Outer layer. Under adverse weather conditions, this layer is supremely important. The outer shell of your layering system blocks wind, sheds rain, and repels snow. Adequate ventilation (like zippered openings) must be provided so that plenty of air can reach the middle insulating layer when needed. The fit should be loose to allow room for the inner layers. Coated nylon is relatively cheap and very effective in shedding rain, but requires full-length zippers to ventilate. In addition, some coatings will survive only a few machine washings. A low-cost outer-shell system could consist of wind-repellent (uncoated) nylon pants and windbreaker, plus a two-piece coated-nylon rain suit. Use the coated garments over the uncoated ones in bad weather. (Under warmer storm conditions, you could use the coated layer alone.) For adequate ventilation, the coated pants should have full-length side zippers and the jacket should have full-front zippers. Underarm zippers may help, but you'll find it's your back that perspires the most. A more expensive (but heavier and bulkier) solution, a parka made of Gore-Tex or similar material, can keep you a little drier and more comfortable, but still requires fully adjustable ventilation. When backpacking with a bulky pack, a coated-nylon poncho is sometimes the best

solution for rain protection. Ponchos can act like sails in a wind, but you can install and fasten snaps along the edge of the poncho to run a tighter ship. Rain chaps used with the poncho can keep your legs dry. Shop carefully for your outer garments; some rain and wind shells contain too many pockets, extras, or styling features that simply add to the weight of what should be a lightweight, functional article of clothing. Remember, too, that some outer garments may need to be seam-sealed. Give extra attention to seams around the pockets, zipper, and hood, which usually have no sealant applied at the factory.

Small men and women are faced with the challenge of finding smaller sizes of thermal underwear, rain gear, and even shorts suitable for outdoor use. Outdoor shops usually do not stock a wide variety of small sizes, since the demand is relatively low. Don't give up, though. Sizings are often notoriously inconsistent. If there's nothing suitable, then talk to the store's buyer about placing a special order. A competent buyer will know which manufacturers offer extra-small clothing and gear. Be prepared to wait some time for your special order. Think twice about accepting a child's size as a substitute. Children's clothing is often made of lighter-weight material.

In addition to the above layers, you'll need protection for your head and hands.

Headwear. Did you ever hear the maxim, "If your feet are cold, cover your head"? It's true; in fact, the whole body benefits when you plug the torrent of heat that leaks skyward from the blood-rich vessels of the head. Under very cold conditions, you can use a layer system here as well. A lightweight balaclava folded down over your mouth allows you to recycle warm moisture from your breath. A second hat or knitted cap adds middle-layer insulation. The outer layer is simply the hood of your parka or other shell. It should have enough of a brim (or wear a visor underneath) to keep rain off your face. Pulling the drawstring narrows the opening to the face, helping to prevent heat loss. Taking off headwear is the fastest way to cool off if the weather warms. You'll want to do that first before shedding other layers. When the sun shines brightly, however, don't forget to put some kind of hat back on to protect from the sun's radiation. A bandanna under your hat shades your neck and ears.

Handwear. Most knitted gloves and mittens suffice for cold, dry conditions (mittens are warmer than gloves). Wet conditions, though, are really a test for handwear. When you're active, water can easily be soaked up by mittens, but not enough body heat is delivered to your hands to evaporate it. Waterproof mitten shells are a first defense (don't forget to seal the seams). Inside that, thick wool or pile mitts provide insulation. You may also want to have a thin pair of liner gloves for tasks that require some dexterity. You can try vapor-barrier protection as well. Plastic bags or disposable rubber gloves work well—you'll be surprised at the difference they can make. Gloves and mittens are items easily lost on trips. The almost negligible weight of a lightweight extra pair is good insurance. Chemical hand-warmer packets help prevent frostbite.

TENTS

Sleeping under the stars on a clear, bug-free night is a glorious experience. But when there's wind, snow, rain, or annoying insects, a tent can be most welcome. In extreme situations, your survival may depend on a sturdy tent. One that's large enough to hold packs as well as people is convenient, but obviously heavier and more expensive. For tents, especially, you'll have to balance the comfort of using a bigger model against the discomfort of carrying it.

Tent costs vary dramatically, and generally you get what you pay for. Cost is based on materials, quality of construction, design, features, and options. When shopping for a tent, consider the following features and options:

- weight and size
- ease of setup
- freestanding ability
- ease of entry and exit
- ventilation
- doors, windows, bug screening, and storm flaps
- vestibule for cooking
- flashlight loops and pockets

Freestanding tents weigh more than tents that need to be staked out, but they can be set up almost anywhere. (Be sure your tent is staked anyway. A sudden wind could blow your unstaked tent into a lake or over a cliff.) Dome tents tend to give with the wind and can withstand strong winds if they are anchored properly. A double-wall design with a full-coverage rain fly (waterproof outer shell) repels rain and also helps keep condensation from accumulating on the inner tent walls. Flat tent walls tend to flap in the wind more than curved walls. Tents with a vestibule or awnings keep raindrops from blowing in through the tent door or windows, and provide a place to cook in bad weather. Almost all tents need to be seam-sealed before use. Don't forget to buy the seam-sealer if it doesn't come with the tent. When comparing manufacturers' specifications, determine if the specified weights include the stakes, stuff sack, and ground cloth.

Always set up your new tent at home before heading out. A missing or broken pole could totally disable a tent, and you won't want to spend half an hour reading the directions in camp anyway. A lightweight ground cloth made of synthetic material helps protect the bottom of the tent from punctures, dirt, and condensation during the night. You should fold or cut the ground cloth to the tent's shape so it doesn't channel rainwater underneath the tent.

SLEEPING GEAR

Your sleeping bag and your ground pad are not a substitute for your bed at home. It may take getting used to what is "comfort" on the trail. Your tent doesn't have a thermostat, so you must rely on a good sleeping bag and sleeping pad. You can also keep warmer by wearing a cap when you sleep, drinking warm beverages before going to bed, and/or taking a moonlight hike to get your circulation moving before you go to sleep. A few restless or chilly nights are normal until you discover the right combination of clothing, keepwarm routines, and sleeping equipment.

SLEEPING BAGS

Don't scrimp on this one. Buy a reputable brand with a lifetime guarantee— your bag could last the rest of your life, with moderate use and proper care.

The warmth of a bag depends primarily on the amount of "loft"—the thickness of the insulating layer. The more dead (nonmoving) air there is between you and the environment, the warmer the bag seems. Another factor is the style (shape) of the bag. Most efficient are close-fitting bags that don't permit your body heat to bypass the insulation between you and the cold environment.

Sleeping bag choices for smaller people may be quite limited. Even so, it's important to get a short bag for two reasons— less weight and more warmth. In an overly long bag, you'll have more trouble keeping your feet warm. Children's bags probably won't be a very good solution. They're usually too narrow at the hips, and don't offer the features or quality of an adult bag.

Different styles of baffles—compartments that hold the insulating fill—are available. Their purpose is to distribute the fill evenly. From a practical point of view, there's not too much difference among them. What matters is that you avoid a quilted bag that is stitched straight through the top and bottom layers, because it lets warm air escape (and cold air in).

Mummy bags are the lightest and warmest style. Rectangular bags weigh more but offer more foot room (nice for the warm-blooded). (See fig. 5-5.) They're also roomier when two bags are zipped together (or when one bag and a ground sheet are used) for a twosome. Bags used in this fashion must have mating zippers.

Common sleeping bag features include a contoured hood with a drawstring to keep the head warm, a filled "draft collar" that helps keep the shoulders and neck warm, and a "draft tube" over the zipper to prevent leakage of body heat there.

Summer-weight bags are rated (in Fahrenheit) from 40° down to 20°, three-season bags are rated from 10° down to 0°, and winter bags are rated from −5° to as low as −50°. These ratings are of help in comparing bags, but may not guarantee your comfort at those particular temperatures. Outer bags and liner inserts are available to increase the warmth of any bag—not a bad way to go if you want a single bag to cover a broad range of seasonal conditions.

Bags filled with synthetic materials (such as Polarguard, Quallofil, and Hollofil) are heavier, less compressible, and more reliable than down-filled bags. Stuffing a synthetic-filled bag into a stuff sack, washing it, and exposing it to heat in a hot car or a dryer breaks down the fibers. Damaged fibers keep the bag from regaining its loft, and warmth depends on loft. Advantages of synthetic bags are their ability to insulate in case they get wet, and lower cost. Synthetic bags are great for extended winter trips, kayaking, and other outings where there's a likelihood of getting the bag damp.

Down bags are lighter and more compressible than synthetic bags. They are ser-

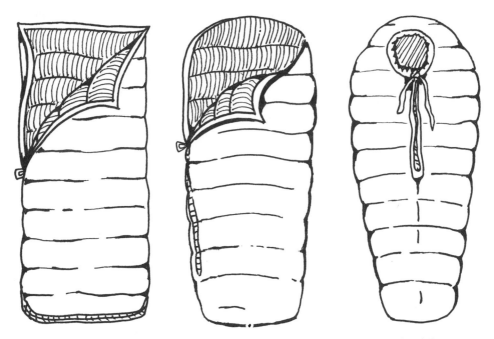

Fig. 5-5. Sleeping bags: Left, *rectangular style;* center, *semi-mummy style;* right, *mummy style.*

viceable over a wider temperature range, rejuvenate after laundering, and are very cozy and comfortable. They're more durable, but much more expensive. When wet, they're practically useless. Down is slow to dry. Gore-Tex shells or outer bags are available to protect them from dew or wind when sleeping without a tent. Down bags don't need to be cleaned very often, but when they do, they should be professionally laundered. Check with your local outdoor-equipment outfitter—it may offer this service.

A shell made of Gore-Tex or Texolite (a punctured aluminized mylar film) or other similar materials can be added to the bag's shell to add warmth and wind protection, but may also make it feel clammy in warm weather.

Here are some tips for getting the best performance out of any sleeping bag:

- Always fluff your bag before using it to get the maximum loft.

- A zipper that opens at both the top and bottom ends of the bag helps you cool off on warmer nights and helps ventilate perspiration.
- Perspiration often condenses on the fibers of the insulating fill during cold weather. Your bag may need some drying time during the day to keep from getting heavier and colder each succeeding night.
- At home, store your sleeping bag by hanging it in the closet; never keep it wadded up in a stuff sack. Make sure it's fully dry before putting it away in an unventilated place.

SLEEPING PADS

Sleeping pads are the foundation of your wilderness bed. No sleeping bag will keep you warm on a cold night unless you're thermally insulated from the ground. Thick pads have more insulating ability at the cost of greater weight, bulk, and expense. Short pads (48 inches long or so) are fine for summer camping if you don't mind sacrificing a little comfort, while the standard 72-inch ones are best for winter.

Closed-cell foam pads (fig. 5-6A) are excellent insulators, do not absorb water, and come in several varieties. Some have contours or ridges that help reduce weight while maintaining as much comfort as possible. In general, closed-cell foam pads are a good value in terms of providing excellent insulation for low cost and light weight. (Avoid open-cell foam pads like mattress cushions. They're good for car camping, but they're water-absorbent and too bulky for backpacking.)

Self-inflating pads (fig. 5-6B) are quite comfortable to sleep on, but more expensive and heavier than closed-cell foam pads of the same thickness. They require more care on the trail to prevent punctures and valve failures (repair kits are available). You can make them last for years if you use a ground cloth underneath them and avoid thorn punctures. The "superlight" 1-inch-thick models are more comfortable to sleep on than most closed-cell foam pads. The 1.5-inch-thick self-inflatable pad is positively blissful, allowing you to sleep

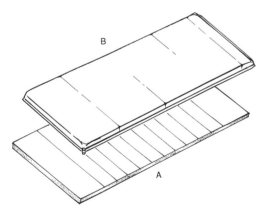

Fig. 5-6. Sleeping pads: A, *closed-cell foam;* B, *self-inflating.*

comfortably on your side. A 1.5-inch-thick pad is the recommended minimum self-inflating model for snow.

For additional sleeping comfort, you can put some extra clothing in your sleeping-bag stuff sack and place it under your knees when sleeping on your back, or under your abdomen when sleeping on your stomach. Any number of soft items can be used as a pillow. If you're using a short pad, place some clothing under your lower legs and feet for extra comfort and insulation.

STOVES AND COOKING EQUIPMENT

The simplest source of energy for cooking is, of course, a campfire. Even in areas where such fires are permitted, however, you will in most cases have a much easier time using a camping or backpacking stove. (If you do plan to use a campfire, you can find many cookbooks that discuss the use of grills and dutch ovens, and various open-fire cooking techniques.) A good selection of lightweight stoves and cookware can be found at most camp supply stores.

TYPES OF STOVES

When choosing a stove, consider first its performance under the conditions—temperature, wind, and elevation—you'll likely encounter during your trip. Also consider the stove's weight, ease of fueling and operation, reliability, and availability of the fuel it uses. To help you choose the right stove, talk to people who use them and to salespeople at camp supply stores. Several outdoor magazines have published comparative information about stoves and reviews of new models. Stoves can be classified by the types of fuel they burn.

Liquid fuel. These stoves burn kerosene, white gas (Coleman fuel), unleaded gasoline, and alcohol. In most cases, the fuel reservoir must be pressurized (with a small air pump) and the liquid fuel must be heated in the vicinity of the burner so it can be vaporized for combustion. The start-up procedure, known as "priming the stove," can be quite a ritual for some models.

Liquid-fuel stoves are economical to operate and have a high heat output. Most are designed to run on white gas, but a few stoves utilize two or three different types of fuel (white gas, kerosene, unleaded gasoline). That is a good feature if you're traveling to a foreign country where kerosene is available but white gas is not. *White gas* is very flammable (which is why it's a good stove fuel), burns cleanly, and evaporates quickly when spilled. *Kerosene* is less volatile than white gas, and slower to ignite and evaporate, but has more heat per volume of fuel. It has a greasy feel, a lasting odor, and a tendency to give off smoke and soot when burning. *Unleaded gasoline* is listed as usable by some stove manufacturers. *Alcohol* is safe to use as a stove fuel and is usually contained in a cup under the stove. When the alcohol is ignited, the surface layer burns and the heat is regulated by a lever that allows more or less air into the cup. Alcohol burns clean, but has the lowest heat output and the highest cost of all the liquid fuels. Cooking a meal seems to take forever. Stoves that burn alcohol appear to be on the decline.

Extra fuel outside of any liquid-fuel stove tank should be carried in special fuel bottles with tight-fitting caps and special seals. For some models of liquid-fuel stoves, the tank is an integral part of the stove, while for others the stove has no tank but is designed to be connected to a fuel bottle. Some stoves have small tanks (you hope you can finish cooking dinner before running out of gas), while others will run full blast for more than 3 hours. Some operate nicely over the entire range from simmer to full heat, while others perform best when operating like (and sounding like) a hissing blowtorch.

Canister fuel. These stoves (fig. 5-7) burn propane, butane, a propane/butane mix, or isobutane, all of which are gases at normal temperatures and pressures. Be-

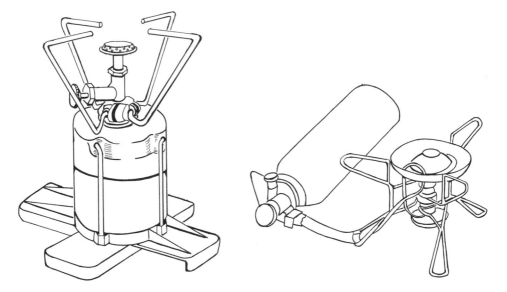

Fig. 5-7. Left, *an example of a canister stove;* right, *a liquid fuel stove. The canister for the stove on the left must remain attached until empty.*

fore use, the burner of the stove is attached to a non-reusable metal canister that holds the fuel. The fuel inside the canister is pressurized, which keeps the gas in a liquid state. It is hard to tell how much fuel is left in a canister (especially from one trip to the next), so you must carry one or more spare cans, depending on the length of your trip. Propane canisters are heavier than butane canisters. Butane, however, must be warmed to operate at cold temperatures. Some canisters have a built-in valve that allows for detachment from the burner between uses, while other types are punctured upon installation and must remain attached to the burner until empty. (Spent canisters, of course, must be packed out as trash.)

Canister-stove use is quite simple—just light a match and open the single valve. To simmer, close down the valve part of the way. These stoves have less heat output than white gas or kerosene stoves and cost more to operate, but are always easy to use.

Solid fuel. Solid fuels include jellied alcohol (Sterno), heat tablets, and charcoal. These fuels are very safe to handle, but all have a low heat output. Stoves using these fuels are of limited use in the wilderness.

Stove stability varies quite a bit among models. The bottom of the stove or the breadth of its tripod legs (its "footprint") determines how stable the stove will be on the ground. Generally, the larger the footprint, the more stable the stove. It is also important to pay attention to the method by which cookware is supported on top of the stove.

Many stoves feature a windscreen that is either part of the stove or an accessory. Some cookware sets are designed to seat into certain windscreens to improve stability and performance. A windscreen, however, should never allow the fuel tank to overheat. Because all stoves are very sensitive to winds, a windscreen should

be considered a mandatory piece of stove equipment.

Stoves that disassemble for transport—such as the MSR brand liquid-fuel stove—must be protected from dirt. Any dirt that enters the pump body or fuel tube will clog the small orifice that helps vaporize the fuel. The use of a cleaning needle may just push dirt particles around. A dirt-clogged burner must be carefully disassembled to clean it well. To avoid complications, always keep the pump body in a clean plastic bag. Never leave it unprotected on your fuel bottle. The end of the fuel tube should be capped securely with a rubber eye-dropper bulb. One-piece stoves with built-in cleaning needles—such as the Coleman Peak 1—may be heavier, but often are more reliable.

USE OF STOVES

All stoves must be considered dangerous, but with a little knowledge and common sense, it is possible to minimize this danger. The most important thing to do is understand how your stove works—read the instruction manual. Some models have instructions printed on the stove itself. Test the stove's operation at home (outside) to see that it works properly before taking it on a trip. The following are some precautions and tips for fueling a stove:

- Never refuel a liquid-fuel stove when the stove is hot.
- Use care when pouring liquid fuel into the stove. Use a small funnel or a pouring cap and add fuel slowly. Check the level in the tank and don't overfill. A filter funnel helps keep the fuel inside your stove clean.
- Leave a little air space above the fuel for stoves that need pumping.
- Refuel away from flame sources.
- Don't pour fuel inside a tent.
- Check the fuel level before starting to cook a meal to ensure that the stove doesn't run out of fuel while you're cooking.

Know how to operate your stove before setting out into the wilderness. (Photo by James Glenn Pearson)

- Replace the cap on both the fuel bottle and the stove before lighting the stove.
- When attaching a canister to a canister-type stove, be careful. The screw threads should be easy to turn (don't cross-thread the fittings) and the gasket surfaces must be clean.
- After the canister is attached, make sure it doesn't leak (listen for a hissing noise). Make sure the on-off valve is closed and the canister is tightly attached.
- Puncture-type canisters must not be removed unless empty.
- Never throw an "empty" canister into a fire. It might not be empty!

Operating a stove can be simple and easy, but hazardous if not done properly. By observing these guidelines, you can prevent accidents and end up with a warm meal:

- Avoid cooking inside a tent. A burning stove consumes oxygen and gives off deadly carbon monoxide gas. If you are forced to cook inside, open the door flap and vents to let plenty of fresh air inside. Some tents have a covered vestibule that can be used when cooking. If possible, prime and light the stove outside and carefully bring it in after the stove is operating properly. Caution: many stove bases get hot enough to melt nylon. They also frequently flare up when being lit.
- Make sure that the stove is in a safe place and is on a stable, level surface.
- Place a pan on the stove to make sure everything is stable enough before lighting the stove.
- For canister stoves, light the match and hold it next to the burner before turning on the gas.
- Do not leave a stove unattended while it is burning.
- When cooking on snow, insulate the stove from the snow with a piece of cardboard, wood, or foam, or with a pan lid.

55

- If the stove has a removable key that operates the flame adjustment, remove it during stove operation.
- Carry spare parts, tools, cleaning needles, and instructions on how to repair your stove. Clean orifice openings regularly.

COOKWARE

Economize, but don't skimp on your cookware and utensils. One pot and perhaps a small water kettle may suffice for one or two people, but fancier meals may require the use of two pots. Most backpacking pots are made of aluminum or stainless steel, and some now come with a non-stick surface.

Some cook sets consist of two pots nestled together with handles that fold down, or no handles at all (a pan grip is used), and a lid that also serves as a fry pan. You can also modify ordinary pans by removing or shortening their handles.

It is very helpful to have your cookware marked with common intervals of volume measurement (1 cup, 2 cups, 3 cups, et cetera). If your pots are not already so marked, you can do it yourself with a hammer and screwdriver.

If you're cooking alone, one spoon can serve for both cooking and eating. In a group, you'll need separate utensils. Be careful when cooking with a metal spoon—don't leave it in the pot when you're cooking or you may burn your fingers. Other common cooking utensils include a spatula and a knife (a pocketknife often suffices).

The stainless steel "Sierra Cup" has been popular with backpackers for years. It is easy to clean; however, it can burn your lips when you drink freshly poured hot liquids, and it allows liquids to cool down too quickly in cold temperatures. An insulated plastic cup, with or without a lid, is easier to use for drinking and keeps your beverage or soup hot for a longer period of time. Some plastic cups with volume markings can double as measuring cups.

If you're cooking only for yourself, you can simply eat from the pot or pan. Otherwise, each person will need a bowl or plate to eat from. A divided plate works well if your menu calls for more than a one-pot meal. As a minimum for utensils, use a pocketknife for cutting food and a spoon for eating. A fork is nice, but not necessary.

Here are a few other useful items: Wide-mouth plastic bottles marked at 1/4-cup intervals are handy for mixing beverages, pancake batter, and pudding. A small wire whip takes the place of your mixer back home for combining dry ingredients with liquids. Don't forget a small can opener (if you have cans), a measuring cup (if nothing else you have measures volume), aluminum foil (for a variety of uses), and a wooden spoon. A bandanna can serve as a mini-tablecloth, dish towel, hot pad, and more. For cleaning up, you'll need a pot scrubber. Some people just use very hot water without soap for washing dishes, but if your food is particularly greasy, you may want to use biodegradable soap.

PACKS

The last "S" in ESSENTIALS refers to packs ("something to carry all of it in"). There are numerous options for the wilderness traveler:

- fanny pack (it's compact, but often too small for even the essentials)
- small day pack (for short hikes)
- full day pack (for longer hikes)
- extra-large day pack (sometimes called a "day-and-a-half pack")
- external-frame backpack
- internal-frame backpack

For the moment, we'll restrict our discussion to the latter two on the above list. The backpack you choose greatly affects how much you enjoy the sport. Fit and style are as personal as with a pair of shoes. What works great for one person may not work for you. Another person's reject may be just what you need, so you decide.

Correct fit is important. Never buy a pack without trying it (or a similar rental) first, preferably on an overnight trip. Select the right size for your body frame, load it up with enough weight of any kind, and walk, climb up and down, tip, turn, and twist. You've found a winner if the pack feels like an extension of your body, moves with you, doesn't poke or gouge, and doesn't make you gasp for joy when you take it off. After prolonged use, you shouldn't have excessively sore spots on the collar, hips, or elsewhere.

When you try out a backpack, realize that the perceived load may vary by as much as ten pounds, depending on how you distribute items inside. Place the heaviest items such as water at shoulder-blade height, close to your back. Don't hang anything out from the back of the pack. Adjust the waist and shoulder straps to distribute weight more or less evenly between shoulders and hips. Other desirable features include padded shoulder straps, a padded waist or hip belt, and a sternum strap (this is tightened across your chest to relieve pressure on your shoulders). Packs tend to leak through the seams and sometimes the material itself, so you may want to buy a waterproof pack cover and/or waterproof stuff sacks to protect your gear.

Internal- and external-frame backpacks (fig. 5-8) are quite different from each other. Internal-frame packs have vertical stays (curved, rigid structural members) inside the pack sack. Internals are relatively compact and fit snugly against your body. They're designed to hold sleeping bags, and sometimes tents and pads, inside. Adjustable straps compress the load and keep it from shifting. For most people, internal-frame models feel more balanced. When you step over boulders, traverse ledges, cross streams, and dodge brush, internal-frame packs move with you, helping you maintain your balance and pace. Drawbacks include generally higher cost, more difficulty in getting at your gear (in top-loading models, particularly), and less air circulation for your back. Internal-frame packs are currently soaring in popularity.

The rigid, exposed frame structure on an external-frame pack keeps the load a few inches away from your body, allowing more air circulation. These packs have fewer adjustments. Sleeping bag, pad, and tent strap onto areas provided for them on the frame, and most other gear fits inside

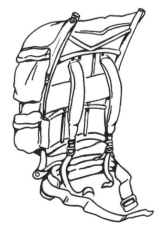

Fig. 5-8. Frame packs: left, *internal-frame;* right, *external-frame.*

the pack's many pockets. Some have a rigid, metal hip support as part of their suspension system. External-frame packs are easier to load and may handle heavy loads (50 pounds or more) better than most internal-frame packs. Unfortunately, they tend to move where inertia leads them, which may not be the direction you want to go. If heavily loaded, they can throw you off balance when you twist, turn, or lift. Gear strapped on the outside tends to snag on branches and rocks. Some models make it impossible for you to tilt your head back and look up. Most external packs are bulky—they can take up a lot of space in the trunk of a car.

As of this writing, manufacturers of both styles are working to blend together the best features of each. Newer internal-frame models have divided compartments for easier loading. They're now handling heavier loads with more comfort. The newer external-frame packs are becoming less boxy and more contoured to enhance stability, while maintaining their carrying volume.

For recreational (as opposed to expeditionary) backpacking, you'll need a pack capacity of 4,000 to 6,000 cubic inches in an internal-frame pack (which holds sleeping bag and possibly tent and pad) and 3,000 to 3,500 cubic inches in an external-frame pack. Don't be tempted to buy a too-large size (what you choose to put in your pack always seems to exceed the capacity anyway). Choose the size that would fit your needs most of the time. You can always use add-on pockets for additional space, or you can rent a pack for times when you require extra capacity.

If your search turns up more than one suitable model of backpack, consider individual characteristics or special features like pack weight, color, extra pockets, ice axe loops, tie-on patches, and versatility (some packs, for example, have top pockets that can be detached and used as a day or fanny pack).

Finally, once you've made your choice,

ask that your pack be fitted properly. The structural members of both internal- and external-frame packs should be carefully adjusted to fit the contours of your body.

Women choosing a backpack should consider the following: Most women need a pack frame that arches away from the head and buttocks. A pack designed for a man's slimmer hips and buttocks tends to tilt forward on a woman, bumping her in the head with each step. A pack designed for a woman is also shorter between the waist and shoulder, has contoured shoulder straps (to keep the pack riding closer to her narrower shoulders), and has a suspension that allows most of the weight to be carried on her hips. The last factor is important because it takes advantage of a woman's lower-body strength and relieves pressure on the shoulders. Most internal-frame packs are designed to do this.

Some backpack brands come in a variety of torso lengths. For women 5 feet-4 inches or shorter, ask for the shorter lengths. The challenge is to get a good fit for the smaller body size and still buy a backpack with a reasonable capacity. Pay attention to the loading style—some styles are more efficient than others.

Whether you day hike exclusively, or want to climb peaks and make side trips on backpack excursions, you'll need a small pack. With regular day packs, most weight is carried on the shoulders (waist belts and sternum straps are stabilizers); with fanny packs, the weight is on the hips. For a summit bid, you may need a pack holding as much as 2,000 cubic inches of necessary equipment such as rain gear, extra clothing, food, water, a first aid kit, and other essentials. On any pack, look for good construction, nonmetal zippers and fasteners (to reduce binding), padded straps, and reinforcements where the straps are sewn in. Cordura material and leather reinforcement make for a heavier but more durable pack. Compressibility is a very desirable feature if the smaller pack has to fit inside a backpack.

RECOMMENDED READING

The best way for you to keep current on equipment and manufacturers is to read equipment articles and reviews in outdoor magazines such as *Backpacker* or *Outside*. These are available on newsstands or by subscription. Back issues may be available at your local library. Hiking clubs may have publications with equipment articles as well.

For buying equipment locally, check your local telephone directory for backpacking, camping, and sports outfitting stores.

RESOURCES

MAIL-ORDER COMPANIES

Campmor, 810 Route 17 North, Paramus, NJ 07652-0997

Early Winters, P.O. Box 4333, Portland, OR 97208; 800-458-4438

Frostline Kits, 2525 River Road, Grand Junction, CO 81505; 800-548-7872

L. L. Bean, Freeport, ME 04033; 800-221-4221

Mountain Equipment Co-op, 1655 West Third Avenue, Vancouver, BC V6J 1K1, Canada

REI (Recreational Equipment, Inc.), Sumner, WA 98352-0001; 800-425-4840

PACK, APPAREL, AND EQUIPMENT MANUFACTURERS

Manufacturers listed below make a variety of styles for both the occasional and serious wilderness traveler. Their products are not necessarily endorsed by the authors and publishers of this book.

Black Diamond (mountaineering products), 2084 East 3900 South, Salt Lake City, UT 84124; 801-278-5533

Climb High (mountaineering products), 1861 Shelburne Road, Shelburne, VT 05482; 802-985-5056

Dana Design (packs), 1950 North 19th Avenue, Bozeman, MT 59715; 406-587-4188

Gregory Mountain Products (packs), 100 Calle Cortez, Temecula, CA 92390; 800-477-3420

JanSport (packs), 2425 West Packard Street, Appleton, WI 54914; 800-558-3600

Kelty Pack Inc. (packs), 1224 Fern Ridge Parkway, St. Louis, MO 63141; 800-423-2320

Lowe Alpine Systems, Inc. (packs), P.O. Box 1449, Broomfield, CO 80038; 303-465-3706

McHale and Co. (packs), 29 Dravus Street, Seattle, WA 98109; 206-281-7861

Moonstone Mountaineering (apparel), 5350 Erickson Way, Arcata, CA 95521; 707-822-2985

Mountain Equipment, Inc. (packs), 4776 East Jensen, Fresno, CA 93725; 800-634-7225

Mountainsmith, Inc. (packs), Heritage Square Bldg. P, Golden, CO 80401; 800-426-4075

The North Face, 999 Harrison Street, Berkeley, CA 94708; 415-526-3530

Simplicity is the answer to outdoor cooking questions. (Photo by Bob and Ira Spring)

CHAPTER 6

Foods and Cooking

Priscilla and Scott Anderson and Carolyn Wood

Old photographs of large group outings such as the Sierra Club or The Mountaineers show lots of people cooking great quantities of food in cauldrons, with wooden tables lined up and piled high with freshly baked bread, beneath giant trees.

John Muir, founder of the Sierra Club, wrote, "My meals were easily made, for they were all alike and simple, only a cup of tea and bread."

The choices of what you eat in the wilderness and how you prepare it have never been broader. You can emulate John Muir and yet subsist quite comfortably on a variety of uncooked foods. Or you can bring along a small camp stove, some lightweight cookware, and all the necessary ingredients to whip up a great feast at the end of each day.

NUTRITION BASICS

The number of calories you need depends on a variety of factors such as your physical size, your metabolism, the length of the trip, and the activities planned. For a short, leisurely trip you may only need to raise your caloric intake over the normal amount by 10 to 20 percent. For long, strenuous trips with a heavy pack, you may need 50 to 75 percent more calories. Uphill backpacking can burn 500 or more calories per hour.

Some people think backpacking is a good way to lose weight, or they may try fasting in the wilderness for health or spiritual benefits. If by traveling your body is demanding more calories, then the wilderness is not the place to cut back on food intake. This energy can come from body-fat reserves, but this is an inefficient and dangerously uncomfortable process. This is especially true if you're far from civilization. If an accident or delay occurs, lack of food or energy reserves could prove disastrous. There's nothing wrong with a low-calorie intake on layover days or days with moderate exercise, but eat heartily on the days your body requires extra energy. If you are on a low-calorie diet, don't stick to it while undergoing strenuous, long-duration exercise. If you're on a medically supervised liquid diet program, consult your physician to determine how to adjust your program. Don't use the wilderness for weight loss—do it at home.

If you know you have special nutritional requirements, take them into account. For instance, a pregnant woman may need to double her protein intake and increase her consumption of milk products. A person with diabetes may need to bring hard candy to be used for medical emergencies (see Chapter 15, Wilderness First Aid, *Diabetes*).

When out in the wilderness, it helps to be conscious of how carbohydrates, proteins, fats, and other nutrition components keep your body fortified.

Carbohydrates are the staple of a hiker's diet. They're easily digested and easily converted into muscle energy. They also keep well and are relatively inexpensive. The majority of your daily calories should come in the form of carbohydrates. They should be consumed frequently during the day to keep your energy level up.

Simple carbohydrates include sugar, honey, jams, candy, and refined flour products. Since they are metabolized quickly, they're most beneficial when consumed immediately before or during strenuous exercise, a small amount at a time. During larger meals, you can combine them with other foods.

Complex carbohydrates include whole-grain products, starchy vegetables, and beans. They keep the muscles working smoothly, give you energy, and provide bulk and fiber. They don't burn as fast as simple carbohydrates.

Proteins provide sustained energy, keep your muscles in good repair, and help keep you warm when you're not exercising. They are digested more slowly than carbohydrates but faster than fats. Common foods high in protein include meat, fish, beans, peas, cheese, milk, eggs, and nuts. Two to three ounces of protein are all you need each day.

Fats metabolize slowly, but yield more energy than either carbohydrates or proteins. When eaten at dinner, fats keep you from becoming hungry during the night and help you stay warm. In very cold weather or at times when food sources are at a minimum, your body relies on stored fat to survive. Increasing your fat consumption is desirable if you have to deal with very cold conditions. However, fats eaten in large quantities at high altitudes may cause indigestion. Good sources of fat include butter, margarine, nuts, cheese, meat fat, and oil. Under normal conditions, less than 25 percent of your daily calories should be from fats.

Vitamins and minerals enable your body to make the best use of the food you eat. By eating a variety of foods, you should get all the vitamins and minerals your body requires. If you are uncertain, you may want to take vitamin and mineral supplements.

Certain minerals (particularly sodium and potassium) are lost through perspiration during strenuous exercise. You can replenish them through your food or by drinking beverages designed to meet this need (see the information on fluids, below). Foods high in sodium include salt, soy sauce, cottage cheese, tomato juice, and cheddar cheese. Foods high in potassium include beans, spinach, raisins, potatoes, oranges, bananas, and milk.

Fiber in foods is important because it helps keep your bodily functions regular. Fiber is found in whole grains, fruits, and vegetables.

Fluid intake can become critically important when you're engaged in strenuous exercise. Most of us have experienced the discomforts of "cotton-mouth," dizziness, weakness, and headaches when exercising heavily on hot days. These conditions are symptoms of dehydration—the loss of water and minerals from the body, mostly through perspiration. It is very important that lost body fluids be replaced by drinking water or other fluids and by eating sodium-rich and potassium-rich foods. Sport or activity drink mixes (Gatorade, ERG, and other brands) containing simple forms of sugar and minerals (also called electrolytes) can be used. They can be purchased at camp supply stores and grocery stores. Check the labels to be sure you're getting what you need rather than just flavorings.

Before you start your hike, be sure to "fill up" with fluids and keep drinking throughout the day. Drinking smaller amounts at frequent intervals is better than one long gulping session. In general, you should consume one gallon of water or other fluids per day. In the desert you may need much more, and in cool or wet conditions you may need less. With experience, you'll learn what your own body requires.

Alcohol is a fluid, but the effects of alcohol should be considered before consuming it on an outing. Taken in excess, it generates a feeling of warmth for a short time, but it actually promotes a net loss of heat in cold conditions. Alcohol impairs your judgment, balance, coordination, and awareness. It also dehydrates the body and decreases your appetite. These effects are multiplied at high altitude. Simply put, excessive alcohol consumption puts you at risk in an environment that magnifies mistakes and misjudgments.

When exercising strenuously for long periods of time, your muscles can only work effectively when your glycogen (internal energy) reserves are high. The best way to achieve this is with a steady intake of carbohydrates throughout the day. Three ounces of carbohydrates every 2 hours is sufficient for moderate exercise. Sport drinks can help provide additional glucose as well as water and electrolytes. When you're on the move, it's better to avoid high-fat snacks such as cheese, nuts, and chocolates. The energy required to digest them is too great, especially at high altitudes.

Even with frequent meals and snacks, your glycogen reserves can be somewhat depleted after a hard day. You can replenish them by eating plenty of carbohydrates during your evening meal. Foods like pasta fit the bill nicely. If you forget to eat frequently, or skip some meals, exhaustion may come within only a few hours. Recovery is slow. It usually takes more than 24 hours to restore your glycogen reserves if they get depleted.

TYPES OF FOOD

Deciding whether you should take fresh, frozen, dehydrated, freeze-dried, and/or canned foods depends on how many days you plan to travel and how much weight you want to carry. Your meals will be more appetizing if you incorporate all of these types of food.

Fresh and frozen foods are the healthiest foods you can bring, but most of them spoil easily and weigh a lot. They are great for weekend trips, but less practical for longer trips. Some homemade breads, energy bars, and cereal mixes will keep for days or weeks and also have high energy-to-weight ratios. By making your own foods in advance, you can control the ingredients, thus eliminating or reducing additives such as preservatives.

Canned foods expand your choices because they do not spoil. However, the weight of the packaging is a consideration on longer journeys (remember that you'll have to pack out the empty cans). Certain flavorful items that will enhance your versatility in meal planning are available in small cans.

Dehydrated and freeze-dried foods offer good alternatives for longer trips. They are widely available at grocery stores and camp supply stores, and by mail order. Some of these foods are laced with chemical additives, but some companies offer healthier alternatives. Dehydrated foods, especially specialty items, tend to be quite expensive.

Dehydrated food can be bought as prepackaged meals (turkey tetrazzini, beef almondine, et cetera) or as individual-item packages. As long as any dehydrated food is properly rehydrated, you can follow recipes as you normally would at home. A disadvantage of dehydrated foods is that some are slow to rehydrate. Pre-soaking helps, and aids digestibility. You can start the soaking process several hours before making camp by mixing the dehydrated food with cold water in a carefully sealed container or water bottle.

If you have the inclination, you can dehydrate your own food at home. The process is fairly simple and can be done in an oven, but better results are obtained from a food dehydrator. Commercial freeze-drying processes remove about 96 percent of the moisture, whereas home dehydration removes about 90 percent. That's not bad, considering the money you will save for the little time invested and the control you have over what goes into the food. Almost any kind of food can be dehydrated.

In some cases, foraging for wild foods can supplement your diet. However, this requires specialized knowledge of plants and their uses. Learning about non-poisonous and edible plants and gathering them in the right areas can add a new appreciation of nature's bounty and beauty. Foraging can be time-intensive, and you may not locate what you want when you want it. Always check with the local rangers first to see if harvesting wild plants is legal in the area you plan to visit. In many parks, cutting or picking any plant is illegal. Even if foraging is permitted in the area you're visiting, consider the effects of overharvesting and limit your gathering to what the environment can tolerate. If huge quantities of people visit an area, it likely cannot tolerate even minimal foraging, due to sheer numbers. Under no circumstances should you gather endangered or rare plants, nor should you gather plants for commercial sale.

Wild blueberries may look tempting, but before consuming any wild vegetation, be sure it has been correctly identified and is in abundant supply. (Photo by George Ostertag)

MENU PLANNING

Planning your meals can be time consuming until you develop a repertoire of recipes. It is important to create a menu and then check off each item as you purchase it and pack it. When formulating menus, you need to consider both nutritional value and weight. In addition to food for the regular meals and trailside snack breaks, plan to purchase some extra food for use during emergency situations. When planning meals, you'll need to consider equipment as well. You can't prepare 3 quarts of a one-pot meal in a 2.5 quart pot! And you won't want to place a massive kettle with a meal for a large group on a tiny Svea stove.

WHAT TO TAKE

When trying to decide which foods to take, consider the length of your trip, the expected climate, the size of your cooking group, meal preparation time, food variety and taste, and the cost.

On weekend trips, you can eat almost anything. Nutrition is not a major concern, except that you must take in enough calories to cover your energy expenditures. Trips longer than three days require more planning regarding nutrition and weight. One and a half pounds of dry weight per person per day is usually enough. However, as you gain experience and tackle more strenuous trips, your nutrition requirements will change. With experience, you will learn what your body requires.

Be sure to study a map of the area where you intend to camp. Know where water supplies are located. Determine whether you'll have to make do with one or more "dry camps." An important factor affecting your selection of food is the amount of water you'll have to carry, since water is heavy and bulky. One gallon of water weighs 8.3 pounds.

Heat reduces your appetite but increases your water needs. Cold increases your need for more calories. When exposed to cold, it's a good idea to eat small carbohydrate snacks frequently. You'll need the extra, quick energy. Hot foods and liquids are more appetizing in cold conditions, and help you stay warm. Never underestimate your needs for food and water. Carrying a few extra pounds is far better than suffering dehydration or hypothermia.

Striving for well-balanced meals should give you plenty of variety. Longer trips require more variety to meet your taste desires and to ensure that your nutritional needs are met. Failure to meet these needs could result in a loss of appetite and possibly a debilitating weakening of the body.

Keeping costs down is another consideration when preparing a trip menu. Perhaps you would put this high on your importance list, but food cost should never be the primary factor in choosing what is right for a trip. If a trip requires a great expense, you should consider whether or not you should go, not how little food you can bring to survive.

SHARED MENUS

Forming a cook group of people who share the same menu cuts down on the amount of weight carried. There's less duplication of cooking equipment, and the weight of the food and equipment is distributed among those who carry it. Cook groups of three or four people work quite well, as many prepackaged meals are designed for four servings. With a large group, consider arranging a group commissary ("central commissary") in which two stoves and two large pots serve up to about fifteen people, and cooking and clean-up chores are rotated among the members of the group.

EATING STYLES

Depending on your preference, meals can be quick and require minimum preparation, allowing maximum time on the trail. Or meals can be more elaborate, with substantial time required for preparation and cleanup. On a longer trip, you may want at least one such meal, where leisurely enjoyment of a major meal is a welcome break from many short "snacks" during long days of hiking.

If you need to get an early start on a given day, keep some breakfast flakes or instant cereal and powdered milk handy in a plastic bag while you start your hike. During your first break, add water to the

Day	Breakfast	Lunch	Dinner	Snacks/Misc
Friday	(Home)			
Saturday				
Sunday				
Monday				
Tuesday			(Home)	

Fig. 6-1. Sample chart for meal planning

cereal and powder and have a quick meal before continuing. High-carbohydrate snacks every hour should keep the furnace burning. If you return to camp late in the day, hot soup and a dehydrated meal are quick and easy.

If your plans are more leisurely, you could enjoy a more elaborate breakfast such as eggs, pancakes, sausage, and biscuits, which take time to prepare and to clean up. A day hike could start at midmorning and you could return by midafternoon. Dinner could be a multicourse meal with salad or soup, a main course of fresh fish and vegetables, and dessert, with time to clean up and relax before going to bed.

Neither type of meal, or variations in between, is better than the other—it's a matter of choice, and you can do both on the same trip. Remember that advance preparation at home can save hours out in the wilderness, where you will lack the conveniences of a modern kitchen.

TYPES OF MEALS

To simplify your menu planning, you can create a chart, such as the one shown in fig. 6-1, which includes the trip days,

the meals required for each day, and space for foods for each meal to be listed in the gridboxes.

A substantial *breakfast* is important. It gives you much of the energy you'll need for the first half of your day's activity. Generally, this meal should consist of carbohydrates (both simple and complex) to get you going and some protein or fat to help sustain you for several hours.

Because time may be limited in the middle of the day, you may decide to base your *midday meal* on whole-grain breads or crackers with spreads such as jam, honey, and peanut butter. Lunch may not be a "square meal," but instead intermittent snacking on high-carbohydrate, low-protein, low-fat foods that digest quickly. A common trail snack is GORP, which stands for "good ol' raisins and peanuts." Today, GORP (or trail mix) comes in a variety of combinations of nuts, seeds, small crackers, dried fruits, and candies. Most prepackaged trail mixes are loaded with fats. You may wish to create your own combinations.

Dinner should include carbohydrates, protein, and fats. There's ample time for your body to properly digest all of them.

	Day 1	Day 2
Breakfast	Oatmeal with fruit Milk Coffee	Western omelet Fruit juice Hot cocoa
Lunch	Jerky Crackers with honey Dried fruit	Bagel Low-fat cream cheese Granola bar
Dinner	Tomato soup Chicken a la king Roll Chocolate pudding	Beef stew Crackers Fruit cobbler

Fig. 6-2. Sample menu

Trail shelters can be found in some rainy regions. (Photo by George Ostertag)

This is also the time to replenish the salts and liquids you have lost during the day. Start your dinner with a hot beverage or soup (unless it's a warm evening, in which case something cool might be more refreshing). To conserve fuel and save time, try "one-pot" meals. The use of spices and seasonings can enhance the flavor of many prepackaged meals. A shake of curry livens up a rice dish. Add onion flakes to your stew. Sprinkle a little sage and basil in the butter or oil before cooking your freshly caught trout. Last, but not least, top the meal off with a satisfying dessert and enjoy a social gathering around the campfire.

Your menu should also include *extra foods* that could see you through an emergency situation. Take foods that keep well and need little or no cooking, in case you run out of fuel. Your emergency supplies might include jerky, granola bars, trail mixes, dried fruits, and additional dehydrated, prepackaged meals. Don't pack foods that are too tasty, or you may be tempted to dig into them unnecessarily. Wrap the food up tightly, store it in the bottom of your bag, and forget about it. You can use the same batch of emergency food for multiple trips, as long as it remains fresh enough.

SHOPPING AND PACKAGING

Once you have planned your meals, create a shopping list of needed foods. Check each item off as you get it, and again as you pack it for the trip. There are a variety of places you can shop: supermarkets, natural food stores, camping stores, ethnic food stores, and mail-order catalogs. Camping stores and mail-order catalogs are a good source for dehydrated foods and meals.

Packing foods takes time. You can't start randomly stuffing food items into your

67

pack wherever you have a little room, or you'll find that you'll still be searching for ingredients while others are enjoying their hot meal. Repackaging and grouping your food supply takes some time at home, but will save weight, shorten preparation time in camp, and make it almost impossible to run out of food on the last day of a trip. Before doing that, decide how much weight you can handle, what containers will work best, and how you will organize your foodstuffs to make them easily accessible.

To keep weight to a minimum, remove all unnecessary store packaging. (Some crackers travel best in their boxes; canned meats, of course, are best left in their cans.) Measure and pack ingredients for individual meals together in a labeled plastic bag, and don't forget to include instructions. If the whole of your food supply ends up too heavy, then examine the heaviest items and ask yourself if there is something lighter that could be substituted.

Most of the containers you'll need are probably around the house already:

Bags. Most food items can be repackaged in plastic or cloth bags. Bags are economical, convenient, light, and reusable, but they don't meet every backpacking need. For example, freeze-dried products are often packaged in foil packets. Don't repackage them. These pouches are moisture-tight and also serve as good containers for rehydrating the food.

Plastic bottles and jars. Dry seasonings can be packaged in film cans or pill bottles. These are light in weight and have tight-fitting caps. Use wide-mouth plastic jars and other plastic storage containers when necessary, but keep these to a minimum, as they are bulky. Plastics can absorb odors, flavors, and oils from the contents, which may foster bacteria. Be sure you thoroughly clean these containers between trips. If the contents are a liquid or powder, be sure to enclose the plastic container in a self-sealing plastic bag to contain any possible leakage.

Squeeze tubes. Reusable squeeze tubes (as opposed to squeeze bottles) are great for semiliquid or semisolid foods such as honey, peanut butter, jam, and mustard. Squeeze tubes are filled from an open end that is later sealed tight by a plastic clip. They can be obtained at camp supply stores and by mail order.

Egg cartons. Plastic egg cartons come in sizes that hold as little as two and as many as a dozen eggs. You can use one to carry fresh eggs as long as you place it in a self-sealing plastic bag—just in case. (If you plan to use fresh eggs very early on the trip, you can break them into a plastic bottle at home, and then simply pour them out when it's time to use them.) Egg cartons can also be used to transport delicate items such as chocolate truffles, if it's worth the trouble.

For the final organization of your foodstuffs, you can employ either of these two methods:

Package by common meals. Select a different-colored stuff sack for each type of meal—breakfast, lunch/snack, dinner—and another sack for coffee, tea, sugar, and condiments and seasonings that could be used during any meal.

Package by day. Group all breakfast, lunch, and dinner foods for a given day in the same sack. You'll still want to keep a separate bag for items that could be used during any meal.

WILDERNESS COOKING

Once you're out in the wilderness, your thorough planning and preparation will pay off. Make sure you have plenty of water, and allow the right amount of time to prepare your meals.

WATER TREATMENT

Unfortunately, the days of blithely filling your canteen and drinking from untested or untreated sources of water are gone. Even in the most remote areas, water may be contaminated with a small protozoan, *Giardia lamblia. Giardia* is transmitted from an infected animal (including humans) whose body waste is deposited in or seeps into a water supply that is then consumed by another animal or person. Giardiasis may result, and may cause severe diarrhea, cramps, nausea, and vomiting. Many physicians haven't had enough experience with the disease to diagnose it correctly. If untreated, the disease may go on for years. Incubation time is 1 to 2 weeks, though some people have gone as long as 2 months before getting sick. Not everyone ingesting *Giardia* shows symptoms of the disease. Some may simply be carriers.

In addition to *Giardia*, there may be other contaminants in the water supply. Always assume that the water found in the wilderness is contaminated and use one of the three basic methods to purify the water:

Boiling. This is the most reliable method of treating drinking water. Most organisms are killed instantly when water reaches the boiling point. Another 5 minutes ensures the purity of your drinking water even at high altitudes. With this method, you need to make sure you have plenty of extra fuel. If you're preparing drinking water, allow extra time for the water to cool.

Chemical treatment. Iodine tablets ("emergency drinking water germicidal tablets") are a convenient way to purify water. There is a slight iodine taste in the water, but it can be camouflaged with flavored beverage crystals. The tablets lose their strength over time. Make sure the

Water filtration is a time-consuming but necessary task. (Photo by James Glenn Pearson)

date is marked clearly on the bottle and replace them every other year. Be aware that some people are allergic to iodine.

Filtering. Water filters are expensive, but filtering can be done almost as fast as chemical treatment and it does not introduce a bad taste. Make sure the filtering apparatus you buy either can be easily cleaned or has a replaceable filter cartridge or element. Filter pores must be 0.4 microns or less in size to be effective against *Giardia.*

THE WILDERNESS KITCHEN

When you establish your campsite, take time to pick out a cooking area nearby that is at least 200 feet away from any water source. You don't want your garbage and waste water to contaminate rivers and lakes. Look for a flat, wind-protected spot to put your stove on. A large, flat rock or rock ledge, or a low area next to a large fallen tree, works well for setting up your wilderness kitchen. If the soil is sandy or soft, or if you're camping on snow, you may need to put some support under your stove to steady it.

Your first step in preparing any hot meal is to start up the stove and heat some water. Hot water is always needed—for preliminary hot drinks or soup, and for your main course or courses. After cooking the main course, you may want to keep your stove busy heating hot water for more hot drinks, dessert, and dishwashing.

For freeze-dried and dehydrated foods, read the instructions carefully. These foods can be quite inedible if not properly rehydrated. Presoaking of some foods may take 15 to 60 minutes, so allow enough time. Food that has been shredded, grated, or powdered usually takes a short time; whole pieces take longer. The higher the water temperature, the shorter the time it takes to rehydrate the food.

High-altitude cooking is always slower because the higher the elevation, the lower the boiling temperature of water (see fig. 6-3). Some packaged-food instructions give cooking-time adjustments for various altitudes. Cooking time for most boiled or simmered food doubles at about 10,000 feet. You may want to keep notes on the cooking time of your favorite foods for reference on future trips. Remember to take extra fuel if you'll be cooking a lot at high altitudes.

Elevation	Temperature
Sea level	212°F
5,000 feet	203°F
10,000 feet	194°F
14,000 feet	187°F

Fig. 6-3. Boiling temperature of water at various altitudes

Cleaning up after a meal is quite simple, and should be done immediately so as not to attract animals into your camp. For some foods, a thorough cleaning in plain hot water is sufficient. For meats or greasy foods or those that stick to cookware, the use of biodegradable soap is recommended. This is especially important for groups, to help prevent the spread of germs. Water used for washing (dishes or people) should be dumped well away from camp, among stones or by a bush, and at least 200 feet from any body of water.

Disposing of garbage is a simple matter—pack it out. If you have a campfire, you can burn paper products; but plastics, aluminum, orange peels, apple cores, eggshells, and the like should be packed out. Garbage in or near a camp is unsightly and trains animals to become camp thieves. Most non-food garbage degrades very slowly, and even some food garbage can take months or years to rot away in a cold and/or dry environment.

It may be impossible to stop hungry critters from visiting your campsite at night. To accommodate them in a way that is best for both you and them (some human foods may be tasty but harmful to animals), remove all food from your backpack and leave all the pockets unzipped. Usually, if an animal can't get access to the contents of a pocket that smells of food, it simply chews or tears into it. Move all food away from your pack to a safe place. Hanging your food in bags several feet above the ground may be effective against the usual bandits such as rodents and raccoons. In bear country, use "bear boxes" if they're provided. Otherwise, certain hanging techniques work best (see Chapter 9, Wilderness Travel, *Close Encounters of the Animal Kind*). In any case, never keep food in your tent in bear country. To discourage any visitation at all, keep your camp clean and free of garbage scraps.

Bon appetit!

RECOMMENDED READING

Bunnelle, Hasse and the editors of *Backpacker Magazine*. *The Back-Packer's Food Book*. Backpacker, Inc., 1981. (Includes information on seasonings for foods, a chart of food values for commonly used camp and trail food items, food additives and chemicals, 300 recipes, provisioning for short to long trips, and more.)

Cross, Margaret and Jean Fiske. *Backpacker's Cookbook*. Ten Speed Press, 1974. (A good beginning book on the basics of backpack cooking. Includes instructions on how to sew stuff sacks and a pot bag. Recipes included.)

Franz, Carl and Lorena Havens. John Muir Publications, 1982. *The On and Off Road Cookbook*. (A book for hikers, boaters, campers, and travelers of all kinds. Humorously written. Includes planning, economizing, equipment, a food values chart, packing and storage, recipes, and more.)

Jacobson, Cliff. *Camping Secrets*. ICS Books, Inc., 1987. ("A lexicon of camping tips only the experts know." Topics are organized alphabetically and range from Anchor to Yard Goods.)

Kinmont, Vikki and Claudia Axcell. *Simple Foods for the Pack*. Sierra Club Books, 1976. (Includes 175 trail-tested recipes using natural, inexpensive ingredients.)

Prater, Yvonne and Ruth Dyar Mendenhall. *Gorp, Glop & Glue Stew*. The Mountaineers, 1982 (Over 165 well-known outdoor experts share their favorite recipes and relate memorable cooking and eating experiences.)

The locations of most bench marks (survey markers) are shown on topographic maps. (Photo by Jerry Schad)

Wilderness Navigation

NELSON COPP AND TED YOUNG

M ore and more Americans are discovering the beauty and tranquillity of our parks and trails, and the fun of wilderness camping and travel. Many of us are seeking out the more remote trails and cross-country routes, yet more people need a good command of the navigation techniques and skills that make such outings safer, more predictable, and more rewarding. As we'll see in this chapter, navigation requires relatively little in the way of equipment. It's primarily a mental effort that keeps one constantly aware of position, direction, and speed of travel. Like the mental effort required in driving an automobile, it requires plenty of practice, but gets easier with time.

As a normal part of living, you're continually faced with challenges of navigating. You're probably quite accustomed to using city navigation tools and cues such as road maps, street signs, and verbal directions. Wilderness navigation is simply an extension of the same route-finding skills you use in the civilized world. Instead of signposts and road maps, you'll use a topographic map, a compass, and the physical features of the land.

Since cues indicating precise location are not always visible in the wilderness and you won't likely be meeting other travelers very often, you'll have to get used to being a little uncertain about your exact position from time to time. This does not mean you'll be "lost." It only means you'll be somewhere in transit between one known position and the next. The more you practice reading the "lay of the land,"

the more comfortable you'll be in the wilderness.

THE TOOLS OF NAVIGATION

MAPS

Topographic maps are almost always best for navigation purposes. These are scale maps with a unique feature—contour lines indicating elevations above (or in some cases below) sea level. "Topo" maps also show bodies of water and watercourses, vegetation types, named geographical points of interest such as mountain peaks, and man-made features. A skilled user of a topo map is able to clearly visualize the topography by carefully studying the patterns made by the contour lines.

Topo maps published by the U.S. Geological Survey (USGS) can be purchased at backpacking and map stores, or directly from the USGS. Private publishers often use USGS maps as a base and update the man-made features on their maps, like roads and trails.

Other maps, such as road maps or trail maps without contour lines, may be of some use for navigation as long as they are drawn to scale. Also useful to some degree are shaded relief maps, giving some rough indication of the topography.

All topo maps are printed with the direction of true north toward the top of the map. From any place on the earth, true north is the direction toward earth's geographic north pole—the north end of its spin axis. Magnetic north, on the other hand, is the direction toward the earth's magnetic north pole, which is located some distance away from earth's north pole in northern Canada. For any place on earth, there's a correction, called magnetic declination, that expresses the angle from the direction of true north to the direction of magnetic north. For North America, magnetic declinations range from about 20 degrees east to 22 degrees west. If you aren't using a compass, the magnetic declination is of no use; if you are, then knowing your declination is essential, as you'll see later.

USGS topo maps come in two types: 15 minutes (scale 1:62,500), in which 1 inch on the map equals about 1 mile; and 7.5 minutes (scale 1:24,000), in which 1 inch on the map equals about 2,000 feet. (The "minutes" refer to minutes of arc in latitude and longitude: 15 minutes covers 0.25 degree of latitude and longitude, while 7.5 minutes covers 0.125 degree.) It takes four 7.5-minute maps to cover the same area shown on one 15-minute map. Knowing the map scale, it is possible to calculate the distance between any two points along a line or curve. For example, if the route on a 15-minute map measures 8.3 inches, the distance is 8.3 inches x approximately 1 mile/inch = approximately 8.3 miles.

Quite often a route will span several maps. Each USGS topo has the names of adjacent maps (usually eight of them) printed on the sides and corners. (Provisional topo maps indicate all adjoining maps at the bottom.)

Figure 7-1 is a close look at the kinds of symbols appearing on USGS topo maps. There are four classes of map symbols: point, line, surface, and contour.

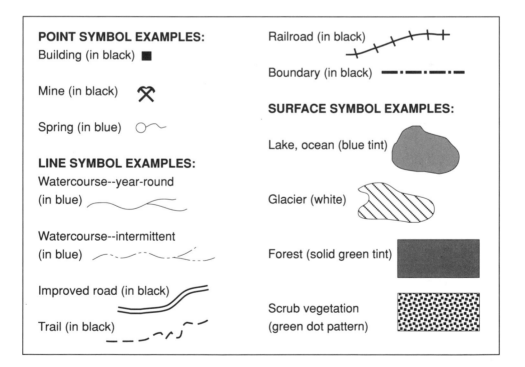

Fig. 7-1. Some symbols used on USGS maps

Contour symbols. Contour lines, typically printed in brown ink on topo maps, are imaginary lines of constant elevation. If you could actually see these lines on the earth, they would curve around the terrain, but always remain level. The elevation difference between adjacent contour lines on the map is called the contour interval. Depending on the type of terrain and the scale of the map, the contour interval can vary from 200 to 20 feet or less. A map with a contour interval greater than 80 feet is generally not very useful for critical navigation. Visualizing the terrain represented on a topo map involves understanding the patterns of the contour lines. Figure 7-2 shows several types of terrain and the corresponding contours.

Although topo maps reflect a great deal of information about the terrain, it is impossible to show every detail. Certain features too small to be detected in the pattern of contour lines may be insurmountable to the traveler. On a map with a contour interval of 80 feet, for example, a cliff or waterfall 60 feet high may not be shown at all if it happens to fall between contour lines. On a map with 40-foot contours, cross-country travel over a gently sloping hillside may appear simple, but not so if the slope is strewn with 10- or 20-foot-high boulders.

Some features on topo maps are necessarily vague. A vegetation pattern indicating forest may represent anything from scattered trees to a dense redwood forest. The pattern indicating scrub vegetation could mean scattered bushes or impenetrable chaparral. A desert wash (a brown stipple pattern on the map) could be filled with anything from sand to boulders. Streams indicated by a thin blue line could be 1 foot wide or 50 feet wide.

Always take note of a map's publication date and the information in fine print at the bottom. The fine print may indicate that the map area was surveyed several

Good navigation skills will lead you to peak wilderness adventures. (Photo by George Ostertag)

years before the map was actually published. Significant changes may have occurred since then. Landslides or simple neglect may have obliterated roads and trails, buildings may be reduced to nothing but half-buried foundations, and vegetation may have changed as a result of a fire, logging activity, or urban development.

COMPASS

The compass has developed over many centuries from a simple direction-finder to a sophisticated tool. In most modern versions used for navigation, the compass needle (a small, bar-shaped magnet) turns freely while suspended in a circular housing filled with a transparent liquid. The liquid quickly damps out oscillations in the needle's rotation whenever the compass is moved or adjusted in any way.

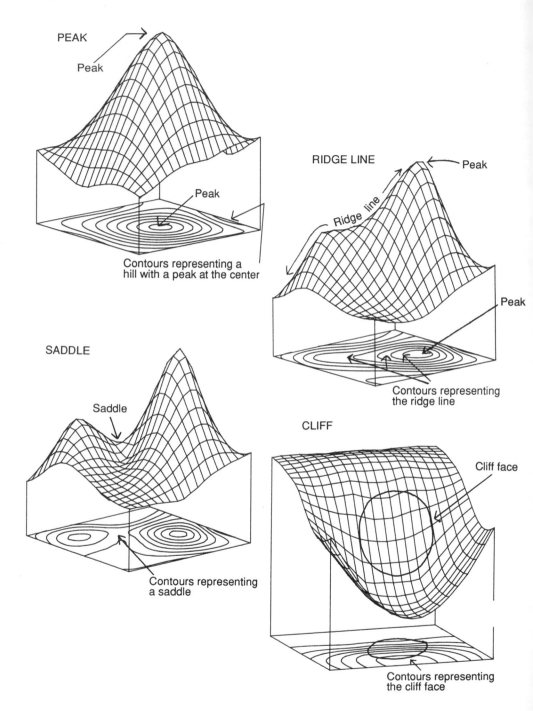

PEAK

Peak

Peak

Contours representing a
hill with a peak at the center

RIDGE LINE

Peak

Ridge line

Peak

Contours representing
the ridge line

SADDLE

Saddle

Contours representing
a saddle

CLIFF

Cliff face

Contours representing
the cliff face

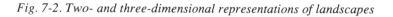

Fig. 7-2. Two- and three-dimensional representations of landscapes

CANYON, VALLEY, DRAW
OR DESERT WASH

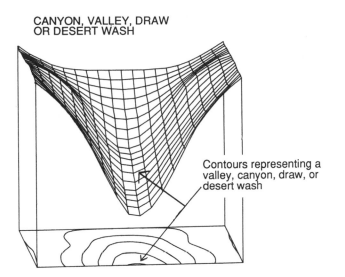

Contours representing a
valley, canyon, draw, or
desert wash

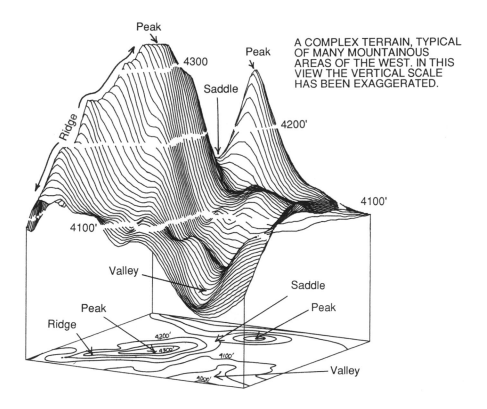

Peak

4300

Peak

Saddle

Ridge

4200'

4100'

4100'

Valley

Saddle

Peak

Peak

Ridge

4200'

4300'

4100'

1000'

Valley

A COMPLEX TERRAIN, TYPICAL
OF MANY MOUNTAINOUS
AREAS OF THE WEST. IN THIS
VIEW THE VERTICAL SCALE
HAS BEEN EXAGGERATED.

77

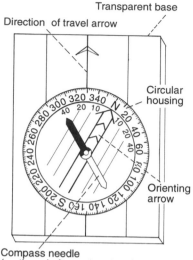

Fig. 7-3. Parts of an orienteering compass

Fig. 7-4. Degree markings on the compass face increase in a clockwise direction.

ALTIMETER

In hilly or mountainous areas where navigation is critical, an altimeter can be a useful third tool. Altimeters are really barometers calibrated to measure altitude (see Chapter 8, The Weather, *Grace Under Pressure*). They can be used to fix your position relative to the contour lines on a topographic map. Altimeter readings are affected by changes in the weather, so it's important to calibrate an altimeter's reading whenever you arrive at a point of known elevation.

We won't discuss the use of altimeters further in this chapter; rather we'll concentrate on navigation techniques using maps alone, a compass alone, and maps and a compass together. While reading the text that follows, it would be helpful to have a topographic map and orienteering compass handy for reference.

For map and compass work in the field, you should use an orienteering compass (fig. 7-3). In this design the circular housing is transparent and rotates on a transparent plastic base. The perimeter of the housing is inscribed with the cardinal directions (north, east, south, and west) and a 360-degree scale, typically in 2-degree increments. The north-pointing end of the needle is usually painted red, and there's a prominent arrow on the base that can be used to indicate your direction of travel or the direction to a prominent land feature.

In some compasses, the needle's north end is coated with phosphorescent paint, allowing readings to be made at night. Most compass base plates include a small ruler in inch or centimeter units to facilitate measuring distance on maps. More expensive compasses include a built-in mirror that helps you make more accurate sightings.

NAVIGATION BY MAP

Considering all the information a map contains, it alone may be all you need to determine your location and plot your course. This works particularly well when distinct features such as road and trail junctions, peaks, passes, or uniquely shaped lakes are within view. This map-alone method of navigation, however, is not effective in bad weather or low visibility. In those cases, a compass is often necessary as well as a map.

The locating process begins with aligning the map so that it corresponds to the landscape in view, and ends with fixing your exact location on the map. You're ready to begin if you can identify features seen on the land with their printed representations on the map. Rotate the map until the features are in the same relative position on the map as they are in view around you.

For example, if you recognize a peak in front of you and a known river junction just below on your right, the map should be rotated and aligned so that when the map is held between you and the peak on the horizon, the peak on the map lies in front of you, while the river junction on the map appears to the right, but closer than the peak. Then find the spot on the map where the river junction is at the same angle to the right of the peak as is the

river junction in your view. That's your approximate location. To further refine your position, look for other nearby distinctive features. Are you standing on top of a ridge, or somewhere along the slope? Is there a meadow or a lake in view? Are there any other high points around you that may help to fix your position?

Once you have located yourself, keep the map within easy reach or carry it in front of you as you travel so that you can periodically relocate yourself. If you're carrying the map, you may want to encase it in a large, transparent plastic envelope to protect it from rain, perspiration, and abrasion.

NAVIGATION BY COMPASS

Basic compass skills involve setting, taking, and following bearings. A compass bearing is simply the angle, as measured by your compass, between the direction of magnetic north (the direction a compass needle points) and the direction of an object or destination. As suggested by the

Fig. 7-5. Locating your position by map alone

scale on your compass's circular housing, bearing angles increase eastward from north, that is, they increase to your right.

SETTING A BEARING

Let's say a friend tells you her favorite fishing hole is on a magnetic bearing (compass bearing) of 60 degrees from a certain parking area. Without a compass, you might have only a vague idea of which direction to hike after you park your car. But if you set a bearing of 60 degrees on your compass, you can simply follow the direction-of-travel arrow on the base of the compass to head in the right direction.

To set that 60-degree bearing, hold the compass flat in the palm of your hand and turn the housing until the 60-degree mark lines up with the direction-of-travel arrow on the base plate (fig. 7-6A). On some compasses, the arrow is labelled "Read Bearing Here."

Turn the entire compass until the north end of the needle lines up with the orienting arrow on the bottom of the circular housing (fig. 7-6B) (the red end of the needle now points to "N" on the housing).

Your compass is now "oriented" to magnetic north, the direction-of-travel arrow is pointing toward the fishing hole, and you are facing in the direction you want to go. Soon you'll learn how to successfully follow that bearing.

Be aware that nearby metallic objects, such as mechanical pencils or pens, a pack frame, a metal watch or ring, or a car can affect the pointing accuracy of a compass needle. Always make compass measurements away from these kinds of objects. A compass can also be rendered useless in certain areas where large amounts of iron-bearing rock is present.

TAKING A BEARING

"Taking" a bearing is the opposite of setting a bearing. In this case, you can see where you want to go, but you don't yet know what the bearing angle is. For example, let's say your goal is to reach a peak visible in the distance. You can see a good route straight ahead and you realize that much of the time you'll be hiking in a forest where your view of the peak will be obscured. First you need to take a bearing on the peak.

To take a bearing, hold the compass in your hand with the direction-of-travel ar-

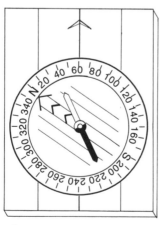

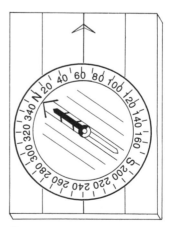

A   B

Fig. 7-6. Setting a bearing

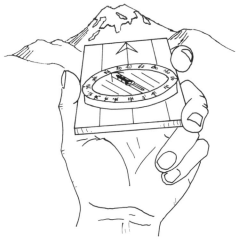

Fig. 7-7. Taking a bearing

row pointing toward the peak (fig. 7-7). You may want to hold the compass near eye level to sight more accurately, but remember to keep the compass level. With the direction-of-travel arrow fixed on the peak, turn the housing until the orienting arrow in the housing lines up with the needle. In effect, you are setting up a measurement of the angle between magnetic north (the direction of the needle's north end) and the peak (the direction indicated by the direction-of-travel arrow).

As you walk through the forest, you can refer to your compass often to maintain your course (fig. 7-8). The degree reading on the compass is not really important, as long as you don't rotate the compass housing along the way. Just keep the needle lined up on the orienting arrow, and the direction-of-travel arrow points your way. Still, it's a good idea to memorize or jot down the degree reading in case your compass housing accidentally gets reset.

FOLLOWING A BEARING

In the previous example, you took a bearing on a peak. You're now ready to start hiking through the forest. Since the bearing is already set on your compass,

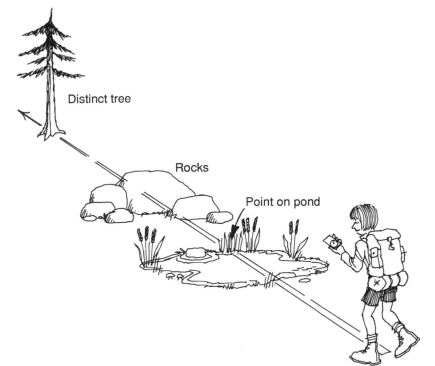

Distinct tree

Rocks

Point on pond

Fig. 7-8. Following a bearing

all you have to do is hike in that direction. But how easily can you follow this bearing? What happens if you must skirt obstacles like dense brush or large boulders? To answer these questions you must learn how to select intermediate points.

Before you start hiking, turn the compass until it is oriented toward north (don't turn the housing). The magnetic needle lines up with the north arrow on the housing and the direction-of-travel arrow on the base plate points in the direction of your hike to the peak.

Now look for an object in the near distance that is between you and the peak, such as a distinctive tree or a pile of rocks. This is your first intermediate point. Walk toward the intermediate point as directly as you can. Moving a little to the left or right to avoid obstacles will not make you lose your original direction. Just keep heading, on average, toward the intermediate point. You should not have to check your compass again until you reach it.

Let's assume that at the first intermedi-

ate point you can't see the peak anymore. No problem—just orient your compass to north again, and look along the direction-of-travel arrow. Then pick out a second intermediate point in that direction of travel to which you can hike without losing your way. You can continue leap-frogging in this manner until you reach your goal.

BACKSIGHTING

Now and then you may lose sight of your next intermediate point. To make sure you are still on the right course, use the technique of backsighting to find the previous point.

Turn around and reorient your compass by lining the south end of the needle with the north end of the orienting arrow (since you are looking 180 degrees back). Now the direction-of-travel arrow will point back toward the previous intermediate point. If it does not, move in a direction either left or right until it does. Now you are on the correct bearing again. It's good

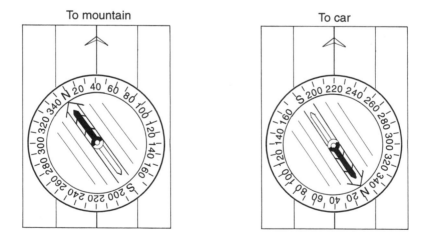

Fig. 7-9. Back bearings. In the diagrams above, 180 degrees was added to the original bearing of 40 degrees to produce a back-bearing of 220 degrees.

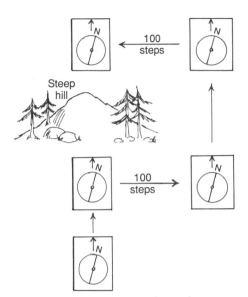

practice to backsight often to make sure you stay on course. It will also help you recognize the terrain for the trip back if you plan to return using the same route.

BACK BEARINGS

Let's say you've spent an enjoyable hour on the summit, and now you want to return to your car. You never took a bearing on the car, in fact you can't even see the car. How do you get back? Easy. Your car is just 180 degrees from your original bearing. Here are two techniques you can use to get back. (See fig. 7-9.)

In the first method, you find the angle that is 180 degrees from your original bearing (if your original bearing is less than 180 degrees, then add 180 degrees to it; if your original bearing is more than 180 degrees, then subtract 180 degrees from it). Reset the housing to this new bearing, orient your compass, and start the journey back.

In the second method, you leave the original bearing set, but orient your compass by aligning the south end of the needle with the orienting arrow (which indicates north).

NAVIGATING AROUND OBSTACLES

Using intermediate points to reach a goal is nice, but sometimes there are obstacles you can't easily sidestep. You might encounter some obstacle you'd rather not try to climb over that also blocks your view of the next intermediate point. You could walk around it, but you're afraid that would throw you off course.

One fairly exact solution to this dilemma is to navigate on a right-angle course (fig. 7-10). First determine whether going to the left or the right will be easier. Orient the compass, and face your original bearing. Notice that the near and far ends of the base plate are perpendicular to your original bearing; this will be your new direction. Start walking in this new perpendicular direction, either left or right, as far

Fig. 7-10. Navigating a right-angle course around an obstacle.

as you need to, counting your paces as you walk.

Let's say you had to walk 100 paces to the right to get a clear shot past the hill. Orient the compass again and walk in your original direction to a point beyond the hill. Then turn left (in this case) and follow a course 100 paces back to your originally projected course. Reorient your compass and continue toward your next intermediate point.

AN EXERCISE IN COMPASS NAVIGATION: FOLLOWING A CIRCUIT

This circuit exercise will give you and your friends some practical experience in taking and following bearings. First, find a rather large, open outdoor area with at least a few obstacles (fig. 7-11). Pick out five or ten points on the landscape that can be linked together in a more-or-less circular course. It's more interesting if some of the points can't be seen from the starting point.

Number and describe the points on a sketch map and give everyone a copy. The

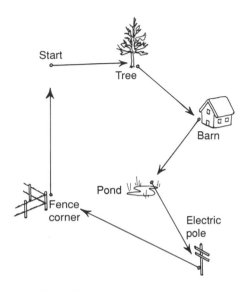

Fig. 7-11. Circuit exercise

object is to take bearings on each successive point, and to navigate to each successive point using compass techniques. Each participant should record the measured bearing on each leg of the circuit. After completing the circuit, the participants can compare their bearings and discuss any problems.

NAVIGATION BY MAP AND COMPASS

As we've seen, the needle of a compass points toward the earth's magnetic north pole. From most places on the earth, this is not quite the same direction as the earth's true north pole. Since maps are drawn with true north up, this means that the magnetic bearings you've been setting and taking will be skewed a little, relative to directions on the map. The difference in degrees between the true north and the magnetic north directions as measured

from any given location on the earth is the magnetic declination.

If you are just using a compass merely as a direction finder independent of a map, then declination is unimportant. When using a map and a compass together, however, you'll have to take declination into account.

On topographic maps, magnetic declination is usually indicated at the bottom left. The symbol includes a vertical line pointing toward a star representing true north, and an arrow labelled "MN" indicating magnetic declination (assumed to be 15 degrees, as shown in fig. 7-12).

Once you know the declination for your map, you may apply either of two methods for orienting your map correctly.

Fig. 7-12. Magnetic declination symbol

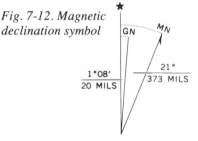

UTM GRID AND 1970 MAGNETIC NORTH DECLINATION AT CENTER OF SHEET

Compass-oriented map method. First place your map on a flat spot. Roughly orient it by looking at the features around you and comparing them to the map. Then rotate the compass's circular housing to line up the orienting arrow with the direction-of-travel arrow on the base plate. Place the long edge of the base plate along the left or right border of the map, with north pointing to the top of the map (don't use any vertical lines drawn inside the map area, since they can represent roads or boundaries that may not really go precisely north and south).

For east declinations (for example, everywhere in the western United States), turn the map and compass together (as illustrated in fig. 7-13A) until the needle points to the number on the housing that matches your declination. Your map now has its vertical dimension oriented to true north, and its orientation is also correct relative to the landscape around you.

Parallel declination lines method. Adding parallel declination lines to a map simplifies navigation technique when using that map in the field. It's much easier if you draw the lines on your map at home before your trip. In addition to your compass, you'll need a sharp pencil and a long ruler or straight-edge.

Turn the compass housing until the scale reads the same value as your declination (this assumes your declination is east). Place your map on a flat, hard surface and rotate the entire compass until the direction arrow on the housing lines up with the border of the map. The long edge of the base plate and the direction-of-travel arrow are now lined up with the correct declination. (You can double check this by making sure they are angled in the same direction as the declination arrow on the bottom of your map.) Place the straight-edge along the long edge of the base plate

and draw a straight line the entire length of the map. Starting from this line, mark 1-inch increments along the top and bottom edges of the map. Then use the straight-edge to connect each pair of these marks until your map—or at least the area you'll be hiking in on the map—is covered with parallel declination lines (see fig. 7-13B).

Map orientation is very simple using this method. Rotate your map so that the parallel declination lines are also parallel to the direction of your compass needle. Make sure the north end of the compass needle points toward the top of the map, not the bottom.

SETTING A BEARING

Let's assume you want to hike to a small lake you can see on the map (fig. 7-14). You'll need to set a bearing on the lake from your present position and then follow that bearing.

If you are using the compass-oriented map method, lay the map on a flat spot and orient it to true north as described earlier. Place one of the back corners of your compass base plate on your current (known) location on the map. This point

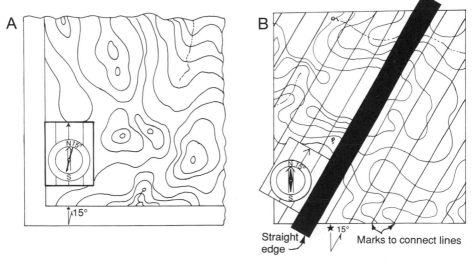

Fig. 7-13. Orienting the map: A, *compass-oriented map method;* B, *parallel declination lines method.*

will act as a pivot. Hold this corner down with your thumb and rotate the entire compass until the front corner on the same side of the base plate is in line with your destination. The long edge of the base plate should now be making a line between the two points. Holding the base plate in this position, rotate the housing until the orienting arrow on the housing lines up with the north end of the needle. You have now set your compass to the correct bearing from your location to the lake. The number of degrees is not important. As in fig. 7-13A, just follow the direction-of-travel arrow on your oriented compass to navigate to the lake.

For the parallel declination lines method, follow the first few steps described above, but rotate the housing until the orienting arrow on the housing lines up with the declination lines drawn on your map. When using this method, always ignore the magnetic needle when you're working on the map. In this case the declination lines you have drawn represent magnetic north. The direction of the needle is not important. (In fig. 7-14B, a magnetic declination of 20 degrees is assumed.)

FOLLOWING A BEARING

Now that you have successfully set the bearing to the lake, you are almost ready to start hiking. First you must choose the best route to your destination. If you start hiking without checking the route, you may end up having to climb steep hills or hike through dense vegetation. So take a few minutes to plan your route, using that wonderful tool—a map.

Take note of any obstacles you may detect on the map and mark them. Then plot your course, which may or may not be a direct route. To avoid tough spots, you can pick out intermediate points, take their bearings from the map, and plot a crooked course, with bearings noted for each leg.

AIMING OFF

If a destination is not large, like a small lake hidden in the trees, you could walk right past it. To reduce that possibility, try to find on the map a prominent stream or an obvious road or trail touching or passing near the lake. If you can find some feature like that, aim slightly off the target lake so that you will cross the more

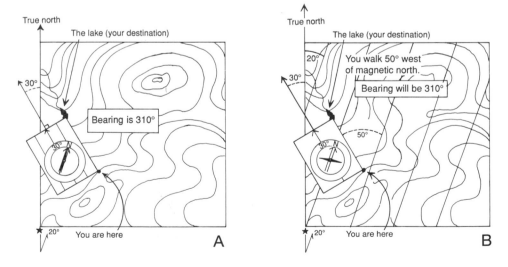

Fig. 7-14. Setting a bearing: A, *compass-oriented method;* B, *parallel declination lines method.*

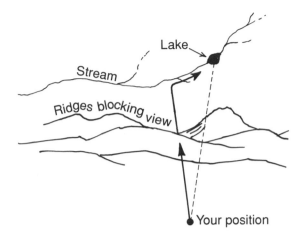

Fig. 7-15. Aiming off. Aim left of the lake, then follow the stream to the lake.

obvious feature sooner or later. When you get there, you'll know which way to turn to find the lake (fig. 7-15).

CHECKING YOUR LOCATION

A good way to keep track of your position, especially during critical navigation, is to frequently recheck your position relative to nearby landmarks and "update" your position on your map. You can do that by keeping your thumb on your current position on the map at all times, or by making a series of pencil marks on the map.

If, for whatever reason, you do lose track of your position on the map, you can use the "triangle of error" technique to rediscover your location (fig. 7-16). First you must recognize three identifiable points both in the surrounding terrain and on the map. The closer the points are to you, the better. Take a bearing on the first point and leave it set on the compass. Transfer it as a line on the map by placing one of the front corners of the compass on the point, holding it with your finger, and pivoting the entire compass until the direction arrow either lines up with the needle, if you are using the compass-oriented method, or lines up with the parallel dec-

lination lines if you drew them on your map.

Draw a line from the first point back along the long edge of the base plate and extend it beyond where you think you are. Repeat these steps for the next two points. The three lines should converge to a small triangle. You should be somewhere inside the triangle!

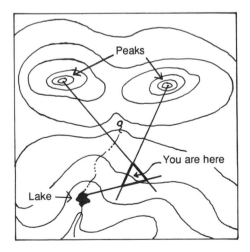

Fig. 7-16. "Triangle of error" technique

87

If the triangle seems inordinately big, then you've erred in taking or plotting a bearing, or you may have mis-identified one of your points, either on the map or on the landscape. If this happens, check your bearings and try it again.

After getting at least a general fix on where you are, it may be useful to do a second triangulation on closer landmarks (if you can identify any) to determine your location more precisely. Once you have a better fix, you may be able to determine your location to a precision of just a few yards by examining the contour lines on your map, and recognizing around you the features they represent.

TAKING CROSS BEARINGS

Suppose you want to hike to a hidden spot, say a desert mine you noticed on the map, which is some distance away from an easily traveled linear feature like a straight wash. Let's further suppose there

are no distinguishing features along the wash to indicate the best place to turn off. But the map shows the mine lying between a distant hill and the wash (fig. 7-17).

Draw a line connecting the mine and the hill and extend it backward to where it intersects the wash. Using your compass, take a bearing of this line on the map. This is the bearing you will want to follow when you reach the right spot in the wash. Set this bearing on your compass.

Then, as you walk down the wash, stop often and point the direction-of-travel arrow on the base plate toward the hill, as if you were going to take a bearing (do not rotate the housing). See if the needle lines up with the orienting arrow. If not, keep walking. As you continue, a place will be reached where the needle will line up with the orienting arrow. You're now on the bearing line you drew on the map. Turn and head toward the mine by following the direction-of-travel arrow.

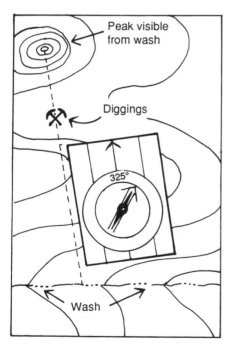
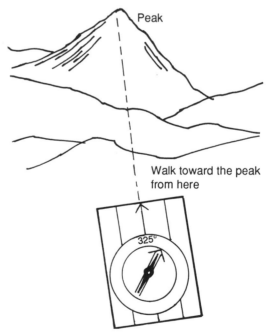

Fig. 7-17. Taking cross bearings

SPECIAL TECHNIQUES

The techniques we've discussed so far are basic ones you will use again and again. There are several other techniques to be aware of for special situations.

USING BASELINES

Aiming off, which we discussed earlier, involves intersecting a baseline, like a road or stream, and then following this baseline to the destination. In the last example (of cross bearings), you were hiking down a wash looking for a bearing line to a distant hill. When you reached the bearing line, you simply had to walk in that direction to reach the mine. There were really two baselines in that example—the wash itself and the imaginary bearing line connecting the wash, the mine, and the hill.

Imagine you've found the spot where the bearing intersects the wash and you're heading toward the mine. But after an hour

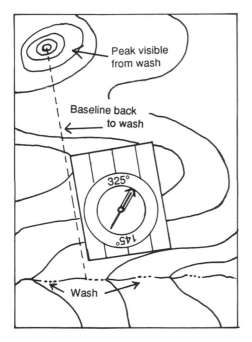

Fig. 7-18. Using baselines

you haven't found the mine and you want to head back to the wash. No problem. There are actually two baselines you can rely on (see fig. 7-18). Recheck the bearing on the hill, which is one of your baselines. Move either left or right until you line up with that bearing and are on that baseline. Now simply walk in the reverse direction, picking intermediate points along the way if needed, until you hit the wash.

The other baseline—the wash—is even easier to find. You know it's behind you when you're facing the hill, so turn around and walk away from the hill. You will soon find the wash and can then return to your starting point (if you know which way to turn when you reach the wash).

Always be aware of the location of at least one baseline—a stream, a road, or some other fairly linear feature—before you start your excursion.

FINDING A FAVORITE SPOT AGAIN

We already covered the triangle-of-error technique that is useful in pinpointing a location. There are other applications for this technique. Imagine you are hiking in the desert and come across a beautiful Indian-made *olla* (clay vessel). You don't want to disturb it but would like to inform a ranger of its exact whereabouts. There are no distinguishing landmarks nearby, only some nearby hills. So how can you find this spot again? You guessed it—take bearings of at least three of the hills and mark the location on your map using the triangle of error technique.

DEAD RECKONING

When visibility is poor, it is often wiser to stay put until conditions improve. However, there may be circumstances in which it is essential to keep moving. You may not have the opportunity ahead to confirm your position very often because of darkness or fog. In this situation, you may use the technique of dead reckoning. While you are still certain of your position, find your destination on the map and mark a number of easily distinguishable points along the way. Draw lines between each of these points, take their bearings, and write them next to each point.

Set the first bearing on your compass and start walking, using intermediate points. If conditions are really bad, you may have to count your paces to determine how far you have gone. Continue doing this from point to point. This technique is risky, since you can easily lose the thread of your course. If you do, you can try to retrace your footprints back to the last known location.

NAVIGATING BY SUN, MOON, AND STARS

Carrying a compass is a necessity on any trip in the wilderness. There are, however, a few tricks you can use that will make you feel like an explorer. The path of the sun can be used as a general direction indicator. For example, at middle latitudes in the Northern Hemisphere, the sun always lies toward the south at midday. Therefore your shadow points north at approximately 12 P.M. (noon) standard time, or 1 P.M. daylight time. On the summer solstice (in late June), the sun rises roughly in the northeast, passes high overhead in the south at noon, and sets in the northwest. On the winter solstice (in late December), the sun rises roughly in the southeast, passes low in the south at noon, and sets roughly in the southwest. During the equinoxes (in late March and late September), the sun rises due east and sets due west.

A good technique, if you're patient, is to put a stick in the ground and mark the end of its shadow (fig. 7-19). Do this several more times at intervals of 10 or 15 minutes. A line connecting these points will be generally east–west; a line perpendicular will be generally north–south.

If you have a watch with sweep hands, you can use it to find rough directions. Make sure the watch is set for standard

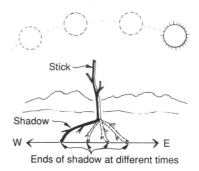

Fig. 7-19. Using the shadow of a stick in the ground to determine general north–south direction

time (not daylight savings time) and face the sun. Move your body to point the hour hand to the horizon below the sun. South will be roughly halfway between the hour hand and twelve o'clock on your watch. This works because the sun moves only 15 degrees in an hour, while the hour hand moves 30 degrees. During the months near the summer solstice, this does not work well near the middle of the day.

During late afternoon, another interesting feat is to use your hand to estimate the time before sunset. Hold your hand at arm's length with fingers parallel to the horizon, and count the number of fingers between the horizon and the sun (fig. 7-20). Each finger represents about 10 to 12 minutes. You can also determine how long

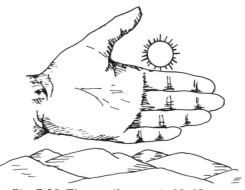

Fig. 7-20. Time until sunset is 10–12 minutes for each finger above the horizon

the sun has been up in the morning using the same method. Since this technique depends upon your latitude, you may want to experiment first; check how long it takes the sun to traverse one finger-width.

Like shipboard navigators, you can also use the stars to indicate directions. The stars move across the sky in the same direction as the sun, east to west. So stars that climb in the sky are somewhere near east, and stars that sink are somewhere near west. Polaris (the North Star), however, hovers in the northern sky all the time.

You can find Polaris by first looking for the Big Dipper. A line extended through the two outermost stars of the Big Dipper's bowl points to Polaris (fig. 7-21). When the Big Dipper is not visible, Cassiopeia usually is. The top of Cassiopeia's W-shaped form points toward Polaris. A further hint is that Polaris' altitude, or angle above the horizon, very nearly matches an observer's north latitude. An observer at Yellowstone National Park (latitude 45 degrees north), for example, would locate Polaris halfway up in the sky.

We've explored the basics of map and compass navigation in this chapter. From simple day hikes to longer wilderness trips, it's important to keep your sense of direction and maintain an awareness of where you are. Carry a map and a compass when you travel in unfamiliar areas, and refer to your map often. With practice, navigational skills become everyday habits.

RECOMMENDED READING

Fleming, June. *Staying Found*. Random House, 1982. (An easy-to-understand book covering the basics of map and compass

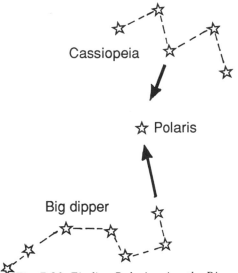

Fig. 7-21. Finding Polaris using the Big Dipper or Cassiopeia

navigation. Lots of helpful illustrations and drawings.)

Kjellstrom, Bjorn. *Be Expert with Map and Compass*. Macmillan Co., 1976. (A valuable reference for information on all aspects of map and compass navigation, including competitive orienteering.)

RESOURCES

USGS topographic maps, and many other maps useful for hikers, can be purchased at outdoor equipment stores and map stores in most metropolitan areas. For large orders of USGS maps, you may want to contact the Branch of Distribution, U.S. Geological Survey, Box 25286, Federal Center, Denver, CO 80225 for areas west of the Mississippi. For areas east of the Mississippi, the USGS address is Branch of Distribution, U.S. Geological Survey, 1200 South Eads Street, Arlington, VA 22202.

At higher elevations, clouds become an extension of the mountaintop landscape. (Photo by Bob and Ira Spring)

CHAPTER 8

The Weather

KEITH GORDON

Although they are often helpful, you don't always need a weatherman. You can be your own! In fact, making educated guesses about the weather is a valuable skill for anyone on a trip in the wilderness. Later this chapter discusses some of the many sources of current weather information that will help you in that effort, but for now let's cover some of the ground rules about the sky.

First, remember that discussions of the weather deal with events and outcomes that are never absolutely predictable. Scientists now consider meteorological systems, as well as many other natural systems, to be inherently chaotic. However, even chaotic phenomena can have probable, if not strictly predictable, outcomes over the short term. That gives one some confidence in a daily weather forecast, even though it seems imprecise and occasionally turns out dead wrong.

All weather phenomena involve air, water, and the transfer of heat energy from place to place. Air consists of various gases plus water vapor. The water vapor content can be highly variable, ranging from almost nothing up to about 4 percent. Within clouds, water is also present in the form of liquid droplets, or ice crystals, or both. The sun's radiant energy is both the source of most of the heat on the earth and the motivating agent of forces that transfer heat from one place to another.

Air tends to expand and rise when warmed, warm air can hold more water vapor than cooler air, and (generally) temperatures within the lower atmosphere

decrease with increasing elevation. If a humid mass of air is cooled sufficiently, the water vapor in it condenses to myriads of tiny, freely floating water droplets. These water droplets are big enough to reflect light, so what is visible is an opaque white mass—a cloud. If a great deal of cooling takes place, heavier droplets or ice crystals may form and drizzle, rain, sleet, hail, or snow may result.

The so-called standard lapse rate, the rate at which temperature decreases with increasing elevation, averages about 3.5° F. per 1,000 feet of elevation (6.5° C. per 1,000 meters) in dry stable air. However, it can be as much as 5.5° F. per 1,000 feet or greater in saturated conditions. If a mass of warmish air holding nearly its capacity of invisible water vapor rises, it cools, more or less at the lapse rate. If the temperature inside falls to less than the dew point for that mass of air, condensation occurs and a cloud forms. The opposite process, exemplified by a cool cloud moving toward a lower, warmer elevation, may result in the cloud disappearing.

Solar heating of the earth's surface and oceans and the rotation of the earth are the driving forces behind the weather machine. As sun rays warm the surface and lower atmosphere, "bubbles" of air expand and begin rising. As long as a bubble is warmer than the air that surrounds it, it will continue to rise. On a larger scale, these bubbles are equivalent to air masses that can move both vertically and horizontally. Whether or not a rising bubble or air mass is destined to become a cloud,

93

the air surrounding it moves in more or less horizontally to take the place it vacated. The process of air moving about, redistributing heat in the atmosphere, is known as convection. The horizontal movement is what is known as wind.

Local topography can influence the course of the winds and affect other factors such as precipitation. Mountains, for example, tend to create updrafts, resulting in greater precipitation on the high windward slopes. The drier air that continues flowing down the lee slopes compresses and becomes warmer. (Think of how hot a bicycle pump gets from compressing air and you'll appreciate this process.) Thus, many arid lands, including most of North America's deserts, lie in the so-called "rain shadow" (usually east) of major mountain ranges. Of course, there's more to the weather than convection on a local or regional scale. A global view takes into account the dynamics of very large air masses, some big enough to cover a good portion of a continent.

GRACE UNDER PRESSURE

The highs and lows pictured on weather maps (fig. 8-1) are representations of huge high-pressure (relatively compressed) and low-pressure (relatively uncompressed) air masses covering the earth. A typical scale used in barometers for measuring atmospheric, or barometric, pressure is "inches of mercury" (the amount of pressure needed to raise a column of mercury metal 1 inch). A barometer at sea level, for example, should measure close to the standard sea-level pressure of 29.92 inches of mercury. In the metric system, the sea-level pressure can be expressed as approximately 1 bar or 1,000 millibars.

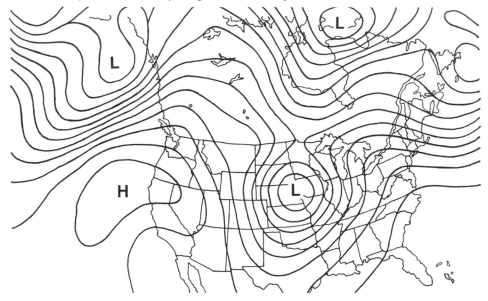

Fig. 8-1. Think of this weather map as a kind of topo map in which the contour lines (isobars) denote equal pressures across the surface of the earth. Generally, air moves from highs (H) to lows (L) across isobars, but the earth's rotation induces a clockwise circulation around a high, and a counter-clockwise circulation around a low. Just as on a topo map, the closer the contour lines, the steeper the pressure gradient. The steeper the gradient, the faster the winds.

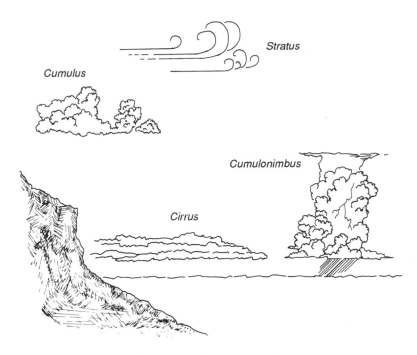

Cumulus

Stratus

Cumulonimbus

Cirrus

Fig. 8-2. Stratus *(layered) clouds are formed by gentle lifting of warm, moist air.* Cumulus *(lumpy, billowy) clouds are formed by vertical air currents. Rain, hail, or snow can fall from these in heavy showers.* Cirrus *(wispy) coulds are the high, gossamer-like formations of tiny ice crystals that often precede the passage of a storm front.* Cumulonimbus *are huge, towering clouds formed by strong updrafts. The friction from air movements within these clouds builds up the electrical charges that are released as lightning. These clouds can unleash great torrents of rain or hail, but are short-lived.*

Significantly higher or lower readings indicate the dominance of either a high or a low nearby. Remember, though, that pressure readings will go down if you climb a mountain. This happens at a rate of about 1 inch of mercury per 1,000 feet (100 millibars per 1,000 meters) of elevation change. If you're carrying an altimeter with you, you're really carrying a barometer. Both instruments measure barometric pressure, but are scaled differently. Altimeters measure altitude above sea level, but must be corrected for the local influence of highs or lows. Barometers, if not read at sea level, must be corrected for altitude. Climb 500 feet and your barometer should show about 0.5 inch less pressure.

If a high dominates your area after initial calibration, your altimeter will indicate lower than your actual altitude. A low, on the other hand, will cause your altimeter to show a higher reading. If you go to sleep with your pocket altimeter indicating 6,000 feet elevation, and a low moves in, you'll awaken at a "higher" elevation. No, you didn't sleep-hike; the weather's changing!

Highs and lows are distributed across the earth's surface and move about in ways

95

that are only partially predictable. In addition, because nature abhors a vacuum (even a partial vacuum), air tends to move from a high toward a low. But the air does not usually move on a direct path. The rotation of the earth causes an apparent force (the Coriolis effect) that induces a clockwise flow of air around a high and a counterclockwise flow around a low in the Northern Hemisphere. (In the Southern Hemisphere, the directions are reversed.) Clouds outlining the spinning vortices surrounding the more intense lows create the elegant, graceful spiral patterns shown in satellite images of our planet.

Around highs, the air is usually stable or even stagnant. Cloudless skies are typical, but dust, smoke, and smog can collect due to the lack of vertical mixing in the air. Within a low, the air is unstable and has a potential for rapid vertical movement. Cumuloform—billowing, towering—clouds (see fig. 8-2) can form, with a likelihood of precipitation or even violent weather.

If you have an idea of where highs and lows are located, and which way they're moving, you might be able to make short-term predictions about the weather in the area you plan to visit. If a high is moving over Mexico, for instance, you might expect warm, tropical air to invade much of the western United States. A high over the Gulf of Mexico or the Sea of Cortez can sling moist air up into the Rocky Mountains and the Southwest desert, triggering thunderstorms and flash floods. A high sitting in the Gulf of Alaska can send a rush of cold, unstable air down the spine of the western states' mountain ranges, generating the kind of stormy weather climbers dread.

During much of the year, the usual "Pacific High" west of California produces clear weather and a steady flow of air west to east inland over the ranges of the western states. Occasionally a high over an interior state like Nevada and a low offshore of the West Coast results in a reverse flow

of air from east to west, causing episodes of dry, hot winds called "Santa Anas."

In the winter months, a high over the Great Lakes region coupled with a low off the Atlantic coast sets the stage for the infamous "Nor'easter," which brings gale-force winds and heavy precipitation down the Atlantic Seaboard and its mountain ranges.

In general, approaching lows feature increasingly lower clouds and the possibility of precipitation, while receding lows feature clearing skies. But lows, which can be squeezed between highs, sometimes travel in series like water in a pipeline, so always beware of the next squirt that might lie just over the horizon.

Start watching the weather on a daily basis, and keep informed of the highs and lows around you. It's part of understanding and enjoying the rhythms of our planet.

BEING UP-FRONT ABOUT THE WEATHER

A front in meteorological parlance is the contact between one air mass and another. There are several types.

A *warm front* means that the leading edge of a moving air mass is warmer than the air mass it is overtaking and replacing. Stratiform—flat, layered—clouds are associated with this type of front.

Figure 8-3 shows the usual sequence of clouds seen during the approach of a warm front: The wispy, high-level cirrus clouds can appear as far as 1,000 miles ahead of the surface position of the front, giving up to two days' advance warning of its arrival. Near the front itself, the nimbostratus clouds are very low. If anything actually falls out of the hazy, gray sky, it is usually steady precipitation in the form of drizzle or light snow.

A *cold front* (fig. 8-4), in which cold air wedges under and replaces warmer air,

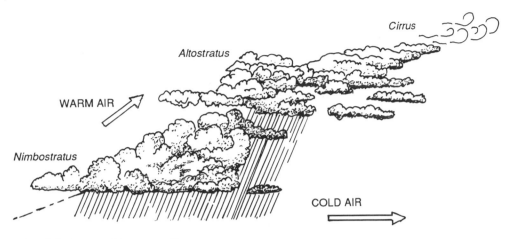

Fig. 8-3. Approaching warm front

produces a different scenario. With the approach of a cold front, the temperature decreases, the wind shifts to a southerly direction, and (if the lifting of warm air is rapid enough) cumulonimbus—billowy, rain-laden—clouds unleash rain or snow. A fast-moving cold front can be preceded by a squall line, a line of thunderstorms.

There's not much warning of the approach of a cold front, though a careful observer would note increasing cumulus clouds and a falling barometer. Some cold fronts can sweep in with only a few minutes' warning, much to the chagrin of big-wall climbers. Cold-front precipitation, however, is relatively brief and the aftermath is usually serene, with crisp, clear air and scattered cumulus clouds in the sky for a while. Of concern to the wilderness trekker is the sudden drop in the freez-

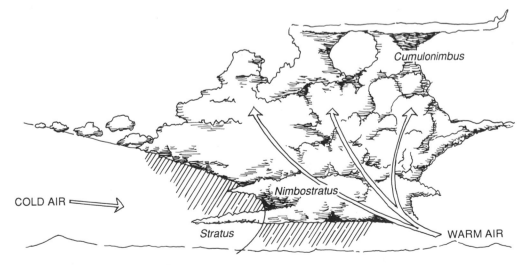

Fig. 8-4. Approaching cold front

ing level, which may leave unprepared campers or hikers stranded in hypothermic conditions.

An *occluded front* is where two or more fronts converge. This can happen when a faster-moving cold front overtakes a warm front. Often described as a zipper being pulled across the sky uniting the two fronts, occlusion may yield the worst characteristics of both fronts.

Stationary fronts develop when opposing fronts balance each other so that no movement occurs. The clouds and weather associated with stationary fronts are often similar to those associated with warm fronts.

In fig. 8-5, a cold front (identified by the icicle-shaped barbs of its symbol) is moving southeast across California. A warm front (with rounded barbs like rain drops) extends across Nevada and Idaho. South of the California–Oregon border, the two fronts have joined to form an occluded front. A stationary front (symbolized by sharp and rounded barbs on opposite sides) lies across New Mexico.

Fronts can, and do, pass without any significant weather being created at all. The air behind a warm front can be only one degree warmer than the air it overtakes. So don't expect a heat wave to follow a snow siege just because a warm front is approaching!

Frontal passage can usually be detected by a shift in the wind. If you're enduring a typical cold-front storm, for example, you'll know the front has passed when winds from the south change to winds from the north. This doesn't mean the show is over, but the end is near.

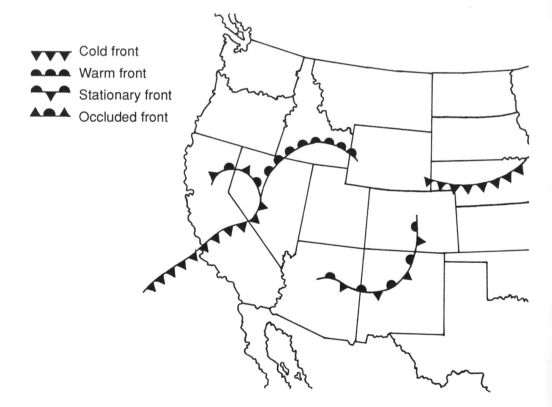

Cold front
Warm front
Stationary front
Occluded front

Fig. 8-5. Symbols used on weather maps for various types of fronts

MICROCLIMATES: WEATHER OR NOT SIZE COUNTS

As we've seen, mountains and other topographical irregularities on the earth's surface can affect the weather. In addition, the presence of a nearby large body of water, like an ocean or lakes, can profoundly alter local conditions. Relatively small areas that experience weather patterns substantially different from those around them are said to have distinct microclimates.

In the mountains, the astute traveler considers the effect of a microclimate when choosing a camping spot. At night, canyons frequently become conduits for cold, dense air flowing down from higher elevations. On calm nights, this chilled air tends to pool in low-lying valleys, often the same spots where inviting lakes beckon the inexperienced camper. The result is a temperature inversion—warmer air overlying cooler air. During the colder months, you may want to avoid canyon bottoms and valleys and take advantage of warmer temperatures higher up on the slopes.

Another local phenomenon associated with mountains is the compressional heating of dry air flowing rapidly down-slope. In the Rocky Mountain and Cascade ranges of North America, for example, this is called a Chinook wind ("snow eater") since it can rapidly melt accumulations of winter snow. Chinooks—and its European version called a Foehn—occur when strong moisture-bearing winds give up most of their precipitation over the windward slopes and blast down the lee side of the ridge line, now drier and warmer. If you are crossing snow or ice fields, be alert for icefalls or avalanche conditions due to the sudden warming.

Sometimes moving air aloft holds moisture as vapor until it collides with or flows over a high peak. The air compresses on the windward side of the peak, rises along the slope, and then experiences a drop in pressure (and therefore temperature) as it goes past the barrier. A long "banner cloud" streams from the apex of the peak, or the peak may be hidden in a "cloud cap." This is why climbers may encounter whiteout conditions when approaching a summit.

When a long chain of high mountains interrupts the prevailing flow of moist,

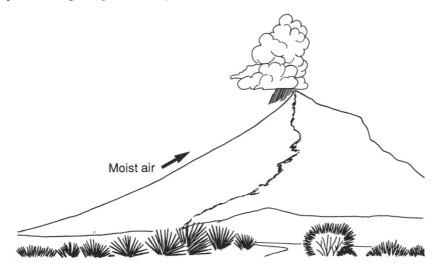

Moist air

Fig. 8-6. Orographic lift

Lenticular clouds often form downwind from a mountain crest. (Photo by James Glenn Pearson)

clear air, spectacular lenticular (lens-shaped) clouds can appear downwind of the crest line. Looking like a phalanx of hovering flying saucers, they are clouds caught at the apex of a stationary wave over, or downwind from, the mountain crest.

Mountains are notorious producers of thunderstorms. Thunderstorms can be dealt with or avoided if you understand their origin and development. Some thunderstorms are initiated by the heating of a broad area of the earth's surface. Others, called orographic thunderstorms, are those triggered by moisture-laden air moving rapidly up mountain slopes (see fig. 8-6). In many of the Western mountain ranges during the summer months, you can almost set your watch to the daily replay of orographic thunderstorms. Heating by the morning sun causes updrafts, the uplifted air chills over the mountain peaks, billowy cumulus clouds build into monster cumulonimbus (thunderheads), and by afternoon the whole show of lightning, gusty winds, rain, and perhaps hail proceeds. Luckily, mountain thunderstorms are born, live, and die in a rather short time, literally drowning themselves out of existence. The unique hazards of lightning associated with these storms will be dealt with in Chapter 12, Mountain Travel. Lightning mishaps are covered in Chapter 15, Wilderness First Aid.

Along the Pacific coast, unique conditions give rise to forms of weather distinct from those of the rest of the continent. The coastal strip often experiences a daily cycle of winds that is purely local in origin. During the day, a sea breeze occurs when cool air over the ocean is pulled inland to replace air rising over the sun-warmed interior land mass. This wind falters, or even reverses, as the inland temperature plummets at night.

If moist air drawn in by the sea breeze flows uphill along a coastal slope and gets chilled to the dew point, low stratus clouds or convective fog results. Another common phenomenon is advective fog along the coast. Here the incoming moist marine air is chilled by cool coastal waters or adjacent land masses and the condensation takes place at surface level, or not

Low stratus clouds along the Oregon Coast (Photo by George Ostertag)

far above it. Often a widespread temperature inversion exists under such conditions, with cool, foggy, or muggy air (often called the "marine layer") underlying warmer, drier air.

Another kind of fog occurs in valleys both close to and far from the ocean. The circumstances ideal for the formation of radiation fog (tule fog) are dominant high pressure; clear, cold, cloudless nights; and almost no wind. As the earth's surface radiates its heat into the atmosphere overnight and cools, water vapor condenses into a fog that hovers just a few feet above the ground. If a temperature inversion is present and there is little mixing of air, this kind of fog can persist for days, as it occasionally does on a grand scale in California's Central Valley, and in high mountain valleys.

WHITHER THE WEATHER

Where can you find the best, up-to-date information about the weather? Try the newspaper first. The weather maps, statistics, and forecasts are fairly exhaustive, if not completely timely. Nowadays, however, there is more current and dynamic information available.

Television weather reports may range anywhere from entertaining to frustrating. If you subscribe to cable TV that offers a continuous weather channel, try that as well. Most PBS-affiliated television stations broadcast a program called "A.M. Weather," which airs around 6 or 7 A.M. weekdays. "A.M. Weather" is produced by professional meteorologists for pilots. Although a bit technical, it should be one of your most trusted sources of information. Consider that pilots and wilderness trekkers have some of the same concerns and traverse some of the same rarefied heights, and you will readily appreciate this short but valuable broadcast.

With a computer and access to a major commercial database network, you can obtain on-line information from the National Weather Service. CompuServe, for one, offers this feature with various levels of detail, ranging from high/low temperatures for selected cities to high-resolution graphic displays of weather charts.

The National Oceanic and Atmospheric Administration (the parent organization of the National Weather Service) maintains a network of more than 380 radio stations across the United States that broadcasts on the VHF FM band in the 162.40 to 162.55 MHz range. These stations continuously transmit weather observations, as well as forecast conditions and information useful to the special needs of listeners in the stations' area, such as boaters, anglers, and hikers.

Once you've gathered the available information, it will be up to you to make your own predictions for the specific area you intend to visit. One clue is the terrain. Most of the mountain ranges of the world are oriented along a north–south or northwest–southeast axis. That means that if a Pacific storm is predicted, the west flanks of mountain ranges are likely to receive the brunt of the precipitation; they face the approaching storm clouds. On the lee slopes, you would expect less precipitation but powerful downdrafts and gusty winds. A warm air mass from the south bearing tropical moisture, on the other hand, might be expected to collide with large obstacles in its path and unleash the heaviest precipitation on south-facing slopes.

In the field, you may have to use your sensory skills to gauge the weather, and perhaps a barometer or altimeter to detect pressure changes. One important clue indicating possible bad weather in the mountains is the appearance of lenticular clouds. If layers of lenticulars develop, followed by lowering overcast, watch out—precipitation is probably on its way.

In general, the weather will probably remain clear if the barometer stays steady or rises. Bad weather is likely on its way if the barometer drops. Barometers, however, are of limited use in the Southwest, where changes in pressure span a relatively small range.

Another way to keep tabs on regional weather is to carry a small Weather Band radio along on the trip.

Be prepared for every type of weather and you'll be able to journey with confidence and appreciate—even enjoy—nature's multifaceted moods. As Mark Twain said, "There is only one thing we can be sure of about the weather ... there will be plenty of it."

RECOMMENDED READING

Lockhart, Gary. *The Weather Companion.* Wiley Press, 1988. (One of the more interesting books on weather legends and lore. Explores the scientific basis for old wives' tales about the weather.)

Schaefer, Vincent J. and John A. Day. *A Field Guide to the Atmosphere.* Houghton Mifflin Co., 1983.

Scorer, Richard. *Clouds of the World (An Encyclopedia of Clouds).* (A beautiful catalog—now unfortunately out of print—of clouds, with detailed explanations of the hows and whys of clouds and how they affect the atmosphere.)

RESOURCES

Pocket barometers. These instruments are handy tools; learn their proper operation and limitations for full enjoyment. They range in price from about $30 to $300, depending on their precision and altitude range. Check at your favorite outdoor or mountain shop.

Pocket Weather Trends. A laminated, full-color slide chart that matches sky conditions and wind patterns for a 12- to 36-hour forecast. Available from Sporty's Pilot Shop, 800-543-8633, catalog #1612A ($4.95).

Weather Forecaster or Weather Cube. These National Weather Service broadcast receivers are available from The Nature Company or Radio Shack (approx. $40).

Fording a stream with the help of a hiking staff; in swifter water, pack straps should be loose and waist belt unbuckled (Photo by Jerry Schad)

Wilderness Travel

NELSON COPP, DON STOUDER, MIKE FRY, BOB FEUGE,
AND CAROLYN WOOD

This chapter focuses on how to travel and camp in the wilderness, with the emphasis on doing it safely and gently. As with any kind of travel in remote areas, travel with friends; there's safety in numbers. The qualities of wilderness areas are preserved when travelers leave no trace of their passage, and are degraded when abused in any of dozens of ways, some of them not too obvious. We can only justify our use of a wilderness area for recreation when we strive to "leave no trace."

LEARNING NEW SKILLS

Inexperienced persons often don't ask questions or attempt to participate in making trip decisions because they may believe everyone else already knows the answers. Actually, being a novice means you need to ask questions about anything you don't understand. Don't hesitate to speak to the leader about a pace that's too fast, or when you need to stop for a pack or clothing adjustment. Taking care of such needs immediately, rather then delaying them, will save time in the long run.

Don't leave your powers of reasoning and judgement at home just because you are in an unfamiliar situation. When you're appropriately assertive, you become a responsible member of the team. You take responsibility for yourself as well as others.

Some women may think that men know more about the outdoors simply because they are male. It's surprising how many men who are novices feel resentful over their female partner's expectation that thcy know how to handle everything. By the same token, men with plenty of wilderness experience are sometimes equally unhappy when they are expected to do all the thinking and call all the shots.

Mastery, possession of skill, or technique requires time, patience, and experience. The key word as you are mastering your new skills is patience. Remember to be patient with yourself and patient with others. At first, everything takes at least twice as long than you think it will. As with other areas in your life where you were once a novice and now enjoy a certain level of mastery, wilderness travel requires you to develop new skills and new perspectives so your experience will be enjoyable and safe.

TRAILHEAD TIPS

Automobiles are by far the most commonly used mode of transportation to and from wilderness trailheads or entry points. Although criminal activity within the wilderness itself is rare, theft and vandalism can be quite common in places where people leave cars unattended for long periods. Try to park in designated areas and let a ranger know how long your car will be parked. Don't forget to lock your car and remove all valuables. For further protection you can disable your car's ignition, or install an anti-theft device on the steering wheel. If you need to use a trailhead that is known to be troublesome, you can have someone drop you off and return to pick you up.

In some areas you may have to contend with theft and vandalism of a different kind. Bears have been known to force their way into cars to get at food they can smell. Marmots, porcupines, and other animals may chew on tires or rubber hoses under the hood.

If your car has recently been prone to mechanical problems, park near a telephone so you can call for help if your car won't start when you return.

Some of the more remote "non-official" wilderness areas that don't enjoy a ban on motorized travel have dirt roads and jeep trails penetrating deep into their interiors. It is tempting for those who arrive in 4-wheel-drive rigs to maneuver as far as possible into these areas on wheels. This can be environmentally damaging, and it's quite often self-defeating. Trying to save a mile or two of walking can result in getting stuck. You may be faced with no easy way to turn around, or hours of tedious digging to free your vehicle from mud, soft sand, or snow.

Not all trailheads have drinking water available, so unless you know for sure that there'll be some, you may want to carry potable water in your vehicle so that you can begin your hike without having to treat water. Bring some water in a large container—one to five gallons, depending on the number in your party and the length of your hike. It's also nice to have some drinking water waiting for you at the trailhead when you hike out.

TRAIL WALKING

We rarely, if ever, think about the act of walking in our everyday lives. When setting off on a long journey through uneven or hilly terrain, however, we must carefully consider pacing, rhythm, rest stops, foot care, and maintaining energy.

Pacing relates to fatigue and frustration. Finding your own pace or travel style on the trail can minimize both. On your first few trips, notice whether you prefer a fast, moderate, or slow and steady pace. You will know in the first 15 minutes on the trail. If the pace is too slow for you, you will feel antsy and want to go more quickly. If the pace is too fast, you will find yourself out of breath and struggling to keep up. Whether "piston legs" or ambler, it is important to realize that you can't change the pace that is the most comfortable for you. The faster hiker finds it irritating to try to slow down and the slower-paced hiker finds it impossible to speed up. Equally important is knowing that once you find your pace and stick to it, you can reach any destination.

Efficient hiking requires a steady, rhythmic pace. When going uphill, shorten your stride but try to maintain a steady rhythm. Try not to lift your feet higher than you have to, except to swing them around obstacles like rocks and tree roots. It's better to expend your energy evenly throughout a day-long hike, rather than moving too fast in the first hour when you're feeling unbridled and strong.

Some hikers, especially those who are physically well trained, experience a "second wind"—a surge of energy that follows an initial period in which the body accustoms itself to the demands of hard exercise. With a second wind you may feel more comfortable going faster, but, again, resist the temptation to do so if you intend to be walking all day.

After about 20 to 40 minutes on the trail, you may want to stop to remove extra clothing and adjust pack straps or shoe laces. Some trip leaders make this first stop a "divided halt," suggesting that men go in one direction and women another, to take care of any unmet needs.

Throughout the day, stop at regular intervals of $1/2$ hour or 1 hour to rest, relieve the pack weight, stretch, or grab a snack. Make these rests brief—5 minutes is good—so that you don't cool down too much or become stiff. Experiment with taking breaks. Some will find that a 10-minute stop every hour works best. Others may decide to stop only when hungry. In unfamiliar areas, you should be keeping track of your position, so rest periods are excellent times to update or confirm your location on a map.

For longer rest stops, such as lunch, put on extra clothing immediately if the weather is cool or cold. The sensation of warmth you get from hiking uphill is from your body's shedding of heat while it expends extra energy. Warm, sweaty skin can turn cold within minutes after you stop.

Don't eat too heavily at any one sitting, or you'll feel like a freight train when you try to move again. Rather, spread some of your lunch over the numerous other breaks.

When walking up very steep slopes, you won't want to become so winded that you can't continue. One solution is to use the "rest step." In this technique you pause briefly every time you begin a new step:

1. Lift your left leg, move it forward, and place it (unweighted).
2. Pause, keeping all of your weight on the right foot.
3. Shift your weight to the left leg and move the right leg forward.
4. Pause, and then continue with step 1.

The rest step is easier to do on a steep slope than on flat ground, so practice it there to gain a sense of rhythm.

Some hikers swear by a hiking staff; others could care less about one. You either love them or hate them. Walking sticks can add more stability when crossing water, extend your reach, test the steadiness of rocks before you try them, and become part of the rhythm of your hiking pace. A staff can be advantageous in areas where balance is precarious, but awkward when you need both hands for climbing or where dense vegetation renders it useless. Pick one where the top is close to the level of your hand when your arm is bent at the elbow. Try one on a short hike. If it feels comfortable, you will eventually find that your walking stick seems like an extension of your arm. It is a silent companion traveling with you, great to lean on as you contemplate new vistas. If it seems like an unnecessary nuisance, don't use one.

Foot blisters simply can't be ignored. Heed the first signs of friction ("hot spots"): adjust your socks, put on moleskin, or do whatever it takes to relieve the pain and prevent damage to the skin.

When extra energy is needed, your body usually tells you so—you get hungry and feel fatigued. Dehydration is more insidious. When you're strenuously exercising, your body usually needs more fluids than thirst dictates. In hot weather, it's difficult for the body to absorb moisture fast enough. In dry, cold weather, a surprising amount of moisture can be lost from hard breathing and from "insensible perspiration" (perspiration evaporating so fast that you don't sense its presence). Sip water or other fluids at frequent intervals, even though you may not feel thirst. If you don't feel the need to urinate every couple of hours or so, you aren't drinking enough fluids and your body will not be working at its peak performance.

If you are hiking with a group, ideally your natural pace should match the pace of other members of a group. Sometimes even spouses and close friends don't have the same pace. The most common reason probably has to do with different lengths of stride. An example of this would be a 6-foot-tall person backpacking with a 5-foot-4-inch-tall person. The shorter person either has to have a naturally faster pace to keep up with the longer strides of the taller person, or they have to agree to not worry about hiking at the same pace. This is also true when there is a difference in physical condition. Realize that sharing your wilderness experience may mean you share lunch breaks and camp time, but not necessarily every step along the way.

If you know you're significantly slower than others on a trip, it's essential you communicate about it. If it's a formal or club-sponsored trip, let the leader know. Slower-paced hikers are most likely only 5 to 10 minutes behind the fastest hiker, anyway. You can verify this easily by having the lead hiker time how long it takes for you to reach him or her after he or she has stopped. Usually an assistant leader stays behind to keep track of the slower members, but if not, and you or others get spread out or separated, you'll want to know where you're going. Normally the leader keeps the group together, but that's not always realized in practice. For safety reasons, it is vital that slower-paced hikers learn to read their trail map. Before setting out, look at the map with your hiking partner or the trail leader and identify possible points of confusion (e.g., where other trails cross your trail). Agree where to meet next, such as when the trail splits off or at the first water crossing. Or you could decide when to meet, such as in an hour. Agree to a trail sign at unexpected points of confusion. This may be a bandanna tied on a bush down the correct trail or an arrow drawn in the dirt or made with pebbles with a word or phrase that identifies it for you alone. Once you have reached your special trail marker, remember to remove it to avoid confusing others using the same trail.

Hikers should yield the right-of-way to horses. (Photo by James Glenn Pearson)

Hikers in groups can get spread apart just as readily when "hot shots" insist on forging ahead. Courtesy dictates that on organized hikes, anyone wishing to go ahead of the leader asks permission first. Trail blazers, the faster-paced ones in the lead, need to be alert to points where there is unanticipated confusion, such as a missing trail sign or a false trail. Leave clear directional signs or wait until your partner or group reaches you. Always stop at the agreed-to rendezvous point or time.

Slower hikers often need as much—or more—time for breaks as faster hikers. It can be most frustrating when a slower hiker catches up to others taking a break, only to have them take off moments later. Feeling pressured to stick with the group, the slower hiker may not have enough time to rest and recover, thus increasing fatigue even more. In the case of a trip designed on a tight schedule, this may be unavoidable. If there's discretionary time on the hike, though, the slower persons should be assertive enough to make their needs and desires known.

Hiking etiquette also requires that you yield the right-of-way to horses and other pack animals. Horses and mules have been tramping the mountains, serving the needs of anglers, trail crews, backcountry rangers, and tourists for well over a century. Remember that trail courtesy dictates that hikers yield the right-of-way. The pack-train leader, who knows his or her animals well, may ask you to move to a position where the animals can pass safely. This can be a tense moment; gather the group to one side of the trail, stand quietly, and don't do anything that may play upon the animals' skittish tendencies. If you are on a hill, the safest side of the trail is uphill. However, this may make you look bigger and hence unfamiliar to the pack animals. Take guidance from the rider or the pack-train leader, who knows the animals' tendencies. Talking in quiet tones to the animals may help put them in a state of ease.

CROSSING STREAMS AND RIVERS

Most trails have bridges of some sort across streams and rivers. Bridges might be elaborate structures or simply a large log with cross-hatches carved in it for better traction. However, some trails require crossing a river on foot. This can be accomplished safely, though fording fast-moving streams can be deceptively dangerous.

First you'll need to choose the best spot to cross. Where water flows through a constricted area, as between boulders, you may be able to hop over safely if the gap is narrow enough. However, the water flows fastest there, so these areas are most dangerous if you fall in. Wider stretches of the stream may contain either deep pools with slow-moving water or fast-moving, shallow water with riffles.

Take the time to thoroughly investigate the stream well above and below where you want to cross. Make certain there are no waterfalls or swift rapids below your intended crossing spot, in case you stumble. If the water is more than knee deep and very swift at the most favorable spots, consider turning back, outflanking the stream via a long detour, or waiting until the water flow decreases. The latter alternative is often practical for streams fed by snowmelt. In the early morning, such streams may be running at a far lower level than during the heat of the afternoon.

When fording fast-moving streams, always wear shoes to protect your feet from sharp rocks. You can keep your boots on, snugly attached to your feet, with or without socks. If you're going to be wading through water quite often, try wearing lightweight boots with uncoated fabric panels and polypropylene socks. The water will quickly drain from the boots and socks, preventing a clammy feeling. If you can carry the extra weight, bring a pair of sneakers and change into them before

109

fording, keeping your boots dry. Applying a lubricant such as petroleum jelly or Bagbalm (a veterinary product for cows with a small, but loyal following among hikers) will keep your feet a little more comfortable. Gaiters will help keep sand and gravel out of your boots.

Before wading in, try to estimate the stream's depth and toss a twig in to gauge the speed of the flow. Loosen your pack straps and unhook the hip belt in case you fall in (your pack is expendable, you're not). Use a hiking staff or a sturdy branch as a "third leg" upstream of you while crossing. Cross facing upstream so your three points of support form a triangle. If the current is swift, choose a path that takes you diagonally across and downstream. That way you won't have to fight the force of the water quite as much as you lift each foot.

More sophisticated methods of stream crossing involve rigging a rope across the stream to assist passage. Never tie yourself to the rope—if you fall, the rushing water may hold you under. Cross on the downstream side of the rope, holding on as you walk across.

You must be especially careful about waterfalls. Every year, people are killed in the mountains by being swept over the lips of waterfalls.

CROSS-COUNTRY TRAVEL

Cross-country, or off-trail, travel can be more challenging and more fun, but often more dangerous and environmentally harmful, than sticking to established routes. By cross-country, we don't mean short-cutting switchback trails—a harmful practice that promotes erosion. Cross-country travel can take a hiker or climber to remote peaks and other secluded destinations to which there are no trails, but it's usually slower and more difficult than

trail travel. Navigational difficulties often increase as well. In a few well-traveled wilderness areas, off-trail travel is prohibited because the impact is too harmful. In some very remote areas, such as parts of Alaska and northern Canada, there are very few trails and hikers routinely travel cross-country.

Make sure your equipment and clothing are up to the task. Wear long pants to protect against rocks, ticks, and low-lying vegetation; and wear a long-sleeve top if scratchy vegetation is likely to be at least waist-high. Sturdy boots will help protect against ankle twists and stone bruises caused by rolling rocks. Gaiters (normally used in deep snow) fastened around your ankles and boots can keep all kinds of debris from entering your boots.

Cross-country travel is more appropriate for smaller groups than hordes of people. Groups should stay close together in order to remain within earshot of each other. Single-file travel is usually most efficient, especially in areas choked by dense brush or vegetation. Don't let tree and shrub limbs that you have pushed aside snap back into the face of the person who follows you. Keep a good distance.

In general, it is best to keep to a single-file, low-impact system. However, there are certain times when you need to learn to make your own choices. When crossing over rough terrain, hopping streams, or scrambling over boulders, leg length, physical condition, and pace make a difference. Learn to identify routes that will work well with your ability, level of comfort, and leg length. It can make the difference between an easy ascent or descent and a difficult one.

Also, when traversing delicate ground or vegetation, too many hikers in a column can cut a deep furrow and hasten erosion. To minimize this effect, members of a party can walk side by side to spread out the impact. When possible, try to skirt delicate areas like wet meadows.

Waterfalls are beautiful to look at, but be cautious when hiking around or above them. (Photo by Jerry Schad)

Plotting a cross-country route, either at home (with maps on the table) or in the wilderness itself, is intriguing and challenging. In most cases, you should try to follow the same route that a trail builder would. Trails are often indirectly routed so as to avoid steep ascents, steep terrain, and obstacles such as rock outcrops—even though that means hikers using them will have to walk farther to get from point A to point B. When planning or choosing a cross-country route, weigh the advantages of ascending or descending a steep hill against the advantages of a longer but more gradual route around the hill. Take into account the nature of the terrain along each alternate route. Try to avoid crossing steep gullies that could contain dropoffs or harbor snow late into the season. Take into account the types of vegetation—thick brush, open forest, or perhaps a lack of vegetation (as on scree)—that might be present on any of the alternate routes.

Whether it is more efficient to travel along canyon bottoms or streams as opposed to parallel ridges depends on the nature of the local geography. Does the canyon bottom or stream meander excessively? Will frequent stream crossings slow you down? Are the ridgelines spiked by rock outcrops, or are they smooth and relatively free of impeding vegetation?

In practice, route finding over rough terrain is an exercise in improvisation. Despite your initial planning, you will find it necessary to change your intended course many times. Just keep your eyes open and your mind focused on the important milestones or destinations ahead on your intended route.

When traveling cross-country, keep safety uppermost in your mind at all times. Shortcuts over difficult terrain may be tempting, but often they're a waste of time and effort if not outright dangerous. Cross-country travel is a mind game involving elements of intuition as well as standard navigational skills. Improvements in skill will only come by experience.

TRAVELING AT NIGHT—A SPECIAL SKILL

Generally, wilderness travelers should always try to arrive at camp or at the car before nightfall. If lost at night, it is almost always better to spend a night out and resume hiking in daylight. For a properly equipped hiker with emergency shelter, extra clothing, and extra food (see Chapter 5, Outfitting: The Basic Equipment, Essentials), an overnight bivouac should present no problems.

Under certain circumstances, it may be preferable to press on at night, assuming one is not lost. Also, experienced persons may elect to travel over familiar trails or terrain at night in order to gain a unique, nocturnal perspective of nature.

Travel at night requires that you see as well as possible. If there's a full or nearly full moon in the sky, you're in luck. When traveling by moonlight, try to preserve your night vision. Generally a trail is more visible to a dark-adapted eye than to one dazzled by a glaring flashlight beam. If you do use a flashlight, hold it low so that you can pick out the shadows of obstacles on the route ahead. Lamps worn on the head are of limited value for hiking because shadows cast by the light are in the same direction as the hiker's line of sight and therefore can't be seen. Two flashlights—one a broad-beam lamp on the head, the other a regular flashlight in the hand—work best.

You'll discover that if you can retain your dark adaptation, your peripheral vision is quite good. This is because the periphery of your retina is rich in the "rod" cells that come into play under low light levels. In order to preserve this advantage while also using some artificial light, some hikers use a red filter over their flashlight (a single or double layer of red cellophane over the flashlight lens or around the bulb works well). This eliminates other colors present in white light that tend to spoil one's night vision.

WILDERNESS CAMPING

SELECTING A CAMPSITE

When you choose a campsite, do so not only with your comfort in mind, but also the care of the environment. Strive not only to observe the "no trace" principle, but also to clean up or restore camping areas that have been abused by others. If not done properly, camping can affect the wilderness far more seriously than any kind of travel through it.

Even when not required to do so, try to use designated or previously used campsites. If possible, your site should be a minimum of 200 feet from lakes, streams, and trails. Avoid camping in areas subject to runoff or rockfall, or below rotten trees. Never camp in delicate areas such as alpine meadows. Sandy areas are preferred over those covered by vegetation. Since cold air often flows downward at night and collects in low-lying spots, a higher campsite may be warmer. Flying insects are often much less abundant in the higher and drier areas as well. Consider also the effects of wind and the position of the sun as it rises the next morning. Camping on an east-facing slope sheltered from a west wind will make it easier for you to get up the next morning.

When camping in popular areas, be a considerate neighbor. Don't crowd other campers. Leave sound equipment, pets, and other reminders of the civilized world at home. Peace and quiet are two of the earth's most valuable resources. Listen to the soft music of the wilderness: the wind, water, and bird song.

When selecting a site for your tent or sleeping bag, remove small rocks and twigs, but avoid wholesale "grading." The century-old practice of cutting branches for bedding is environmentally harmful, and unnecessary today now that lightweight sleeping pads provide us with all the cushioning we need. During mild weather, sleeping under the stars can be carefree and enjoyable. Cold, rain, or mosquitoes, however, may dictate the need for a tent or a tent substitute like a bivouac sack, a tube tent, or a tarp rigged overhead. In harsh conditions, there's no substitute for a sturdy tent.

You can help eliminate the annoyance of mosquitoes and other biting insects by applying insect repellent, using netting in a tent, wearing a head net, or moving to a breezy spot where the insects can be blown away.

SANITATION

Another problem you will deal with at the campsite is sanitation. Because most of us are so accustomed to the accessibility and ease of use of modern bathrooms, "toileting" in the wilderness can be a major area of concern. The techniques of eliminating body wastes and maintaining privacy—especially when part of a group—can be problematic.

Urination is not a complicated issue, since urine is normally biologically sterile, although it causes odor problems too close to camp (try to keep your toilet downwind from camp). If "nature calls" routinely around 2 A.M. at home, then it likely will in the wilderness, too. Since the bathroom may not be a convenient few feet away, one technique is to use a "tent bottle." This is common on mountaineering expeditions, when weather conditions may not allow you to go outside.

Women can use a "tent bottle" along with a special funnel designed for a woman's anatomy. Some backpacking shops and mail-order companies carry these funnels. Set aside a one-liter plastic bottle with a narrow top and spray-paint the bottle, except for an area masked from top to bottom, to clearly mark the bottle and also provide a clear space to view its contents.

113

A one-liter bottle handles about two average "pees." Set up your private indoor bathroom before you go to sleep: Have your pee bottle and funnel, a small pack of tissues, a couple of pre-moistened towelettes, a self-sealing plastic bag, and your flashlight (a headlamp works best) nearby. Stay off your sleeping bag when first practicing the technique. After filling the tent bottle, screw the top back on immediately! Let the tissues catch any drips from the funnel and then leave the funnel out to dry. Stash the tissues and towelettes in the plastic bag. Next day, empty the bottle, rinse it if possible, and let it air out.

Wherever existing facilities are not available, travel a good distance away from camp and any source of water (usually 200 feet or more) to deposit solid body waste. Dig a small "cat-hole" 6 to 10 inches deep, squat down, and when finished, fill in the hole with soil and then tamp it down. The specific technique will come by trial and error. The squat position may be difficult if you are accustomed to only sitting in chairs, and can become unbearable if maintained for a long time. If there's a tree with low, strong branches nearby, another technique is to hold on and balance over the hole. If you can find a small log or a rock in a private spot with soft soil beside it, you can dig a hole there and use the log or rock as a kind of a toilet seat while extending your buttocks over the hole. A third technique is to dig the hole near something you can lean back into. This is tricky and it is better to put something soft between your lower back and the log or rock to prevent scrapes. A fourth technique is to try balancing with your hands behind you and your feet in front of the hole. It's best to pack out all toilet paper or burn it in a safe manner. Be careful if you do any burning—fires have been started by campers leaving smoldering paper buried in dry leaves or pine needles.

Many people report that half of their internal plumbing system refuses to function smoothly while on wilderness trips. Of course, no one ever dies from a few days of constipation. In some cases, it is due to a change of diet. Some people are susceptible to "inhibition constipation," which is probably triggered by being uncomfortable about toileting in the outdoors. Inhibition constipation can be overcome by first understanding that you are not the only one who has experienced it. Try drinking something warm shortly after waking up. Take the time to find a pleasant spot far enough away from camp that affords absolute privacy. Allow yourself plenty of time to relax and let nature take its course. If you're on a trip with a tight schedule, then plan to wake up earlier so you'll have enough time. You can even prepare your latrine the evening before. Be careful where you dig a hole, though. You won't want some unsuspecting member of your party tripping in the night.

Women have another area of hygiene to consider: menstruation. The decision whether or not to travel in the wilderness during menstruation depends on your experiences at home. If cramping and flow are normally no problem, you'll find your menstrual periods in the wilderness are only slightly inconvenient. By taking self-sealing plastic bags for used sanitary products, extra tissues, and moistened towelettes, you'll handle any situation with aplomb.

Always pack in a full supply of sanitary products! Even women with menstrual cycles like clockwork may find that altitude, heavy exercise, or just plain excitement can alter the normal pattern. Even if you don't end up using most of your supplies, there may be a less-prepared woman in the group who might be very grateful for your foresight.

In the event you are caught short of supplies, extra panties, socks, T-shirts, bandannas, or handkerchiefs can be used. Fold the piece of cloth to fit, and secure to underclothes with safety pins, if they're available. If you have an allergy to wool, don't use wool socks or you may find yourself with two problems to overcome! When your improvised items are used up, you can wash them out at least 200 feet away from any source of water, or you can bag them up in a sealed plastic bag, carry them out, and wash them at home.

The best way to dispose of your used sanitary products is to simply bag all used items securely and carry them out. As with used toilet paper, avoid burning them. Some products don't burn completely anyway, since they're made of other substances in addition to paper.

While there used to be many options regarding getting rid of garbage, now there are only two: use trash cans where available, and pack out all garbage from areas where garbage cans are not available.

WASHING UP

How to live without the conveniences of the bathroom is a major concern of beginners, but life without your shower is simple to master. Generally, on shorter trips you won't need to wash your whole body, your hair, or your clothes, but on longer trips bathing can be a welcome refresher. Often, you can find a good swimming hole to wash off the day's dust (don't use soap, though). For day's-end freshening, there are moist towelettes in various sizes available in drugstores, usually in the baby supply section. They come in handy packets of a dozen towelettes, scented and unscented. Remember, for this type of convenience, you will be carrying in extra weight that you have to carry out.

The simplest bathing facility is the largest cooking pot you already have along. There are plastic fold-up basins that can serve as a mini-bathtub for foot washing and clothes washer, but this extra weight is probably only necessary on longer trips. Fill with water and move to a site a minimum of 200 feet from the main water source. With a sunny site, you can wash with cold water. If you have enough fuel,

heat some wash water or use any clean hot water left after washing dishes. Use only biodegradable soap, and use it sparingly.

For full luxury, you can bring a portable plastic mini-shower bag, which, when filled with water and left on a sunny rock for a few hours, gives you a warmish adequate shower. You can also fill the shower bag with water you've heated—this is quicker and ensures the water is warm enough, but it does use fuel. The 1.5-gallon shower bag is fine for a two-person shower, including hair washing, if you are each conservative in your use of water. Remember to put your shower set-up in a place where the runoff does not go into a stream or lake. If possible, stand on a rock to keep your feet clean. Arrange your after-shower clothes for easy access. Pick a sunny and hopefully draft-free site. You can rig a shower enclosure with your poncho, some rope, and a couple of trees.

CAMPFIRES

Many hikers look forward to the pleasure of a crackling campfire. Remember though, that in many wilderness areas they're prohibited, or regulated by fire permit. Actually, you rarely need a fire. Cooking needs can be easily be met by your camping stove alone (see Chapter 5, Outfitting: The Basic Equipment, *Stoves and Cooking Equipment*). A candle lantern, used as a substitute for a fire, can add a nice warm touch. Your high-tech clothing should keep you reasonably warm.

Being cold at night is a common complaint. Aside from improvements in equipment, here are a few things you can try to make yourself more comfortable in cold conditions:

- Put on warm clothes before you feel cold.
- Find a wind-sheltered spot or orient yourself so that your head is downwind.
- Eat some protein and fats before or

after going to bed (this speeds up your metabolism during the night).

- Exercise before going to bed or do isometric exercises inside your bag.
- Wear plenty of dry clothing, especially the insulating variety, inside your bag.
- Wear a wool cap or down hood to prevent heat from leaving your body through your head.
- Place a bottle of hot water (make sure it doesn't leak) near your feet.
- In an emergency situation, you can sleep close to others to benefit from their body heat.

If you do have a fire, make it a small one. Bonfires are "out" these days. Besides, you'll enjoy the closer companionship of your friends as you crowd around the glowing embers of a small fire. Whenever possible, use the stove units found at some designated campsites, or use existing rock rings at other sites where fires are permitted.

CLOSE ENCOUNTERS OF THE ANIMAL KIND

Encountering wild animals in their natural habitat during wilderness travel enhances everyone's enjoyment of the wilderness. If you're quiet and observant, you'll increase your chances of spotting wildlife and observing their interesting behavior. Animal encounters may involve bears, bighorn sheep, mountain goats, bobcats, mountain lions, and snakes, as well as the more common deer, birds, coyotes, marmots, rabbits, and squirrels. Unexpected encounters with wild animals can be so surprising and so exhilarating that you may forget the wilderness is really their home and that you are an intruder. As a considerate intruder, you have a special obligation to the animals as summarized by the oft-repeated credo, "Take only pictures, leave only footprints." In other words, do not disturb wild animals or their habitats. This means you must not feed, harass, or handle wild animals (even if they're injured), or disturb the nest or den of a wild animal.

No matter how cute or how tame a wild animal appears, you should never feed it. When animals develop a taste for human food, such as the goodies in your pack, they can easily come to depend on it. Reliance on unnatural and unpredictable food sources may reduce the animal's chances for survival in the wild. By accepting food handouts, wild animals quickly lose their fear of man, their natural predator. This process, called habituation, can become destructive. A classic example of habituated animals are the black bears of Yosemite National Park who raid trash cans and campgrounds for food, undeterred by human presence. These animals have become pests to humans, which requires either their evacuation to remote areas or their destruction. The very act of feeding a wild animal can be dangerous. Some animals do "bite the hand that feeds." If bitten, you risk rabies, serious injury, and even death.

Never harass wild animals, even if it seems the animal would suffer no harm. Harassment includes throwing rocks at them, chasing them, and invading their habitats, except where such actions are necessary for self-defense. Photographers are often guilty of unwittingly harassing animals to get better shots. In doing so, they risk retaliation. A harassed mother bear can charge and even kill a person if she feels her young are under attack. It's better to remain quiet and silent and simply observe or photograph these animals from afar.

The practice of handling wild animals, even if they appear tame and friendly, carries some risk as well. Handling can promote harmful habituation of the animal and also increases your risk of being bitten. It may lead to injuring the animal as well. Handling young animals (especially birds and eggs in nests), could result in parental abandonment.

In the wild, you'll occasionally come upon an injured or abandoned animal. Being compassionate, you'll want to intervene and assist the animal. According to many naturalists, however, human intervention is not the best course of action. Animals have natural defensive abilities that may be thwarted by our actions, leaving them even more defenseless later on. A doe, for instance, will deliberately abandon a young fawn to lure a would-be attacker toward her and away from the fawn. In such situations, the fawn (which has no odor) simply lies down and waits motionless for the doe to return. Human intervention can destroy this natural defensive strategy and cause the doe to forsake the fawn. Injured animals in the wilderness should be left alone to nature's course. This can be a heart-rending decision, but it's best in the long run.

BEARS—A SPECIAL CONCERN

A sudden encounter with a bear in the wilderness is both exciting and potentially dangerous. In the temperate regions of the western United States and Canada there are two types: the grizzly bear and the black bear. Encounters with each type must be handled differently to minimize the chance of injury.

Within the North American continent, the modern range of bears has shrunk to encompass the larger mountain ranges of the West and a few areas in the East (fig. 9-1). The black bear is found in almost all mountainous regions of the western United States and beyond.The grizzly is mostly limited to regions in and around Yellowstone and Glacier national parks in the United States—though there have been sporadic sightings of grizzlies in the Cascades, some as far south as the Mount St. Helens area—and in many provincial and national parks in western Canada. Alaska

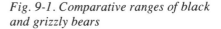 Black bear range   Grizzly bear range

Fig. 9-1. Comparative ranges of black and grizzly bears

is prime habitat for black bears and grizzlies, as well as for the coastal variety of grizzly known as Kodiak or Alaskan brown bear, which grow to enormous size.

Bears are omnivorous—they'll eat almost anything, including nuts, berries, bark, insects, fish, and small animals. A bear's diet changes with the seasons and the climate. Bears spend much of their waking hours foraging far and wide for food, moving mainly along established trails or stream banks, or through "wildlife tunnels" in dense vegetation. In dry seasons, bears will readily invade populated areas to find food.

Much of the human–bear conflict stems from our underestimation of a bear's mental and physical prowess. Bears are not far behind primates in the order of intelli-

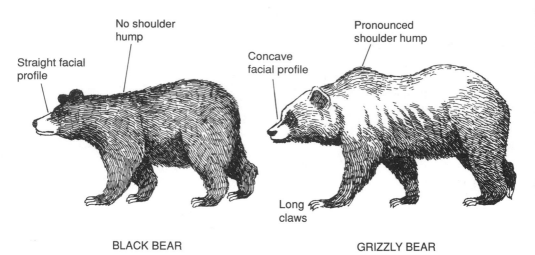

Fig. 9-2. Comparative physical characteristics of black and grizzly bears. Black bears, despite their name, range in color from black to brown to cinnamon. Grizzlies are generally brown in color and larger than back bears.

gence. They're not dumb animals. Instead they're extremely curious animals that tend to investigate whatever piques their curiosity. While humans rely primarily on their visual sense, bears rely on their very keen sense of smell. Bears will readily investigate unusual smells, not necessarily those related to food. They'll check out sunscreen lotion, toothpaste, and lipstick, to name a few. Relative to humans, bears are superior in strength, probably poorer in vision, and probably equally endowed in hearing. Despite their ponderous appearance, they're quite capable of outrunning humans, climbing trees, and swimming.

Is it foolish for women to go into an area frequented by bears during menstruation? There appears to be no clear answer. Experiences vary. Plenty of women have visited bear country while menstruating with no incident. Bear-keepers at zoos report no additional precautions are taken, or recommended, during menstruation. On the other hand, there have been several reports of menstruating women being fatally mauled. Whether their scent was stronger at that time and attracted the bear, or whether it was the fact that their paths

just happened to cross, no one will ever know for sure. A basic precaution is suggested in the book *Bear Attacks: Their Causes and Avoidance* (by Stephen Herrero, Nick Lyons Books, 1985): wear tampons, not external pads.

Black bear or grizzly? Figure 9-2 shows some anatomical differences between black bears and grizzly bears. The black bear is shy, preferring to avoid humans unless it is habituated, protecting its young, or desperate for food. Compared to the grizzly, the black bear is much less prone to violent, deliberate attacks on humans.

A grizzly bear must always be regarded as a potential threat. Grizzlies may interpret a sudden encounter with a human as a threat, and charge, maul, and kill with little warning. What seems threatening to a grizzly may not coincide with your idea of a threat.

The best way of preventing a bear attack is to avoid surprising or threatening the bear. Also, do not do *anything* to threaten any type of bear cubs, since the mother is certainly nearby and will just as certainly defend her cubs vigorously and aggressively. If you somehow provoke a mother bear with cubs, do not defend yourself, and do not run, but retreat as quickly and unthreateningly as possible.

In grizzly country, it's wise to make noise (sing, talk loudly, ring bells) on the trail. Look for signs of grizzly presence like claw marks on trees, bear scat (feces), and bear prints. If you do spot a grizzly, it's best to circle about widely (staying downwind of the bear), or simply abort the hike if you have to. With grizzlies, you have little control of the situation, so aborting the hike may be the wisest course of action.

Black bears are not prone to attack. Their occasional attacks on humans are most likely to be predatory—a child or small adult may be viewed as prey to a large, hungry black bear. If that happens, don't be passive! Defend yourself—kick, yell, throw rocks, swat it with a branch. The bear will usually back down. Don't climb a tree, since black bears can prob-

ably climb a tree as high up and quicker than you.

If a grizzly attacks, however, it is usually responding to what it considers a territorial dispute. You have only two alternatives: You can quickly climb a nearby tree to a height of about 30 feet, or you can "play dead" (see fig. 9-3). Playing dead removes the perception that you are a threat. Never charge a grizzly or run from it. The passive response may result in some mauling, but generally the bear will not continue the attack once it has asserted its dominance. If the bear continues to be aggressive, then you must change tactics and do whatever is possible to save your life. Your best strategy, of course, is early detection and avoidance.

Camping techniques in bear country. When selecting a campsite in bear country, it's best not to camp immediately alongside a trail or a stream, because bears travel in these areas searching for food.

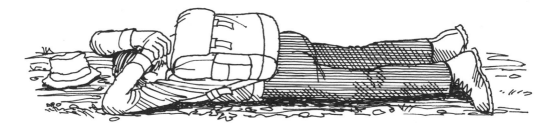

Fig. 9-3. Positions for "playing dead" during a grizzly bear attack: Top, *hands behind neck, with arms protecting the face and side of the head;* bottom, *fetal position, lying on one's side.*

119

Fig. 9-4. Bear-proof box with double latch and chain

Fig. 9-5. Cable for hanging food

Bears also like to investigate regularly used campsites, usually at night. If you detect tracks, scat, or other signs of a bear in the vicinity of your selected campsite, move to a safer place.

It's safer to sleep inside a tent in bear country, because the tent wall provides some separation should the bear decide to claw at smells emanating from the tent. All food and smelly items should be placed in stuff sacks and stored downwind at least 100 feet from the campsite. In certain campgrounds, you can store your food supplies in bear-proof boxes (fig. 9-4), or on cables (fig. 9-5) or poles (fig. 9-6). If these are not available (in most designated wilderness areas, they are not), you can use the "counterbalance method" of hanging

food from trees, recommended by the National Park Service (fig. 9-7) or the "loop and stick" method (fig. 9-8).

Regular counterbalance method. Find a tree with a sturdy limb that is not dead or close to other limbs, and that stands about 20 feet high and extends out at least 10 feet from the trunk (see fig. 9-7). Next, divide your food into two equal bags of no more than ten pounds each, and attach a nylon rope $^1/_8$ inch or larger and at least 50 feet long to the first sack. To the opposite end of the rope, tie a rock that is light enough to toss over the limb but heavy enough to fall to the ground after it has crossed the limb. Before tossing, ensure that the rope isn't snarled. Toss the rock

Fig. 9-6. Pole for hanging food

A

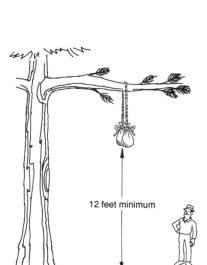

B

1 inch maximum diameter

4 inch minimum diameter

8 feet minimum

14 feet or more to ground

E

F

12 feet minimum

over the end of the limb at least 8 feet away from the trunk of the tree. Pull the rope to elevate the stuff sack, remove the rock from the other end of the rope, and replace it with another food sack or a rock that weighs the same as the food in the first stuff sack. The sack or rock should be tied at a point on the rope that allows both weighted ends to be suspended about

12 feet from the ground. Stuff excess rope into either or both stuff sacks. Find a long stick (or use a ski pole or hiking staff) to shove the second sack upward and also to retrieve the stuff sack later.

Alternate counterbalance method. An alternative to the stick is a second rope, looped through the strings of the first stuff

C

D

G

Fig. 9-7. Regular counterbalance method: A, select tree; B, select branch; C, divide food into two equal bags; D, attach rope to first bag and toss over branch; E, hoist first bag and tie on second bag so that F, both can be suspended about 12 feet above the ground; G, use a long stick to shove one bag upward for retrieval.

sack before it is hoisted. The second rope can be used to pull the first bag down to a counterbalanced position with the second bag. To prevent a bear from using this rope to pull the food bag down, pull the second rope free. When you want to retrieve the food, simply pull the two ends of the second rope together and pull them both downward. This action will lower the

first stuff sack while raising the rock or second stuff sack. Once the stuff sack is released, the counterbalanced rock or second stuff sack should come down easily. But watch your head!

Loop and stick method. An alternative to the counterbalance method is the "loop and stick method" shown in fig. 9-8. First, se-

123

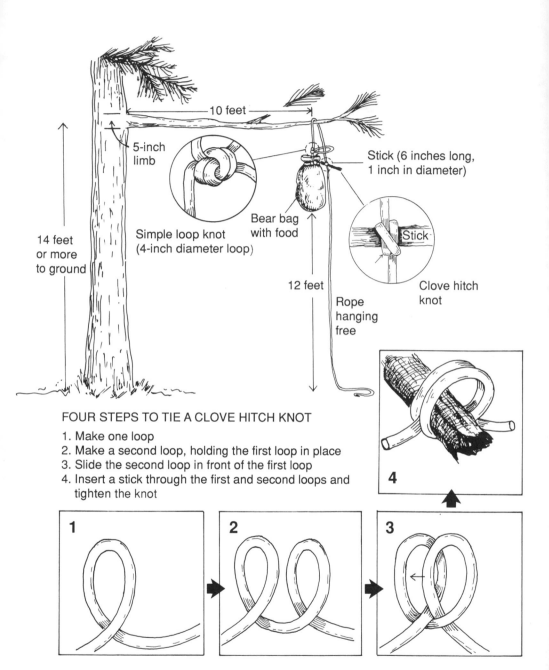

10 feet

5-inch limb

Stick (6 inches long, 1 inch in diameter)

Bear bag with food

Simple loop knot (4-inch diameter loop)

14 feet or more to ground

12 feet

Clove hitch knot

Rope hanging free

FOUR STEPS TO TIE A CLOVE HITCH KNOT

1. Make one loop
2. Make a second loop, holding the first loop in place
3. Slide the second loop in front of the first loop
4. Insert a stick through the first and second loops and tighten the knot

1

2

3

4

Fig. 9-8. Loop and stick method: tie loop knot next to food bag before tossing rope over; thread rope through loop; tie a stick high up on the other end of rope; allow stick to lodge in loop; let rope dangle.

lect a tree limb of the same dimensions as in the counterbalance method. Throw a rope over that limb and tie one end of the rope *securely* to the stuff sack. Just above the stuff sack, tie a 4- to 6-inch loop (using the simple loop knot shown in fig. 9-8). Thread the other end of the rope through this loop and pull on it until the stuff sack reaches the limb. Reach as high as you can on the rope and tie a stick onto the rope using a clove hitch knot (also shown in fig. 9-8). Lower the bag until the stick lodges in the loop and let the remainder of the rope dangle. Bears will play with the rope, but the "loop and stick" will keep the bag securely hung until you wish to retrieve it.

If there are no trees in the area, you can try wrapping all odorous materials in two or more plastic bags, taking care to seal them tightly. Stuff the bags into a deep crevice in rocks, well away from camp. This may or may not work, but it may be the best you can do. Never simply give up and sleep with the food—this practice may invite a midnight bear encounter!

At the campsite itself, try to eliminate food odors (see fig. 9-9). All cooking should be done downwind and away from the main campsite. Food residue should be buried deeply or burned completely. Fish remains should be buried well away from camp, and fish odors should be washed from hands and clothing. Dishwashing water also should be buried downwind, well away from camp.

It's thrilling to see bears in the wild, and even more pleasing to not have an unpleasant encounter or lose your food. By understanding bear behaviors and being prepared to act accordingly, you can ensure that the only bear victories will be in Chicago!

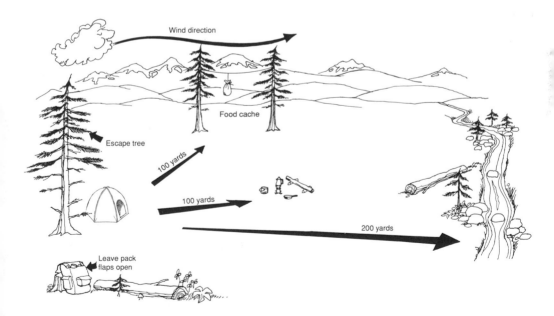

Fig. 9-9. An ideal campsite in grizzly bear country. An "escape tree" can be useful in grizzly country, as grizzlies are not good climbers.

125

SAFETY CONCERNS

In wilderness areas, there are often hazards that you could encounter and should be prepared for, though most travelers do not experience these misfortunes. Below are some of the concerns associated with wilderness areas.

POISON OAK/POISON IVY POISON SUMAC

Poison oak, poison ivy, and poison sumac thrive in moist ravines and canyons, as well as on hillsides and even hilltops (if protected from intense sunshine), below about 5,000 feet elevation. The maxim "leaves of three, let it be" is a good one. Learn to recognize these poisonous plants, and to distinguish them from other three-leaved plants (wild blackberries, for example) that are harmless.

By wearing long pants and a long-sleeved shirt, you can keep skin contact to a minimum. In winter, and sometimes in very dry conditions, poison oak loses its leaves but still retains some of its irritating resin. It's a good idea to learn to recognize the stem color and structure of the plant before you do any cross-country hiking among the leafless plants. If you know you've been exposed to poison oak/ivy, treat the area as instructed in Chapter 15, Wilderness First Aid, *Environmental Hazards in the Wilderness*.

POISONOUS SNAKES

Poisonous snakes of various kinds thrive in a broad range of environments. Water moccasins and coral snakes can be found in the southern United States, and copperheads in the eastern United States. Perhaps best known of poisonous snakes, however, are rattlesnakes. They will often be found in rocky areas, or near canyon bottoms where the small creatures they prey upon are abundant. You're most likely to see them out and about when temperatures are in the 75° to 90° F. range. Remember that snakes may enjoy sunning themselves or relaxing where you might also choose. Be especially careful in these areas.

Normally not aggressive, rattlesnakes will usually buzz unmistakably if you approach too closely. When in snake country, scan the path ahead, and never put your feet or hands in places you cannot see without probing ahead with a stick. Wear long pants and ankle-high boots, since a snake's strike would likely occur on the lower leg.

Learn to identify the types of poisonous snakes that inhabit the areas you plan to hike in. Remember that, like most other wild animals, a startled snake would prefer to leave the area quickly if an escape route is available. Step rapidly away from the snake, and it will probably slide away in the opposite direction as fast as it can. Rarely are hikers bitten by poisonous snakes. If you are bitten, refer to the instructions in Chapter 15, Wilderness First Aid, *Environmental Hazards in the Wilderness*.

TICKS

When hiking along overgrown trails or "bushwhacking" (traveling cross-country in brushy terrain), check yourself frequently for ticks. These small, blood-sucking parasites feed on wild animals such as deer and domestic animals such as horses, dogs, and cattle. They lie in wait on tips of shrub branches along hiking or game trails, lodging on warm-blooded creatures that come along.

If you're in tick country, wear long pants and a long-sleeved shirt. You can tuck the hems of your pants into your socks for further protection. Wear a scarf around your neck, and a hat. Scan your clothing for ticks and brush them off before they crawl out of sight.

If a tick successfully hitches a ride on a human host, it usually crawls upward to some protected spot underneath clothing before choosing a spot to attach itself onto. By visually checking yourself often, and by being aware of the slightest irritations on your body, you can intercept the tick before it decides to bite. If it does bite, you will almost certainly be aware of an itchy irritation.

Ticks can be difficult to remove when attached. For instructions on removing ticks and treating their bites, see Chapter 15, Wilderness First Aid, *Environmental Hazards in the Wilderness.* Lyme disease is carried by ticks. A red "ring" spreading outward from the bite may indicate Lyme disease, which can produce arthritislike joint problems. See your doctor for tests and antibiotics treatment.

OTHER FORMS OF WILDERNESS TRAVEL

In addition to hiking and backpacking, there are other non-motorized ways to propel yourself across the land: mountain bicycling, mountain running, skiing, and snowshoeing. The latter two are thoroughly discussed in Chapter 14, Winter Mountaineering, *Winter Travel Techniques.*

MOUNTAIN BICYCLING

The new all-terrain bicycles, or "mountain bikes," are becoming popular as a means of travel over backcountry terrain. Mountain bikes allow you to cover greater distances than you can normally cover on foot, while providing similar sensations of fun and accomplishment.

Mountain bikes, however, are not welcome everywhere. In fact, they are banned outright from all federally designated wilderness areas and many parklands. The Mountaineers opposes the use of mountain bikes on national park trails and in wilderness areas. In areas other than national parks and wilderness areas, off-road vehicles (ORVs) such as mountain bikes should only be permitted on trails or on off-road areas expressly designated for their use. In some areas, mountain bikes

Mountain bikes are a great way to explore dirt roads. (Photo by Jerry Schad)

are allowed on all dirt roads, but no trails. In other areas, particularly on most national forest lands, mountain bikes can be used almost without restrictions. Still, nonmotorized mountain bikes should be allowed only on trails designated for their use by the appropriate land management agency. They should be prohibited off-trail or on hikers-only trails. Even with these restrictions, the possibilities of mountain-bike travel are almost endless. There are hundreds of thousands of miles of dirt roads and trails open to mountain biking throughout the western United States.

There are many styles and models of mountain bikes to choose from. If you plan to ride mostly off-road, consider a sturdy bike with fat tires. If you're going to spend some of the time on paved roads as well, then get a bike that incorporates some of the features of a road bike. Some hybrid touring/mountain bikes have rims that can accommodate narrow tires for road riding, as well as 2-inch-wide knobby tires.

For years, trails were the sole territory of hikers and horseback riders. The established etiquette involving hikers and equestrians now has been modified to include mountain bikers as well. To help standardize riding practices, the National Off-Road Bicycle Association (NORBA) has developed a riding code:

1. I will yield the right-of-way to other nonmotorized recreationalists. I realize that people judge all cyclists by my actions.
2. I will slow down and use caution when approaching or overtaking another and will make my presence known well in advance.
3. I will maintain control of my speed at all times and will approach turns in anticipation of someone around the bend.
4. I will stay on designated trails to avoid trampling native vegetation and minimize potential erosion to trails by not using muddy trails or short-cutting switchbacks.
5. I will not disturb wildlife or live stock.
6. I will not litter. I will pack out what I pack in, and pack out more than my share whenever possible.
7. I will respect public and private property, including trail-use signs and no-trespassing signs, and I will leave gates as I have found them.
8. I will always be self-sufficient and my destination and travel speed will be determined by my ability, my equipment, the terrain, and the present and potential weather conditions.
9. I will not travel solo when bike packing in remote areas. I will leave word of my destination and when I plan to return.
10. I will observe the practice of minimum-impact bicycling by "taking only pictures and memories and leaving only waffle prints."
11. I will always wear a helmet whenever I ride.

When venturing into the backcountry on a mountain bike, check the regulations before you go! Remember to take all of the essentials you would take on a hike: extra water, food, clothing, sunscreen, first aid kit, map, and compass. You'll also need some simple repair tools, tire irons, and patches. A helmet is just as essential for safety on dirt roads and trails as when you ride on paved roads.

You'll be covering ground considerably faster on a bike, so don't forget to check your position on a map often. You may need a map that covers a larger area than the ones you are accustomed to using while hiking.

As with any kind of travel in remote areas, travel with friends; there's safety in numbers. The skills and techniques of mountain biking over rough terrain require considerable practice.

MOUNTAIN RUNNING

Mountain running, or "adventure running," in wilderness areas is popular among a dedicated group of hard-core athletes. A trained runner carrying minimal gear can easily cover two or three times as much distance over trails than a lightly burdened day hiker can. A good technique used by some is to mix running and walking. The easier stretches of trail (the smoother, flatter, or slightly downhill parts) are run, while the rougher, steeper stretches are walked.

Running a trail allows you to get to and from remote areas quickly, but it also exposes you to danger if you are not aware of your limitations or are careless about preparation. As on any wilderness outing, you need to carry enough survival gear to cover emergencies. Small backpacks that strap on tightly and hip-hugging fanny packs that don't bounce can be used to stow minimal gear such as extra clothes and food. You can carry water bottles in your hands or in a special carrier secured to the back of a belt. Water can also be carried in a plastic tube or sack worn around the waist or on the lower back. Some water storage systems have a plastic tube you can drink from while "on the run."

Traveling with companions is especially important when on running excursions. Usually the amount of survival gear you can carry is quite meager, and you may need outside help fairly quickly if you run into a serious problem.

RECOMMENDED READING

Brainerd, John W. *The Nature Observer's Handbook*. Globe Pequot, 1986.

Fletcher, Colin. *The Complete Walker III*. Alfred A. Knopf, 1984.

Gillette, Ned and John Dostal. *Cross-Country Skiing*. The Mountaineers, 1988. (Includes how-to and instructional photos on all aspects of cross-country skiing.)

Herrero, Stephen. *Bear Attacks: Their Causes and Avoidance*. Nick Lyons Books, 1985. (A good blend of anecdotal and research information. Highly recommended for those who plan a backcountry trip in the grizzly territories of the U.S. and Canada.)

Maughan, Jackie Johnson and Ann Puddicombe. *Hiking the Backcountry: A Do-It-Yourself Guide for the Adventurous Woman*. Stackpole Books, 1981. (Now out of print. Excellent, in-depth treatment.)

Meyer, Kathleen. *How to Shit in the Woods: An Environmentally Sound Approach to a Lost Art*. (A lighthearted, but serious account of how to take care of toilet needs while enjoying the outdoors.)

Niemi, Judith. *The Basic Essentials of Women in the Outdoors*. ICS Books, Inc., 1990. (Encouraging and practical.)

Prater, Gene. *Snowshoeing*. The Mountaineers, 1988. (Helpful information about all aspects of snowshoeing.)

Sloane, Eugene A. *Complete Book to All-Terrain Bicycles*. Simon & Schuster, 1985. (Helpful guide to all aspects of mountain bikes.)

Van der Plas, Rob. *The Mountain Bike Book*. Bicycle Books, 1990. (Helpful information about choosing, riding, and maintaining off-road bicycles.)

Curious children find the wilderness an exciting place. (Photo by Marge and Ted Mueller)

CHAPTER 10

Children in the Wilderness

MARIANNE RINGHOFF

Hiking and camping with children can be most enjoyable for all concerned. Kids are natural explorers, filled with enthusiasm and curiosity. When you're accompanied by little ones, your world seems a bigger and more wonderful place. By sharing in their experiences, you become like a child yourself—liberated from the cares of adulthood, at least temporarily.

Children learn quickly by observing, and they readily imitate your behavior. Be a positive role model. Also be receptive to your children's moods. Tailor your activities, whenever possible, to their interests. A successful outing—one that is both enjoyable and a learning experience—is one that your children may remember for the rest of their lives.

PREPARATION

CONDITIONING

Children may be physically more resilient than adults in some ways, but they still need plenty of conditioning prior to a big trip. It's important to properly prepare a child's mind as well.

Walking is the easiest form of conditioning. Walk to the park, walk around the neighborhood, walk on the beach, climb some hills. Stick to a routine—walk in bad weather as well as good. But always make it fun. Let them catch raindrops and look for a rainbow. Sneak in a natural history or science lesson while you're at it. And practice some of the routines you'll follow when on the trail, for example, shedding and adding clothing as the weather changes.

Children have short attention spans, so vary your routines to keep things lively. March to a song, count trees or fence posts, spy on birds, or challenge them to a race. This is a good opportunity to give them some freedom—let them choose the direction of travel, or let them play tag on the beach or in the park. Pique their curiosity and follow through in answering their questions.

DESTINATION AND ROUTE

The trip destination should be appropriate for both your children's and your own interests, and not beyond the scope of your experience and training. Do include your kids in the process of planning. Ask them what they would like to see and do. Plant the seeds of anticipation. Start by gathering information about the places you'd like to visit. Aside from queries to tourist bureaus and parks, try your local library. Consult or borrow geographic, natural history, and guide books. Some libraries now have video departments with tapes offering previews of the popular parks. Kids can get bored with "just hiking" but get highly motivated when activities are different, such as climbing, skiing, and snowshoeing. Let the kids participate in the

decision-making process.

When planning for a day trip, allow for some exploratory time. On an extended trip, be sure to allow for one or more lay-over days. The immediate area around a campsite can seem like a whole universe to a little one. Let the child gain some familiarity with the surroundings; allow him or her to bond with nature. Be sure to modify the ratio of adults to children when hiking with a group. Older children are more independent than younger children, and having the right number of adults can be critical.

SURVIVAL TRAINING

The most important aspect of pre-trip planning is teaching your children how to avoid getting lost, and what they should do if they do get lost or separated. In a

Fig. 10-1. The STOP method: Sit; Think; Observe; Plan.

larger group of kids, the "buddy system" works well. By having children pair up, each buddy always knows the whereabouts of the other. If someone leaves the group for any reason, he or she must tell the buddy and also the parent or leader.

On the trip, each child should carry at least one item of bright-colored clothing, a whistle, and a plastic trash-can liner in addition to other items that might be in his or her pack. The first two items are quite effective for signaling to would-be rescuers, while the third serves as emergency shelter.

Children should be taught that the first thing to do when "lost" is to STOP—Sit, Think, Observe, and Plan (fig. 10-1). They should be secure knowing that their parents, and possibly others, are out looking for them. They must realize that the farther they wander, the more lost they will become.

Project Hug-a-Tree (see Resources at the end of this chapter) offers an excellent program to schools and clubs on basic survival for children. By "hugging a tree," a lost child avoids panic and does not wander aimlessly. The child is trained to blow a whistle rather than use his or her voice, and to listen for any response. If an aircraft passes overhead, the child "makes himself big" by wearing brightly colored clothing and lying flat in a clearing. The child is trained to use a plastic trash-can liner as a sunshade and, with a hole cut in it, as an impromptu shelter from rain and cold.

Prepare a tracing and imprint of your child's boot or hiking shoe, to be used for a search in case the child becomes lost. Here's a good way to do it: Place a piece of paper on soft ground. With your child wearing his or her hiking shoes, spread ink on the lugs or sole pattern of either the left or the right shoe. Have the child

OBSERVE   PLAN

carefully step on the paper with the inked shoe and leave it in place while you make a pencil tracing of the sole rim. To clean the sole afterward, blot it with a rag and then let your child scuff through some sand or dirt.

EQUIPMENT

FOOTWEAR

When choosing footwear, remember that kids don't just walk. They will invariably spend much of their time running, jumping, and climbing. Don't hobble them with boots that are too heavy and uncomfortable. On the other hand, you'll want shoes with enough support to handle rocky or uneven ground.

High-top sneakers often work fine, especially for the younger child starting out on short, easy day hikes. Once the child is ready to hike longer distances or over rough terrain, though, the proper choice of footwear becomes important.

Today you can choose among a wide variety of lightweight hiking boots in children's sizes. These boots break in quickly, offer good foot support and traction, and sell for a moderate price. They're comfortable and stylish enough to be worn at home or school as well. Don't forget to allow a break-in period—your child should wear them on at least a couple of shorter walks or hikes before the main event.

When choosing a boot size, consider your child's rapidly growing feet. Have your child try on boots using two socks on each foot—medium- and heavy-weight. There should be enough room to wiggle the toes but not enough room to allow the heels to slip when the boots are snugly laced. Have the child squat down to check for heel slippage, and have him or her walk down an incline to check for cramped toes in front. Check that neither the big toe nor the little toe gets pinched on the side (boots with square toe-boxes usually prevent this problem).

Before the trip, make sure that toenails are clipped short. On the trip, carry foot fleece (soft wool) for placing between the toes if needed, and moleskin for "hot spots" and blisters. Check your child's feet during rest stops, and be receptive to any complaints. Don't allow a hot spot to develop into a blister—apply moleskin at the first hint of redness and discomfort.

CLOTHING

Temperatures can change quickly in the wilderness. Dry, sunny conditions on a south-facing slope can instantly turn into damp, chilly conditions on a north-facing slope with the rounding of a single switchback on the trail. A single thundercloud blotting out the sun's rays produces an instant nip in the air. Taking off extra clothing in warm weather is a minor inconvenience. But not having enough clothing in cold conditions can precipitate an emergency situation.

A three-layer clothing system works well with children, as with adults. Generally, the first layer is for comfort, sun protection, and a small amount of insulation. The second, insulating layer retains body heat, while the third, protective layer sheds rain and wind. Pile on or remove the layers as appropriate. Remember that a child's body has a larger surface-area-to-mass ratio than an adult's, therefore a child loses body heat more rapidly. Warm headgear (a knitted cap or balaclava) and mittens are lightweight, essential items for cold conditions.

For sunny conditions, don't forget to protect your child's delicate skin from the sun's ultraviolet radiation. That means long-sleeved tops, a wide-brimmed hat or a cap with a bill, and sunscreen on all exposed parts of the body such as the back of the hands.

Collecting all this specialized clothing may be quite costly. But kids' clothing seldom wears out before being outgrown, so your child can be the recipient or the donor of hand-me-downs. Consider sewing identification labels into your child's outdoor clothing; this could be helpful for searchers if your child ever becomes lost.

DIAPERS

This essential item for very young ones merits considerable creative thought. For an extended trip, cloth diapers are less bulky to carry than disposables. They can be used with diaper liners which usually contain most of the waste. You can bury the waste as an adult would, and wash (not directly in a stream or lake, but well away from the water) and reuse both the liner and cloth diaper. If disposables are used, they must be carried out. If a disposable's inner lining is cotton, it can be removed from the plastic and burned. The plastic itself should be carried out.

"Biodegradable" diapers are appearing on the market. However, in the harsh climate of many wilderness areas, it may take years for them to disintegrate. Even if you bury them deeply, animals may locate and dig them up. Ask yourself how you'd feel if you discovered the remains of diapers at a prospective campsite.

SLEEPING BAGS

Children sleep "colder" than adults, so the choice of a sleeping bag should reflect that fact. Usually a child will sleep warmer in a lighter, more compact mummy bag than in a roomier, rectangular-style bag. Some children cannot tolerate the confinement of a mummy bag. Most junior-size bags fit children up to about 5 feet in height. The leftover length, if any, can be tied off or tucked under as a mattress. When choosing between down or synthetic fill (see Chapter 5, Outfitting: The Basic Equipment, *Sleeping Gear*), take into account the issue of bed-wetting as well. Down sleeping bags lose their insulating qualities when wet, and they are difficult to launder.

To prevent a child from creeping out of a sleeping bag at night, cinch the top cord down to shoulder size. Any extra cord can be secured in such a way to prevent the child from getting tangled up in it, yet allowing easy access if it's necessary to open the bag in a hurry. One effective way is to wad up the excess cord into a plastic film cannister. The tight-fitting lid will pinch the cord, keeping it inside.

PACKS

Any child old enough to walk can wear a pack. Start out with a small "play" daypack for your toddler. You can put special toys and snacks into it for trips to the park or to the babysitter. The child gets used to carrying things on his or her back, and feels helpful to boot.

Most kids old enough to use daypacks for school can easily graduate to a pack with a rigid frame. Junior-size, external-frame packs often have adjustments that will accommodate a fair range of growth. When checking for fit, load up the pack and adjust the straps so that the waist belt lies on the hip bones. The weight of the pack should be borne by hips as well as shoulders. A well-padded waist belt may be needed for a thin child; a broad frame will be necessary for a heavy child. Make sure there are no buttons, zippers, or extra folds on the pressure areas of the hips that may cause chafing. See how easily the pack's closures (zippers, cinch cords, velcro) allow your child to get at items stored inside.

Shoulder straps should attach to the frame about 1 or 2 inches below the top of the shoulders. While you are on the trail, check from time to time to see if the pack is riding comfortably. Sometimes the waist belt will slip down below the hips and result in too much weight on the shoulders.

CARRIERS

One of the best ways to get children interested in the outdoors is to start early. For pre-toddlers, this usually means that you'll be purchasing a child carrier. Newborn infants, who lack the ability to hold

A good backpack-type carrier can soothe even the crankiest baby. (Photo by Bob and Ira Spring)

their heads up, should be transported in a sling-type carrier worn on the front of the parent's body. From roughly age 4 months and up, most children are comfortable in a standard backpack-type carrier. The better models have a capacity of up to 40 pounds. In addition to providing a good view of the surroundings, the rocking motion of a carrier can soothe even the crankiest baby.

When shopping for a carrier, make sure you try it on with the child in it. Have someone check for pinching on the child's arms and legs. Look for any stray belts, buckles, or snaps that can get into little mouths. Some kind of head support is desirable if the child is very young. Make sure the pack is comfortable and does not throw you off balance when you walk.

The child in a backpack-type carrier should face forward with his or her head high enough to see over your shoulder, but not higher than your head. When on the trail, avoid the possibility of the child climbing out by making sure all belts are securely fastened and snug. Some carriers feature a "kickstand" that will support the pack upright on the ground. In that position, the pack can serve as a high-chair in camp, but you must never leave your child unattended in that way.

FOODS

Get the kids involved in the fun of pre-trip menu planning. Consider their likes and dislikes, and try out the meals before your trip. Kids burn up an amazing amount of energy during a trip, and therefore they always seem to be hungry. That means plenty of snacks should always be available to feed to them. Chocolate-covered raisins, peanuts, candy, granola bars, and fruit rolls are tasty, nutritious in varying degrees, and rich in the calories that kids need on the trail. Have the kids mix their own GORP at home before you leave. You may be surprised what they put in it!

Weight and packaging of foodstuffs is especially important on family trips. Your younger kids won't be able to carry the weight they use and consume, and that will add to your burden. Remember the importance of fluids—bring plenty of water with you if none is available along the trail.

For the main meals at camp, quick and easy preparation is an important consideration, particularly if you run into bad weather. Finger foods will keep the little ones busy while you are preparing the main course or courses. Encourage the older ones to get involved in the kitchen chores. It's amazing how kids will do things willingly in the backcountry that you can't get them to do at home!

HEALTH AND SAFETY

Have you ever had a child hand you some beautiful arrangement of vegetation that just happened to be poison oak? Kids are so adventurous they can get into just about anything before you realize it.

With some instruction beforehand, your children will know that if they see "leaves of three," they should "let it be." But if they do blunder into poison oak (or ivy or sumac), you can wash the affected parts of skin with a mild soap. That will reduce or eliminate the allergic reaction that usually follows some hours or days later. If a rash does appear, old-fashioned calamine lotion helps relieve the itching (see Chapter 15, Wilderness First Aid, *Environmental Hazards in the Wilderness*). Don't allow your kids to use sticks for cooking; they may be from poison oak plants or contain toxins.

Syrup of Ipecac in your first aid kit is useful in inducing vomiting if your child has swallowed something poisonous. The Sawyer Extractor, a suction device, is useful for treating poisonous snakebites and all kinds of insect bites and stings (again, see Chapter 15, Wilderness First Aid, *Environmental Hazards in the Wilderness*).

Be sure to keep your children's immunizations, such as tetanus, up to date. While on the trip, sunscreen applied to all exposed skin will prevent much potential misery. Perhaps the most important, but often overlooked, preventative measure is constant vigilance. You and your children must develop a sense of awareness of each other, and of the hazards that exist in the wilderness.

A LOST CHILD

What should you do if your child is missing? First, don't panic! Second, use a whistle to call to your child. If there's no response, retrace your steps and mark the spot you last saw your child. If there's no further response to signaling, send for help. Include information such as your child's physical description, his or her clothing, the type of footwear, and the time and point where the child was last seen (see Chapter 16, Search and Rescue, *The Case of the Missing Hiker*).

ON THE TRIP

As long as your child has had adequate preparation, the real trip will be just another adventure, though a bigger one. Remember that having shorter legs means more steps must be taken, so your child will probably tire more quickly than you do. Start out slow, then gradually increase the pace to match the ability of the least able child in your party. Don't let the more energetic ones run ahead of the group—you'll never be able to keep track of everyone that way.

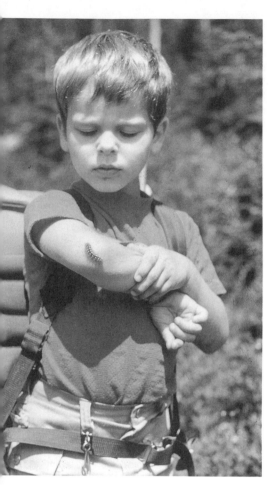

A caterpillar examines a young hiker.
(Photo by Marge and Ted Mueller)

By all means, make the trip interesting and educational. Start good wilderness habits (safety, conservation, picking up after one's self) early—they will last a lifetime. Aim for a positive experience with nature. Share observations and feelings, and be responsive to your child's interests. Use games to energize and to calm. Bring photocopies or printed material on plants, animals, and animal tracks. Encourage questions, and if you don't know the answer, try to find it together. Most important, don't push. Let nature be the teacher.

SUGGESTED CHILDREN'S GAMES

Sames and differents. This game involves things of various shapes and sizes, including leaves, rocks, trees, and clouds, that bear some resemblance to each other. Have the child look at one object, then have him or her discover another object that is similar in some way.

Nature's shapes. With heavy paper, cut out different shapes, such as circles, squares, rectangles, and triangles. Have the child match the shapes to natural features, small and large.

What am I? Blindfold the child in a safe area. Have him or her use all the senses except sight to discover the world around him or her. Ask questions like: "What do you hear?" "How does that feel? Soft? Rough? Sticky? Wet? Smooth? Warm? Cold?" "What does that taste like?" (Use edible foods, of course.)

Next stop. Count steps to the next rest stop or destination. Identify a point ahead on the trail, and allow the child to hike "on his or her own" to reach it. Let your child measure the time taken during a rest stop—a great way for him or her to learn how to tell time and get a sense of the passage of time.

Night walks. Visit a place at night that you saw earlier in daylight. What is different about it? This may be a little scary for some kids, but most love it.

RECOMMENDED READING

Burton, Joan. *Best Hikes With Children in Western Washington and the Cascades.* The Mountaineers, 1988.

Burton, Joan. *Best Hikes With Children in Western Washington and the Cascades, Volume 2.* The Mountaineers, 1992.

Doan, Marlyn. *Starting Small in the Wilderness*. Sierra Club Books, 1979. (A good introduction for the beginning family hiker.)

Foster, Lynne. *Take a Hike: The Sierra Club's Guide to Hiking and Backpacking*. Little, Brown & Co., 1991.

Henderson, Bonnie. *Best Hikes With Children in Western and Central Oregon*. The Mountaineers, 1992.

Keilty, Maureen. *Best Hikes With Children in Colorado*. The Mountaineers, 1991.

Lewis, Cynthia C. and Thomas J. Lewis. *Best Hikes With Children in Connecticut, Massachusetts & Rhode Island*. The Mountaineers, 1991.

Lewis, Cynthia C. and Thomas J. Lewis. *Best Hikes With Children in the Catskills and Hudson River Valley*. The Mountaineers, 1992.

Lewis, Cynthia C. and Thomas J. Lewis. *Best Hikes With Children in Vermont, New Hampshire & Maine*. The Mountaineers, 1991.

McMillon, Bill and Kevin McMillon. *Best Hikes With Children: San Francisco's North Bay*. The Mountaineers, 1992.

McMillon, Bill and Kevin McMillon. *Best Hikes With Children: San Francisco's South Bay*. The Mountaineers, 1992.

Mooers, Robert L. *Finding Your Way in the Outdoors*. Outdoor Life, 1972. (Easy reading with the use of many diagrams.)

Rawson, John Boswell, ed. *The U.S. Armed Forces Survival Manual*. Wade Publishers. (A complete guide to survival in any circumstance.)

Silverman, Goldie. *Backpacking With Babies and Small Children*. Wilderness Press, 1986. (Practical information, with answers to questions you usually forget to ask.)

Zatz, Arline. *Best Hikes With Children in New Jersey*. The Mountaineers, 1992.

RESOURCES

Camp Fire
4601 Madison Avenue
Kansas City, MO 64112

Project Hug-a-Tree
6465 Lance Way
San Diego, CA 92120
(Send a self-addressed, stamped envelope for free information.)

SOME MANUFACTURERS OF CHILDREN'S EQUIPMENT

The Baby Bag Company
P.O. Box 566
Cumberland Center, ME 04021

Gerry Baby Products
12520 Grant Drive
Denver, CO 80233

Tough Traveler, Ltd.
Geneva Road
Brewster, NY 10509

Coastal travel requires special preparation, but spectacular scenery makes it worth-while. (Photo by Bob and Ira Spring)

Coastal Travel

DON STOUDER AND EMILY TROXELL

Today, visiting a crowded beach is as "wild" an experience as many people ever get. But that's no reason to sell the coastline short—it's still one of the world's most magnificent areas. For every overcrowded beach, there's a quiet lagoon or a rocky shoreline where nature reigns.

This chapter gives a look at the coast, some travel techniques, and ways we can minimize our impact on this unique part of our world.

THE DYNAMIC COAST

No matter if the beholder is a biologist, geologist, artist, surfer or beachcomber, the thin edge of a continent has much to offer. For biologists, the coastline is interesting as an ecotone, a boundary where diverse biological habitats converge (this particular boundary is the intertidal zone). Geologists look at wave-battered cliffs and see the structure of the earth laid bare. Artists, surfers, or anyone, for that matter, can appreciate the power and dynamism of the waves. The slowest kind of dynamic change on the coast is geological in nature. The most common kind of rock found along the coastline is sedimentary—sandstone, shale, conglomerate—the product of river silt and sand deposited in low-lying areas on land and offshore long ago. This type of rock, which is inherently weak, is constantly exposed to severe erosion by wave action. Other types of rock, volcanic among them, resist the battering of the waves somewhat better, but eventually succumb and crumble like all the rest.

More rapid change, still in the geologic realm, involves the movements of sand particles. These particles are tiny bits of hard minerals eroded from rocks that lie inland. Carried coastward by rivers, they bide their time along the shoreline before being dragged offshore by wave action or perhaps being blown inland. Unfortunately, the sources of our beach sands are being choked off as the natural courses of rivers are blocked upstream with dams. Would-be beach sand simply accumulates behind dams, forcing some communities to import vast quantities of river sand and dredging spoils to maintain their beaches.

The ebbs and flows of the tides cause rapid and repetitive changes in the environment of the intertidal zone (fig. 11-1). In the past, some cultures attributed the rise and fall of the ocean waters to the breathing of a gigantic sea monster. Today the explanation is, in a way, even more romantic: tides are a consequence of the moon's attraction to the earth. The basic fact is that the moon's gravitational pull produces two watery "bulges" on the earth—one on the side facing the moon, the other on the side facing away from the moon. As the earth turns on its axis once per day, we pass through the bulges twice a day, and that gives us two high tides and two low tides. Because the moon keeps moving around the earth (taking roughly one month to complete one orbit), the

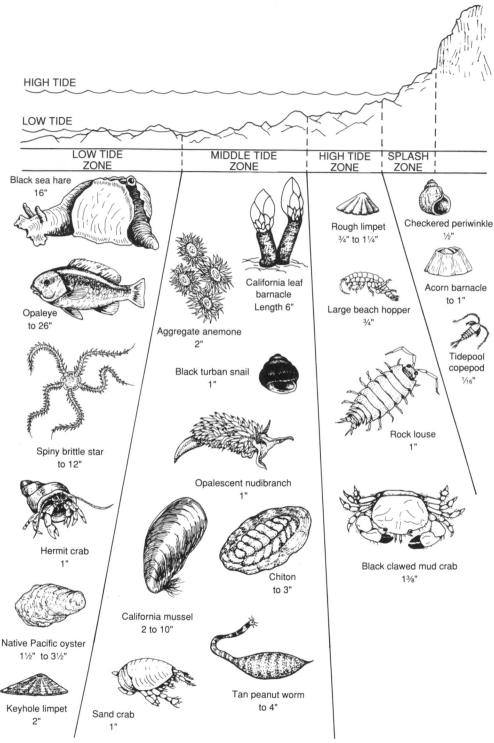

HIGH TIDE

LOW TIDE

| LOW TIDE ZONE | MIDDLE TIDE ZONE | HIGH TIDE ZONE | SPLASH ZONE |

Black sea hare
16"

Opaleye
to 26"

Spiny brittle star
to 12"

Hermit crab
1"

Native Pacific oyster
1½" to 3½"

Keyhole limpet
2"

Aggregate anemone
2"

California leaf
barnacle
Length 6"

Black turban snail
1"

Opalescent nudibranch
1"

California mussel
2 to 10"

Chiton
to 3"

Tan peanut worm
to 4"

Sand crab
1"

Rough limpet
¾" to 1¼"

Large beach hopper
¾"

Rock louse
1"

Black clawed mud crab
1⅜"

Checkered periwinkle
½"

Acorn barnacle
to 1"

Tidepool
copepod
1/16"

Fig. 11-1. Typical life forms of the intertidal zone

142

double high-low cycle repeats over a period of not exactly 24 hours, but roughly 24 hours and 50 minutes.

The rise and fall of tides are actually very complex. The sun's gravitational pull has some effect: during new and full moons, the solar influence adds to that of the moon, and we have higher high tides and lower low tides (spring tides). During first and third quarter moons, the solar influence diminishes but does overcome the moon's pull, so we have less extreme highs and lows (neap tides).

Despite these general rules, tidal periods and heights cannot be accurately predicted without sophisticated mathematical modeling. The results of these calculations are found in tide tables. Newspapers carry daily or monthly tidal predictions. Most bait and tackle shops and marine outlets offer a yearly tide-table booklet. Tide information is essential for hikers who plan to explore coastlines hemmed in by cliffs.

In a very immediate sense, the coastline environment is dominated by the ocean waves. Waves are born in the high winds of storms, and can travel to distant shores. On the open ocean, waves may differ in speed, in height, and in spacing. The time interval between successive waves (the period) is controlled by both the spacing (the wave length) and the speed. The typical period is 10 to 15 seconds. If waves of diverse character travel a great distance together, they tend to coalesce in the form of swells. And when a swell encounters the increasingly shallow water close to shore, it curls over as a breaker. A multitude of breakers is surf. Surfers are aware that the waves seem to come in "sets." There's no magic formula for predicting sets; in fact, there's always a lot of natural variation in the sizes of waves. Hikers on the shoreline should always be wary of the rogue wave that may sweep in unexpectedly.

When water in a breaking wave runs up along the shoreline, it must return to sea again. Frequently it does so as a narrow, outgoing stream called a rip current, riptide, or undertow (actually, this type of water action has nothing to do with the tides). Rip currents can be dangerous to those unfamiliar with them. If you're caught in one, don't try to swim against it—it will wear you out. Instead swim parallel to shore, even if that action takes you away from shore temporarily. You'll eventually come to a place where the current goes toward the shore.

TRAVELING THE COAST

The coast almost always has a cooler, windier, and more humid environment than areas even a short distance inland. The sun's rays are more intense due to reflection from sand and water. You're quite likely to get your feet wet, and the salt-laden water or spray may be damaging to the gear you carry. Keep these things in mind when you plan a coastal trip.

You can leave the mountaineering boots at home. Light hiking shoes (properly treated to repel water), sneakers, sandals, and even bare feet all work fine on the easier terrain. Rocky shorelines require something more substantial. For very wet areas, mud boots with rubber lug soles are ideal. Be sure to wear thick socks with these boots for extra cushioning.

In terms of clothing, remember that you must protect yourself against both the wind and the ultraviolet radiation from the sun. Keep most of your body covered, wear a hat and sunglasses, apply sunscreen to exposed skin, and remember that even the most innocent of overcast days can pack a bad burn (especially in spring and summer). Dress in clothing that will give you many temperature-regulating possibilities. A layering system works best (as described in Chapter 5, Outfitting: The Basic Equipment, *Clothing*). You can wear shorts on warm days, and the rest of the time, any comfortable, loose slacks that dry quickly will work well. Top-quality rain gear is essential for wet or misty conditions. Storms on the coastline often bring wind-driven torrents of rain, and there's no easy way to dry out your inner clothing if it gets soaked. If you're well prepared for rain though, there's no better time to be on the beach. Only then can you fully ap-preciate the savage beauty of the coast and the awesome power of the breakers (from a safe viewing distance, of course).

Be sure to include an ace bandage in your first aid kit. A twisted knee or sprained ankle is a very real possibility when traveling over slippery or jagged rocks.

Narrow, rocky, heavily forested coastlines can become impassible at high tide. (Photo by Marge and Ted Mueller)

There's water everywhere, but not a drop to drink—so don't forget to take plenty of drinking water or a means of treating available freshwater. Remember that freshwater streams near the ocean are often slightly brackish due to their low elevation and proximity to salt water. Some coastal areas have streams with high levels of tannin from the redwood or cedar forests. Neither tannin-laden nor brackish water are harmful to drink, if properly treated (see Chapter 6, Foods and Cooking, *Wilderness Cooking*), but they may be an unsettling brown color and/or have a slightly unpleasant taste. You can use powdered drink crystals to mask these minor problems.

Topographic maps are a must for unfamiliar coastlines. They indicate the precise shape of the coastline and the height of the bluffs, and they show sandy beaches and shoals. They're important for plotting escape routes if an emergency occurs. While it's possible to backpack for miles along parts of the Pacific coast, there are many places where you must leave the beach and walk on forest trails to get over headlands. Tide tables are just as important for routes that involve tight passages between the cliffs and surf. By using maps and tide tables, you can safely backpack wild coastal areas and avoid having your route rendered impassable by a high tide.

Finally, consider the potential effects of exposure to salt water or salt spray. Whether you're day hiking or backpacking, good pack features include tough, waterproof material, padded shoulder and hip belts, and non-metallic zippers, buckles, and closures. If you want to take along nonessential items such as a camera and binoculars, carry them in a sealed plastic bag and avoid contact with salt water and sand.

Some coastlines (such as those in Olympic National Park in Washington) are true wilderness areas. There and in other areas where remote camping is allowed, you may have a whole beach or cove to yourself. Observe the following common sense practices: consider the prevailing direction of the wind when seeking a sheltered spot. Use heavy rocks to secure tent stakes driven in sand. Camp well above the next high tide or tides (remember that tidal differences are greater during spring tides, less during neap tides).

The hazards of coastal travel are many and varied, and sometimes unexpected. For example, poison oak, poison ivy, and rattlesnakes may be found in the ravines or on the bluffs just behind the beach. The coastal bluffs themselves are often very unstable—don't camp or spend a lot of time beneath steep cliffs. The seemingly solid brink of a cliff can crumble in the blink of an eye if you walk too close to the edge.

You'll want to minimize your chances of encountering unfriendly marine life. Stingrays, batrays, and jellyfish like to hang around in the surf and shallows, especially when the water is warm. Sea urchins, found in the rocky intertidal zones, are equipped with brittle purple spines that can break off if stepped upon. If severe pain results from any of these encounters, seek medical attention.

THE FRAGILE COAST

Because much of the life found along the coast is fragile and inconspicuous, you must exercise great care during your visit. Footprints left on the beach "wash" away eventually, but not so the effects of a heavy-footed traveler. Here are some basic guidelines:

- A large group of people should spread out when crossing fragile beach areas. Each person should try to step on the ledges and rocks that do not have creatures attached to or living on them.
- Look at the creatures, but let them live their lives undisturbed.
- Many of the tidepool creatures are

nocturnal. They hide under rocks by day. It's okay to turn over rocks to find these animals, but don't allow the animals to remain out of the water for long periods. Return the rocks to their original location so that the animals' habitat is unchanged.

- Take nothing from the sea coast and bring nothing (permanently) into these environments. Each natural object plays a role in the healthy functioning of the ecosystem there. Even small shells and shell fragments have a use: shells are used by hermit crabs as homes, and anemones use the fragments to coat their bodies when exposed to the air.

There's a sense of peace and serenity on the shore. Perhaps you've had the experience of sitting on the beach, sand between your toes, sun-warmed rock against your back, watching and feeling the ocean ebb and flow with every wave. There's a sense of comfort and serenity—a sense of coming home. At day's end, the sun bathes the bluffs and dunes in a golden radiance and then disappears under a glistening horizon. Your world, at least for the moment, is at peace.

Tidepools host fragile, miniature ecosystems—particular care should be taken when exploring these delicate areas. (Photo by Jerry Schad)

RECOMMENDED READING

California Coastal Commission. *California Coastal Access Guide*. University of California Press, 1983. (Information on all the scenic and recreational facilities of the California coast, including descriptions of several hundred public accessways.)

Hinton, Sam. *Seashore Life of Southern California*. University of California Press, 1987. (This popular guide to intertidal life in Southern California also includes a "Selected References" list of books about other areas along the Pacific coast.)

Kozloff, Eugene. *Seashore Life of the North Pacific Coast*. University of Washington Press, 1983.

Meinkoth, Norman. *The Audubon Society Field Guide to North American Sea Creatures*. (An excellent field reference filled with color photos.)

Climbing a snowfield (Photo by Bob and Ira Spring)

Mountain Travel

MIKE FRY AND BOB FEUGE

The restless wanderings of the earth's crustal plates exert forces—up, down, and sideways—that create the three-dimensional landscapes known as mountains. Most of the North American continent's Western mountains (especially the Sierra Nevada range, the Rocky Mountains, and much that lies in between) have been thrust upward along faults and folds. Others, like the Cascade mountain range, are evolving through repeated violent episodes of volcanism.

The titanic forces of colliding and grinding plates are just the opening salvo. Mountains collect extra rain and snow, and the erosive forces of running water and creeping ice tear at their flanks, opening up ravines, widening canyons, and creating jagged crests.

When mountains are formed, every aspect of the regional environment is altered. Weather patterns can be affected hundreds of miles away. On the Pacific coast, for example, moist air moves inland over the coastal mountain ranges, dropping most of its moisture on the west-facing slopes. Once over the mountain crests, the air blasts down the east-facing slopes, warming and drying as it approaches the relatively arid lands beyond.

Mountains make possible a great diversity of habitats that support a wide variety of plant and animal life. Timberline and alpine zones occur at high altitudes where the short summer growing season is not long enough to allow trees to repair the damage caused by severe winter storms. A lone, dead snag high on a ridge may indicate that a milder climate existed there in the past, but mostly the plants and animals of these airy retreats keep a low profile. At lower elevations, biological richness and diversity increases. Here, the lush forests and cascading rivers are prized for commercial as well as recreational use. Wild areas containing old-growth forest are increasingly restricted to the national parks and designated wilderness areas. Unfortunately, much of North America's forested lands (including many national forests) have been sacrificed to commercial logging and massive water projects. Alpine and timberline wilderness areas have fared better because of their more limited resources.

MOUNTAIN TRAVEL CONCERNS

SEASONS

Most backpackers visit mountain areas from the spring through early fall. In the alpine and timberline zones, these "warm" seasons may be compressed into a period of just a few weeks, so you may have to time your visit carefully. A severe winter may have left high passes blocked by snow even into August, and swollen streams at a lower elevation may have knocked out bridges, or rendered certain streams impassable. Be sure to inquire with the local agency (park service or other authority) before your visit.

In the Sierra Nevada, which is fairly

typical of the big mountain ranges of North America, early summer is the best time for flowers, but the worst for mosquitoes. Midsummer through early fall usually brings fine weather—notwithstanding the occasional thunderstorm—to the Sierra Nevada and the Cascades. This is not the case for the Rocky Mountains. Violent thunderstorms, typically occurring in the afternoon, are common there. Usually, sunny weather prevails each morning, but cloud buildups over the higher peaks by noon signal that all prudent hikers seek refuge from the rain, wind, and lightning by early afternoon.

Early autumn—anytime from late September through October—is the best time to enjoy the fall colors of trees such as aspens, cottonwoods, and maples. Mountain weather in the early fall is usually calm and stable, but this is also the period when the season's first heavy snowstorm is likely to arrive.

Deer-hunting season in the national forests and other public lands usually runs from late September into October. Since there's a lot of space for hunters to wander throughout the wild, this is not necessarily a serious conflict for hikers and backpackers. However, you should be extra careful to wear bright colors and make your presence known if you decide to visit areas frequented by hunters. Better yet, you can stick to state and national parks, which usually prohibit any kind of hunting.

ALTITUDE EFFECTS

Air at higher altitudes tends to be both thinner and drier. Both of these characteristics affect the local climate. Temperatures tend to be much cooler than in the lowlands, and they also can swing from warm daytime highs to bone-chilling nighttime lows.

While trying to keep cool in the midday sunshine, you may be tempted to shed as much clothing as possible. Don't. When the sun stands very high in the sky, as in a clear summer sky, the ultraviolet radiation is intense. The bombardment comes from all directions, as UV readily reflects off of snow, rocks, and water. It also scatters in thin clouds, so a cloud cover is no guarantee of protection.

Unprotected skin at high altitudes burns very quickly. Areas of the body that normally receive a lot of sunlight, including the nose, the tops of the forearms, and the backs of the hands, are affected the most. Often and liberally, apply one of the more powerful sunscreen lotions, and cover up with a long-sleeve shirt and a brimmed hat. To protect your hands, you can wear lightweight cotton gloves.

In the mountains especially, don't neglect the health of your eyesight. Use sunglasses or goggles with 100-percent UV-absorption characteristics. Exposure to high-intensity sunshine and excess UV can cause such temporary distresses as snow blindness or sun blindness, while repeated episodes of UV overexposure may trigger serious vision problems later in one's life.

The thin mountain air is refreshing once you get used to it. During the first couple of days on the trail, though, you may be gasping for breath when working hard, so plan easier days on the early part of a trip. When exercising heavily, be sure to exhale completely so that you effectively remove carbon dioxide from your respiratory system and leave plenty of room for incoming oxygen. By concentrating on your exhale, you will naturally breathe in enough air on the inhale.

Some people who cannot acclimate properly to high altitudes (sometimes as little as 8,000 feet) develop altitude sickness. The surefire antidote is to remove the victim to a lower altitude (see Chapter 15, Wilderness First Aid, *Environmental Hazards in the Wilderness*). During altitude acclimation, many people tend to fall into an alternating cycle of rapid breathing and very slow breathing while at rest or asleep. This is nothing to be alarmed about; it is a normal part of the respiratory system's adjustment to a new balance between oxygen intake and carbon-dioxide output.

SNOWFIELDS AND ICE

In the mountains, the north sides of high passes may be choked with snow all year-round. In the morning, and again late in the day, these slopes may be icy on the surface. A slip and a fall on such a slope could result in a long slide. With an ice axe and crampons (see Chapter 14, Winter Mountaineering, *Winter Travel Techniques*), safe passage across such icy slopes may be possible; otherwise, you must bide your time and wait for the snow to soften in the afternoon.

Sometimes snow can be advantageous for travel on cross-country routes if deep, consolidated snow covers brush, boulders, or downed logs on the less steep terrain. There are potential hazards though, especially when the snow cover is too soft, thereby allowing a hiker's leg to plunge into holes. Be especially careful when you cross "snow bridges" across streams, as these could collapse if the temperature is too warm and the snow too soft.

Ice-covered lakes pose another obvious but insidious hazard. It can be all too tempting for an inexperienced person to venture out on what may appear to be thick ice. If the ice breaks and you tumble into icy water, it's almost impossible to haul yourself out. Without a rope to toss or special equipment, a would-be rescuer can easily fall into the same trap and face the same consequences—death by hypothermia in a matter of minutes. By simply staying on the shore, you won't have to worry about these possibilities.

Glacier travel is an integral part of wilderness travel in the northwestern United States, western Canada, and Alaska. Because it is potentially dangerous, considerable planning and training is required to have a pleasant, safe outing. Ropes should always be used, regardless of how simple the crossing appears. All members of the team should have critical equipment such as ice axes, crampons, avalanche beacons, and other items when traversing glaciers, particularly if the snow/ice conditions are marginal. Readers of this book should get training on glacier travel and should travel with experienced mountaineers on their first attempts at negotiating a glacier field. Additional information on glacier travel is available in *Mountaineering: The Freedom of the Hills*, published by The Mountaineers.

When trails are obscured by snow, you may have to follow blazes (indentations chipped into trees) or other markers, if they're available. Where snow is present, a trail hike can often turn into a cross-country ramble, so keep your map handy and be prepared to use your navigational skills.

LIGHTNING

In many mountain areas, the pattern of crystal-clear mornings, afternoon thunderstorms, and evening clearings repeats like clockwork for days on end.

If you're planning to cross a high pass or climb a peak in a thunderstorm-prone area, the obvious thing to do is get an early start, and get off the peak well before the storm moves in.

If you care to know the distance between yourself and a bolt of lightning, use the rule of thumb that every 5-second interval between a visible streak of lightning and the audible thunder means a mile of distance. Sometimes there's not much advance warning, though.

First there's a billowing cloud above, then hail, then the first lightning strike somewhere nearby. Your hair may stand on end, and sparks (corona discharge) may jump from eyeglasses, pack frames, or other metallic objects. If this happens, you're clearly in trouble—a lightning strike is imminent. Immediately assume a position as low as you can. Sit or crouch low on your pack or other insulating object to avoid ground currents. After the strike, move quickly downhill. If you feel

151

Stay on trails to protect delicate plant life when crossing alpine meadows. (Photo by Bob and Ira Spring)

the charge building again, get into a low position, as before. Ice axes, tent poles, and metal hiking sticks should be carried horizontally or abandoned if lightning is a threat.

Any tall object, reaching above its surroundings, is a highly probable target for a lightning strike. Obviously you do not want to be that object. Sharp-edged objects also have a tendency to attract lightning discharges. A good strategy, then, is to find a safe haven in a low spot close to but not directly under an object such as a tree that would bear the brunt of a strike.

A 30-foot-tall tree would probably protect you if you're 20 or 30 feet away from it.

When seeking a low spot, don't position yourself in a soggy basin, along a creek, along the base of a cliff, close to cracks in the rock, or at the entrance of a cave (the center of a spacious cave, if dry, is okay). These places are likely to conduct ground currents traveling along the paths of least resistance on the surface of or through the earth.

FRAGILE ECOSYSTEMS

The short growing season of the alpine and timberline zones poses severe challenges to the survival of the unique plants and animals existing there. Most park agencies rightfully prohibit campfires in these areas. Leave that dead wood to build soil, or for someone to use in an emergency. Those sticks lying on the ground could be hundreds of years old, and they cannot be replaced tomorrow.

When below timberline, restrict your campsites to forest duff (pine needles, no shrubs or grasses), bare soil, or sandy areas free of vegetation. Never build a campfire on duff, however, since duff can smolder for a long time, possibly triggering a wildfire. Mountain meadows, especially just below timberline, are attractive-looking as campsites, but most assuredly not appropriate for that use. Many of the mountain parks prohibit camping in meadows, or 200 feet from sources of water or trails. Carry a full 2-gallon water bag to a campsite high on a sandy ridge or along the timberline, and you'll have all you need for a comfortable night at a dry campsite. With dramatic views at sunrise and sunset, this can be as good as wilderness camping gets.

Hiking through a canyon in the desert Southwest (Photo by Carol Murdock)

Desert Travel

HAL BRODY

The desert has a certain spiritual quality not found on the seashore, in the mountains, or along the rivers. There's an overwhelming sense of stillness, solitude, and space. The isolation and quiet is restful, and you never have to put up with the hordes of people you often meet on the mountain trails. With its meager vegetation and clear, dry air, the desert is full of mind-expanding perspectives.

Going cross-country in the desert is relatively easy—there's usually no bushwhacking involved. There's often not much to screen the view either, so even a slight elevation gain yields tremendously broad vistas. When camping, you needn't be concerned about bears getting into possessions and food, though rodents can be a minor problem.

When you travel through the desert, you can see its geologic structure laid bare, revealing a kaleidoscope of shapes and colors. But the desert is full of other surprises as well. It's a real thrill to come upon a rare cactus, a trickling spring, a hidden palm oasis, or an ancient Native American artifact.

To help you understand the desert and desert travel, let's first look at the anatomy of the North American deserts.

NORTH AMERICAN DESERTS

The desert regions of North America have little (about 10 inches or less) and irregular rainfall. Other common features are high summer daytime temperatures; low humidity; wide swings in temperature from day to night; frequent sunshine and clear, blue skies; soil that is low in humus and high in minerals; and a ground surface that gets easily eroded by wind and water. Under these severe conditions, plants and animals have had to employ unique—and sometimes bizarre—strategies in order to survive.

In addition to true deserts, there are semiarid areas that have many similarities to deserts. The Four Corners area of southeastern Utah, southwestern Colorado, northwestern New Mexico, and northeastern Arizona is perhaps the best-known example. The true North American desert can be divided into four regions based on distinct kinds of vegetation.

The Great Basin desert (dominated by the grayish Great Basin sagebrush—or "purple sage") is the largest and most northern of these divisions. It comprises southeastern Oregon, southern Idaho, most of Nevada, western Utah, and a small amount of northern Arizona.

Second largest and southernmost is the Chihuahuan desert, indicated by a particular type of agave (spiny, succulent plant). This desert lies mostly in northern Mexico, but occupies a small area of southern New Mexico and western Texas.

The Sonoran desert is the third largest, covering most of southern Arizona, southeastern California, and much of Baja California and the adjacent Mexican state of Sonora. More complicated assemblages of vegetation, including the ocotillo (a spindly, spiny plant), the giant saguaro cactus, and fan palms represent the many subregions of the Sonoran desert.

Smallest of the North American deserts is the Mojave (also spelled Mohave), which extends through parts of southeastern and eastern California into southern Nevada and western Arizona. The Joshua tree, a type of giant yucca, dominates the higher elevations of the Mojave Desert.

In general, the most interesting places to explore in any of these regions are the mountains that rise from the desert floor, the storm-carved canyons and dry river courses (washes) that infrequently carry runoff from these mountains, and the enigmatic, salt-encrusted sinks that collect the runoff. Wherever water has forced its way through soft earth (often old seabed sediment), fascinating "badlands" are formed.

You can find plants almost everywhere in the desert—animals too, but their activities are usually secretive and nocturnal. Generally, you'll encounter many more varieties and quantities of spiny plants in the southern deserts than in the northern (Great Basin) desert.

DESERT TRAVEL

As in all wilderness travel, water is criti cal. In the desert, water availability and abundance is subject to the whims of nature. Although many natural water sources exist in the desert, you cannot necessarily trust maps that show springs and permanent streams. Springs dry up, seasonally or permanently, and cartographers have a tough time keeping up with such changes. Check with rangers or people at other agencies such as the Bureau of Land Management regarding water availability in the area you plan to visit.

More often than not, you'll be unsure of the availability of water, and you'll have to plan on carrying all you'll need for both drinking and cooking. A rough rule of thumb is 1 gallon per day (per person), but this refers to sunny, mild weather.

Actual requirements could range from as little as 2 quarts on an overcast winter day in the high desert to more than 2 gallons on a 100° F. day in the low desert. Since water weighs 8.3 pounds per gallon, your mobility may be severely limited if you're forced to carry all the water you'll need. Carry your water in leak-proof containers (such as sturdy plastic bottles). If you're planning an out-and-back trip, consider stashing some of your water on the way in. Unless you trust your memory absolutely, make a written note of where you placed the water on your map, so you can find it on the way out.

Because it's possible to hike in almost any direction in the desert, it's very tempting to do so. If you're accustomed to staying on marked and maintained trails in the mountains, you may not realize how easy it is to become lost or disoriented out in the open. Navigational skills are important in the desert, as is a constant awareness of major landmarks around you. Don't allow yourself or others to become separated from the group. The desert's corrugated surface can conceal a separated person as surely as a dense forest.

The desert harbors a wonderful variety of beautiful yet potentially distressful cacti and shrubs. These plants survive heat and drought, and hungry and thirsty animals, through various strategies. Being sharp is one. If you can't be watchful and careful of their sharpness, then you deserve what you get! Cholla-cactus balls, which fall from the parent plant to become new plants, sometimes end up attached to your arms or legs. If you do get snagged, slide a comb between your skin and the ball and then pull outward. In a pinch, a rock in each hand will usually do the trick. Small pliers or hefty tweezers can usually grip individual spines well enough for removal.

When traveling over steep, rocky slopes, climb or descend diagonally, rather than straight up or down. Any rocks kicked loose will then pass to the side of your

Many hikers are drawn to the stark, remote regions of the Southwest. (Photo by Carol Murdock)

comrades rather than collide with them. If a rock is set in motion, yell "rock!" to warn those below.

Some people are quite anxious about rattlesnakes in the desert. (Actually, there are more of them in the mountains.) Between late fall and early winter, most desert-dwelling snakes are in hibernation. When they're out and about at other times, they're usually not aggressive unless provoked. Most will retreat if given the opportunity. Still, you should always avoid placing your hands and feet in places you can't see clearly (see Chapter 9, Wilderness Travel, *Safety Concerns*).

Desert washes are particularly prone to flash flooding. Runoff can be funneled into places far from where the rain falls, resulting in a wall of water packing enormous momentum. There's usually some forewarning in the form of a low roar, but often not enough time to get to higher ground. Unless you're absolutely certain no rain will fall either locally or upstream, don't sleep in a wash.

In all seasons except summer, the weather in the desert is often quite gentle. Expect daytime highs in the 60s to 80s F. Winter nights however, can get downright frigid—low 30s in the lower deserts, 20s in the Mojave, even less in the higher elevations of the Great Basin. Even the driest parts of the desert can get occasional heavy rainfall, while snow dusts the upper-elevation Mojave and Great Basin deserts regularly. Hypothermia can be an unexpected threat.

Springtime weather in the desert can be

quite fickle, ranging from high winds with mild temperatures to ovenlike heat. If the weather service says a warming trend is building with predicted temperatures in the 90s or higher, you should consider either cancelling your trip or scaling back the miles you expect to cover.

The time from late May through September is usually too hot for strenuous activity in the desert. You should also be wary of early May, however, as the daylight hours are long, and the sun's high angle at midday steals away the shade.

CLOTHING AND EQUIPMENT

The desert can be extremely tough on the feet. The stiff and spiny vegetation, the rocky terrain, and even soft sand present unaccustomed challenges. Boots with leather uppers provide excellent protection from cactus as well as good support. When walking over rocks of all shapes and sizes, your feet and ankles need as much support as possible, especially if you're carrying the weight of a full backpack. Before wearing boots made of flimsier material, consider that a cactus spine can penetrate nylon boot material with almost the same ease as a sewing needle passes through nylon fabric.

To avoid bruises and scrapes from climbing over rocks and scratches from cactus, wear loose-fitting or stretchy long pants. They don't hinder your stride, and they help protect your legs from the ravages of the sun as well.

Shade is hard to come by in the desert. A sun hat is a necessity to keep from "frying your brain." Gray matter is very sensitive to heat. It will be the first part of your body to malfunction when overheated. Without a hat you risk sunburn, headache, nausea, and dizziness.

When the sun's up, your eyes should be

Cholla cactus, nemesis of desert hikers (Photo by James Glenn Pearson)

shielded by ultraviolet-blocking sun-glasses, and your skin should be covered by long-sleeved and long-legged gar-ments—especially if you're fair-skinned. These precautions will become more ur-gent as the earth's ultraviolet-blocking ozone layer continues to be attacked by certain gases—byproducts of modern in-dustry—that have migrated into the upper atmosphere.

You must be prepared for cold tempera-tures, rain, and even snow in high deserts, so travel with the appropriate clothing and sleeping bag (see Chapter 5, Outfitting: The Basic Equipment). Have lightweight rain gear with you, and a tent as well if you'll be camping away from the car.

DESERT SURVIVAL

If you need to locate water in the desert in an emergency, here are some techniques. As you survey the desert landscape for possible water sources, look for a line of trees or bushes that may indicate water at or near the surface. A clump of grass or sedges is a good indicator as well. An-other likely place would be the base of a steep canyon wall. Flocks of birds can sometimes be seen circling over waterholes, especially during the morning and evening. Take note of the type of veg-etation around a source of water. If peren-nial grasses or cattails aren't present, then the source probably dries up during the summer. When you find water, mark it on your map with the date. That way you can build a valuable history of water sources in your favorite areas.

Tanks or tinajas (naturally formed, wa-ter-filled depressions in rock) often serve the needs of desert animals. If the water supply is especially low, don't draw water from them unless you have to. Large tanks holding thousands of gallons are good sources, though the water will probably need filtration or chemical purification. Spring-fed pools should be used only for drinking. Water in running streams, how-ever, can be used for limited washing.

White clothing helps keep desert hikers cooler. (Photo by Hal Brody)

Never do any washing in a natural water source; always carry the water far from the stream, and wash with a small amount of biodegradable soap. Swimming in pools of the larger streams is a real treat in hot weather!

A few areas of the desert contain springs with unpalatable (salty or alkaline) or even poisonous water. Beware of water sources close to mine tailings (spoils). If the water has a normal amount of algae and crawl-ing or wiggling critters, it's probably not poisonous. Beware of stagnant water with nothing alive in it! Tracks of animals com-ing and going to drink are another positive sign—unless there are a lot of skeletal remains in the area. If in doubt about the water quality, check first with local authorities or rangers.

If you find yourself in the grip of a heat wave and low on water, start thinking and planning immediately. Rest in the shade during the hottest part of the day, and make haste to get back to your car (or other point of safety) in the cool of the evening and early morning. Drink your remaining water as your thirst dictates. Saving your water is not the best solution if you're slipping into dehydration. Don't waste time on schemes to extract water from cactus— you'll sweat out more water than you extract from the plant. Avoid eating too— digestion uses water.

HIGH-TEMPERATURE STRATEGIES

It makes good sense to stay out of the desert during summer, yet it can be frustrating to be "locked out" of your favorite desert areas for three or four months each year. Below are some strategies that make summer desert backpacking not only feasible but actually enjoyable. These strategies are quite applicable to the hot and dry conditions often found elsewhere in the arid West. Remember that the hazards of summer desert travel are severe and should never be taken lightly.

If you'd like to try high-temperature hiking or camping, then work up to it slowly. Start in the spring, with trips in the 90s F. Try camping near your car, and experiment with hikes that take you only a short distance away. Never let yourself become isolated from a source of water—either stay close to a stream or spring, or carry a supply that is adequate for any emergency, as discussed earlier.

Conditioning. Good aerobic conditioning is a prerequisite for any kind of high-temperature exercise. For 3 weeks before a trip, practice "heat conditioning" in conjunction with normal exercise. Evidence of proper heat conditioning is profuse sweating. If the weather won't cooperate, then wear sweat clothes or other heat-re-

taining clothing while exercising to induce heavy perspiration. This practice trains the body's sweat glands to dilate quickly in response to overheating, and the blood to circulate near the skin so as to liberate the body's internal heat. Psychological acclimation to heat is another benefit of heat conditioning. You become more comfortable with the feeling of simply being very warm. Forty-five minutes per session, 3 or 4 days per week seems to be adequate. Never withhold fluids while exercising or afterward; ignoring thirst is a dangerous practice.

Clothing. In a high-temperature environment, head-to-foot clothing offers protection from the radiant heat of the sun, and from high winds that might evaporate perspiration too quickly. White, loose-fitting cotton clothing and a white, broad-brimmed hat does the job well. In the absence of wind, some air circulation is needed to evaporate moisture from the skin, and thereby cool it. Consequently, cut slits or holes in your clothing where the sun doesn't shine—from armpits to elbows, from crotch to knees. Holes in the hat also help. Shirts that can be easily opened in the front when walking with the sun at your back are a real advantage. Skirts solve the air-circulation problem too, though they're awkward when climbing or scrambling.

Electrolyte maintenance. The body must have a proper balance of electrolytes to function at peak efficiency. The electrolytes to be most concerned with are potassium, sodium, magnesium, and calcium. These, of course, are lost in part through perspiration. Normally you replace any losses by eating a normal diet. But being active at high temperatures means perspiration losses of up to 2 gallons per day, and consequently a very rapid loss of electrolytes. Fatigue and muscle cramps are the typical signs of electrolyte depletion.

The solution is to use one of the com-

In desert areas shade may exist only in caves. (Photo by Jerry Schad)

mercial sport drinks or "thirst quenchers" designed to replace electrolytes. Gookinaid ERG (Electrolyte Replacement with Glucose) is a product sold in ready-to-mix powder form with an "isotonic" mix that ensures that it is quickly absorbed by the body, and extra glucose (sugar) that gives a boost of energy. Other sport drinks may be overly sweet or too concentrated; however, you can experiment with dilutions.

Emergencies. Even if you do everything right, you can overheat. Watch each other closely for signs of heat exhaustion. In fact, a victim is often the last to notice the adverse effects of an overheated body and brain. Early signs are fuzzy thinking (slurred or incoherent speech, perhaps) and a loss of balance and sure-footedness.

Act very quickly if this happens: Steer the victim to a shady spot, or create your own shade with the lightweight tarps that each person carries. Place the victim on three or four of the "sit-upons" (small, insulating pads) that you each carry, and use the others as fans if the air isn't moving fast enough. Remove excess clothing to ensure the maximum cooling effect of evaporation. If a water source is nearby, immerse the victim (if possible), or shuttle water from the source to pour over the victim's body. If there's no water source nearby, then at least "mist" the victim using two or three spray bottles that the group should carry. Meanwhile, coax the victim into drinking as much fluid (laced with electrolytes) as he or she can take.

ON THE ROAD

Automobiles are essential tools for reaching the edge of the desert wilderness, but when broken down they can leave

161

you miserably stranded. The following suggestions are meant to help you with the reliability of your transportation. Since overheating is a common problem in the desert, we'll focus mostly on that.

First, it's better to travel in two or more cars rather than one. If one breaks down, someone can go in another car for help.

Any car used in the desert must be in good mechanical condition. Before going, have your cooling system in good working order—a water-cooling system should be pressure-tested. Your radiator should be filled with a mixture consisting of water and a coolant designed to withstand higher-than-normal temperatures. Check the condition and tightness of the fan belts, but also carry spares and the necessary tools to install and tighten them. It's wise to carry an extra 5 gallons of water in case you lose your radiator water through a ruptured hose. This should be clean water just in case you need to drink some of it.

As you're driving, you should monitor your temperature gauge or warning light. If overheating is indicated, stop your car and engine as soon as it's safe to do so. Check your fan belt; if too loose, it will slip and reduce the effectiveness of your fan and/or water pump. Check the coolant level at the overflow tank—determine if and where you are losing coolant. Do repairs if necessary and, once the engine has cooled down, add water back into the system if needed. (Never remove the radiator cap while the engine is hot! You will get a face full of dangerously hot steam.)

If the problem is due to a ruptured hose and you don't happen to have the right hose to replace it, radiator-hose repair tape can get you moving again. Wrap, as tightly as possible, the ruptured section of hose, and don't forget to loosen or remove the radiator cap so as to greatly reduce pressure in the system. By doing this, the tape will prevent the coolant from escaping, but the coolant will slowly boil off. On the road again, you must check the coolant

level every half-hour or so and add as required. The repair tape is, of course, a very temporary quick-fix.

A less likely cause of overheating is a stuck thermostat, preventing coolant from reaching your radiator. This can be cured by simply removing the thermostat once the engine has cooled (learn how to do this ahead of time).

If, after stopping with a hot engine, everything looks OK, then all you can do is proceed at a slower speed (with the air conditioner off, since it draws from the cooling system too) as soon as the engine has cooled. Slower speeds mean less power output and less heat production. By turning on your car's heater (uncomfortable as it may be), you can draw off some additional heat from your engine. Watch your temperature gauge and take it easy, especially on the uphills.

Extra motor oil, jumper cables, and a gas-tank patch kit should be carried. It's easy to puncture your gas tank while bouncing over rocky roads, especially if you yield to the temptation to cover those endless desert miles too quickly. If you need to carry extra gasoline, do so in an approved container. These containers are more safely (and legally) carried if securely attached to the outside of a vehicle, rather than packed inside.

Have a tow rope and shovel stashed in the car and know how to use them. Getting stuck in the sand happens to almost every desert adventurer sooner or later. A 1-foot-square piece of plywood will allow your jack to lift more efficiently in soft sand. Strips of old carpet placed under the tires can help you escape problem spots. Soft-sand roads can be more easily negotiated by deflating your tires to about 15 pounds per square inch of pressure, but the process of pumping them back up to recommended pressure can be time-consuming, even with a battery-operated tire pump.

Hone your tire-changing skills and make sure your jack is operational and your spare tire is pressurized. Your jack is a powerful tool for getting your car off a big rock or anything else that might keep the weight off your wheels.

If your car breaks down irreparably, stay with it unless it's obvious you can walk for help. In an emergency you can call attention to yourself by using the car's horn, lights, and mirrors. The spare tire, when doused with gasoline, burns with copious black smoke for a long time. If you need shelter from the sun, dig out enough room under your car to comfortably lie on your insulated sleeping pad. Store water in your body, not in your water bottles. Don't drink radiator water unless it contains only water, and filter it, when possible, if you do.

PRESERVING THE DESERT

More so in the desert than almost any other place, it's important to pack out paper items like toilet tissue and sanitary supplies. Paper, like everything else, decomposes very slowly in the absence of water. If buried around a campsite, paper can be unearthed by the winds, by animals, or by an unfortunate hiker, thereby announcing the earlier presence of careless humans.

When you break camp in the desert, return the site to its natural appearance. Scatter or remove campfire rings or blackened rocks and sand. A "buddy burner" is all you really need at night. Here's how to make one: Cut a strip of cardboard as wide as the height of a small can such as a tuna-fish can, line the inside of the can with the cardboard, and fill it to the top with melted paraffin. A buddy burner of this size will burn for about two hours, even in a strong wind, and have a flame sufficient for a group of fifteen—not much heat but enough warm light to chat by. A larger-diameter can yields a larger flame, and a deeper one burns longer.

A buddy burner provides a surprising amount of heat and light. (Photo by Carol Brody)

The toughness of the desert is, in a way, just a façade. The desert ecosystem is actually quite fragile. Desert plants grow very slowly and are always struggling for survival. Any damage we inflict can remain like scars on the land for decades. In some areas of the desert, you can still see tank tracks left by U.S. military training efforts during World War II. In other areas, grazing cattle have displaced the native wildlife and pulverized the vegetation. One insensitive person with an off-road vehicle can do a tremendous amount of destruction in only a few minutes. Even hikers can do damage.

One little-known life form that needs our protection is cryptogamic soil, a brittle crust made up of lichens, mosses, algae, and fungi. It appears as a lumpy ground cover about 1 inch thick, and black, green, or white, depending on the organisms it contains.

Cryptogamic soil is an important link in the desert ecosystem because it stabilizes and builds fertile soil by preventing erosion and fixing nitrogen. Spongy and resilient when wet, it becomes vulnerable when dry, which is most of the time. Crunched to a powder when stepped on, it can blow away with the next breeze. Hikers needing to cross areas covered by cryptogamic soil can minimize the impact by using a single set of footprints while walking single file. Please avoid cryptogamic soil when selecting a campsite.

If you find something of interest in the desert, your grandchildren and their grandchildren will probably find it fascinating, too. Leave it there for others to see and enjoy. Artifacts of past human habitation are an especially sensitive issue. Native Americans lived in many of our deserts up until very recent times, so things like pottery shards are still in relative abundance. In the desert they provide an almost magical reminder of past civilizations and spiritual heritage. On the mantel at home, they're just old pieces of clay. In many desert areas, it's illegal to remove anything at all. So should it be for all our wilderness areas.

In *Desert Solitaire*, Edward Abbey offers us a powerful insight into the nature of the desert wilderness: "Despite its clarity and simplicity . . . the desert wears at the same time, paradoxically, a veil of mystery. Motionless and silent it evokes in us an elusive hint of something unknown, unknowable, about to be revealed. Since the desert does not act it seems to be waiting—but waiting for what?"

Searching for that "unknowable" is what keeps us going back to the desert again and again.

RECOMMENDED READING

Abbey, Edward. *Desert Solitaire*. Ballantine Books, 1968.

Larson, Peggy. *A Sierra Club Naturalist's Guide: The Deserts of the Southwest*. Sierra Club Books, 1977.

Schad, Jerry. *California Deserts*. Falcon Press, 1988.

Zwinger, A. H. *The Mysterious Lands*. Truman Talley Books, 1989.

CHAPTER 14

Winter Mountaineering

DAVE USSELL AND BOB FEUGE

The mantle of white enshrouding the winter landscape is simultaneously an invitation to experience one of nature's most beautiful spectacles and a warning to be more wary and respectful than usual of the dangers that await the unprepared. Fortunately, preparations are not as difficult as they may first appear.

An outing in the snow is enhanced by breathtaking scenery, a virtually unspoiled wilderness, and a dearth of insects and dangerous creatures. The stillness and tranquility of the winter landscape is seldom spoiled by hordes of fellow travelers. The winter traveler is not restricted to staying on trails, if, indeed, trails can be found at all.

CLOTHING AND EQUIPMENT

Winter travel places stringent demands on clothing and equipment. Certain advantages claimed for equipment used during the warmer three seasons can be more pronounced when the same equipment is tested during the fourth season. A case in point is the performance of internal- versus external-frame packs. An internal-frame pack's streamlined design sheds snow, hail, and wind more easily than an external-frame pack does. Its body-hugging shape does not impair the wearer's balance as much as an external-frame pack.

With no exposed metal, internal-frame packs are easier and safer to handle with bare skin under extremely cold conditions.

WINTER CLOTHING

Clothes retain body heat in cold conditions, but less clothing allows for evaporative cooling in warmer conditions or when generating a lot of heat through exercise. The winter traveler must be prepared for both, and must do so with a limited wardrobe that is multipurpose and efficient. Thus the layering system discussed in Chapter 5, Outfitting: The Basic Equipment, *Clothing*, becomes critically important.

The winter traveler should be prepared to put on any combination of layers that:

- trap warm air
- hold in body moisture (when not exercising heavily)
- keep winds from removing body heat
- resist the passage of water from outside to inside
- allow ventilation and encourage the passage of moisture from inside to outside (when exercising)
- allow freedom of movement
- provide some protection from abrasion and penetration

These layers, ideally, would be light in weight, low in cost, and easily repaired.

Several synthetics do a good job of letting body moisture escape from the skin. The names of some commonly available examples are polypropylene, Capilene, pile, bunting, Synchilla, and fleece. Wool is the only common natural fiber that can provide significant warmth when it's wet. Most kinds of wool are too scratchy to be considered an acceptable choice for underwear. For this reason, Capilene and polypropylene are some of the most popular choices, but some synthetic underwear may have a tendency to retain body odors, even after laundering.

For warmth, almost any material that traps air and minimizes its motion can be potentially useful. Wool, duck or goose down, and synthetic materials such as Quallofil, Polarguard, and Hollofil work well, with various advantages and disadvantages. The synthetics have the advantage of providing some warmth when wet, whereas down provides more warmth for the same weight, but is ineffective when wet.

To block the wind, a nonporous synthetic shell (outer garment) is best. There are many materials suited to this task, including nylon (Taslan) and Gore-Tex. The design of the shell should include adequate provision for ventilation. Jackets or parkas lined with an outer shell are fine for urban use, but they don't offer enough versatility for use under changeable winter conditions. Consider as an alternative a pile jacket and a separate shell garment. This affords comfort in moderately cold conditions (using just the jacket) and/or in windy conditions.

The use of vapor-barrier materials, such as plastic, urethane-coated nylon, or rubber, can be advantageous in certain situations. When the temperature is extremely low, a vapor-barrier layer under a jacket can add as much as 15°F. of apparent warmth, although effective ventilation must be assured by such features as underarm zippers for use while exercising. Vapor-barrier mittens and socks are usable over a much wider range of tempera-

ture and activity. A simple way to test the effectiveness of vapor barriers is to wear plastic bread bags between inner and outer socks. As a result, your feet may feel slightly clammy, but will most likely stay warmer while out in the snow.

With the right combination of long underwear, a layer or layers of insulating garments, and a wind- and rain-resistant shell, comfort can be achieved under almost any conditions. Of course, it must be remembered that heat losses also occur from the extremities and from the head—more than 30 percent from the head alone. Polypropylene liner gloves and a ski mask or balaclava are good first layers. On top of those should be insulating layers consisting of a wool/polypropylene hat and gloves or mittens. A hood and nonporous overmitts can be used for extreme conditions. Hoods work best when they are attached to a jacket or parka. Outer gloves should have a non-slip surface in the palm area and a large gauntlet with a tightening arrangement to minimize drafts. It is common practice on winter expeditions to keep gloves on lengths of cord attached to the wearer in some way to avoid loss if they are removed for any reason.

It's worth mentioning that sometimes winter conditions can be more dangerous on warmer days. Sunshine or higher temperatures may cause snow to melt on contact with your clothing. If seams are not sealed properly or the outer material is porous, your clothing may absorb a lot of water, which then greatly reduces the effectiveness of the insulation when the sun sets and the temperature begins to fall.

It is very important on any winter outing to have at least two sets of clothing, particularly those garments that stay close to your body, such as long underwear. At all times, at least one set of clothing should be dry or at least in the process of being dried. Few things can ruin a winter trip faster than wet, cold clothing!

Wrap your extra dry clothes in plastic bags and seek opportunities to dry moist or wet clothing when your travel itinerary and/or sunshine permit. Many tents have loops inside to accommodate stringing up clothes lines. A candle lantern can do a remarkable job of drying clothes under adverse conditions.

PACKS

Proper gear and clothing is often neglected by winter mountaineering novices who, by not taking extra clothing and other items, foolishly count on near-perfect weather and no delays. It's better to take along a larger day pack or backpack than needed for the warmer seasons. This reduces the temptation to leave important things behind and makes carrying the extra load more comfortable. For cross-country ski touring in particular, a pack must allow the arms to move freely past the body while poling. When loading a backpack for overnight use, put the heavy items close to the back, not near the top. Pack medium-weight items at the bottom, and afterward stuff the lighter items anywhere they'll fit. Use plastic bags or coated nylon sacks to protect all items from snow and to group items by use.

BOOTS

Boots used for winter mountaineering should keep the feet dry and warm. A hiker should never try to keep feet warm by putting on more socks to the extent that circulation is reduced—that will only make the feet colder. Conventional leather boots must be sealed with a sealer specifically designed for that purpose. Gaiters (the knee-high size is best) are helpful for not only keeping boots dry from the outside, but also for keeping snow from spilling into the boots from the top. Certain expensive gaiters have such features as full boot-upper coverage, Gore-Tex material, and insulation.

On long trips, even properly sealed boots can become soaked. What do you do then? A neophyte might handle the problem of wet boots by merely setting them aside in camp and putting on some warm booties. By morning, the boots would be frozen solid. A better choice would be to slowly dry the boots near a campfire. Another alternative is to put on a dry pair of inner socks, and then vapor barrier socks (plastic bags will do). On top of that, put on the outer socks (hopefully dry ones) and then the wet boots. On boots handled like this, "steam" has been seen within a few minutes, although it is unreasonable to expect the boots to dry completely by this method. To further the drying process, either place the boots in a plastic bag and sleep with them, or put a trash bag in the bottom of your sleeping bag (to protect the bag) and sleep with your boots on. This approach may not produce the most comfortable of nights, but life will be easier in the morning.

Plastic mountaineering boots with removable inner boots are an excellent choice for the fourth season. They're rugged, warm, and waterproof, and will easily accept crampons, gaiters, and snowshoes. The inner boots alone can be worn in the tent. On the negative side, they're fairly stiff, heavy, and expensive. Stiffness in a boot can be an asset in many climbing situations, however. Even when walking on flat terrain, the snow "gives" a little, which compensates for the lack of flexing in the boot.

Walking in deep, soft snow with a pack and boots alone is an exhausting process. With each step a hiker can sink to as far as the crotch, and forward progress is excruciatingly slow. This is called post holing. The solution is to lower your pressure on the ground by spreading your body weight over a larger area by wearing either snowshoes or skis. It's also possible to lighten or eliminate any load on your back by placing your gear in a lightweight sled specially designed to be towed behind a skier or snowshoer.

Cross-country skis, unlike snowshoes, require special boots. When shopping for skis, you're really looking for a system of skis, bindings, boots, and poles. Each kind of ski boot is designed for use with a particular type of binding, and bindings are attached to the skis by special tools. The outfitter can help sort through the many options and help you choose the right system.

Ski boots for day tours or ski backpacks should be durable and warm, have good torsional rigidity yet some forward flex, and extend just above the ankle bone to provide lateral support and ankle protection. Boots with uppers made of Gore-Tex or other synthetic fabrics are OK for light uses; leather boots are much better, as long as they're treated for waterproofness with the appropriate silicone or beeswax sealant.

SNOWSHOES

Snowshoes are usually selected based on the user's weight (with gear) and the type of terrain to be covered. Snowshoes with an upturned lip are best for powdery snow. Flat and open terrain allows larger snowshoes to be used. In steep, rough, or brushy terrain, the large snowshoes are more of a hindrance than a help. Smaller snowshoes with various lip curvatures are available for these conditions. Your local outfitter can offer advice about appropriate sizes and types of bindings. Older snowshoes consisted of little more than a wooden frame with a rawhide weave. Many newer snowshoes have a lightweight aluminum frame, reinforced neoprene pad areas, quick disconnect bindings, and a fixed or movable toothed grip for climbing slopes.

CROSS-COUNTRY SKIS

The bottoms of cross-country skis are designed to grip the snow when one's full weight is applied, and to slide smoothly on the snow when less weight is applied. This allows you to "kick and glide" forward on the snow. Proper ski length and stiffness is important since the middle, or "kick" part, of the ski bottom must be in contact with the snow during the kick, and should be off the snow during the glide.

Generally, the length of a properly fitted ski should reach from the floor to the wrist of your raised arm. During ski fitting, you should also stand on the skis: a piece of paper should easily slide under the kick part (middle) of the ski when both skis are equally weighted, but each ski should touch the floor when all your weight is on it.

For ski travel in mountainous terrain, "off-track touring skis" are needed. These have a narrow "waist," a wider "tail," and an even wider "tip." Skis without these characteristics are suited for use on groomed tracks or race courses, but not for true cross-country travel. For general ski touring, skis should have enough "camber" (flex) so that they can be pressed together, bottom-to-bottom, with one hand.

Unless one is willing to spend the time required to gain enough experience in waxing, start out skiing with no-wax skis— skis with a relief pattern on the bottom to grip the snow when kicking. This term is a bit of a misnomer, since even they can benefit from the application of a glide wax (paraffin candle wax will do) to the tip and tail portions. Waxable skis, with no relief pattern, require the application of a "kick wax" on the kick portion of the ski to provide the needed grip.

Metal-edged skis are best for technical demands of steep, icy slopes, but they are usually not required for skiing in softer snow. Metal-edged skis are heavier and less flexible, and wet snow tends to freeze and stick to the metal edges.

When wearing a heavy pack, you may need to have skis that are either wider (to provide additional flotation) or metal-edged (for stability).

"Skins" are an optional but very useful aid in ski touring. Today they're made with mohair (goat hair), nylon, or polypropylene fibers. One side has short hairs facing one direction, and the other side has a reusable adhesive. When the sticky side is applied to the bottom of the skis, the hairs grip the snow (but not ice) and keep the

Cross-country skiing opens new worlds to the outdoor enthusiast. (Photo by Jerry Schad)

skin from backsliding when climbing steep hills. Skins, of course, prevent efficient gliding, but this can be an advantage when it's necessary to keep your speed down on steep downhills.

Ski poles are essential to maintain balance, and also to assist with forward propulsion. Aluminum alloy poles, preferably a high-grade aircraft type, are best. If bent, they can usually be straightened in the field. Fiberglass poles, while cheaper, can shatter. Generally, the poles should just fit under your underarms when the tips are touching the floor.

ICE AXE

For winter mountaineering, there are not many pieces of equipment as useful as an ice axe (fig. 14-1). For a person falling on a steep slope, the ice axe is the only piece of equipment that can arrest the slide in a rapid and controlled manner.

Select a longer axe if your travels are mostly on gentle inclines, and a shorter one if you're climbing a lot. Consider that "height" will change a bit when one sinks into the snow while walking. Lightweight, metal ice axes are very strong and moderately priced, and require little maintenance. But they're always cold to the touch under winter conditions. Carbon-fiber axes are strong and absorb shock well, but are very expensive and not so forgiving if a boulder should bounce off the shaft. Ice axes with wooden shafts are less strong and less expensive than the others. Hickory

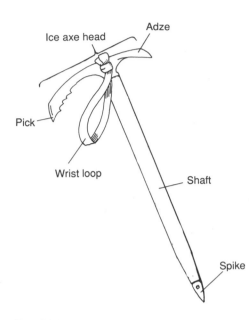

Fig. 14-1. Parts of the ice axe

shafts are usually preferred to ash.

Gouges in wooden or synthetic axes are greater cause for concern than in metal. Holes should never be drilled in axes for any kind of attachment. Most ice axes already have a hole in the head for utility use. The axe should be kept free of rust and deposits, and sharpened when needed. Sharpening of the pick, adze, and spike should be done with a file rather than a grinder, so as not to cause excessive heat that could affect the temper of the metal.

CRAMPONS

For icy conditions, there's no substitute for crampons, boot attachments whose sharp, metal points are designed to penetrate and grip hard snow and ice (fig. 14-2). Crampons are attached to boots with either a full strap binding or a step-in attachment that slips over the toe-end welt of the boot and attaches with a strap around the ankle.

Crampons typically have ten primary (downward-pointing) points and two forward-pointing points for climbing. Like the ice axe, they should be kept sharp at all times. If they are used for aerating lawns in the summer, don't forget to clean and sharpen them afterward! Protective sheaths for the points are commercially available, but can usually be improvised with tape and old inner tubes, or something similar.

SLEDS

There are a few decisions to make in selecting a sled for toting gear. All of the standard considerations of weight, material, cost, and ease of operation and maintenance apply. In addition, some ridges or runners of some sort (which function like that of a keel on a sailboat) must be on the bottom to allow easy forward motion and tracking, but limit lateral motions. A special, semirigid harness must be used to maintain the separation of traveler and sled when descending.

SPECIAL CLIMBING GEAR

Winter climbing involves most of the usual rock-climbing gear discussed in books on technical climbing. Somewhat unique to winter climbing are the ice axe, ice screws, and "deadmen." Ice screws take the place of pitons, nuts, and chocks for use as anchors on ice. A deadman should

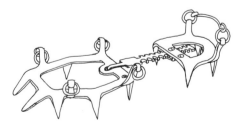

Fig. 14-2. Crampons

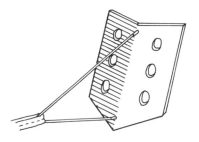

Fig. 14-3. Deadman anchor

not be confused with a dead man. Both happen to be difficult to move, but a deadman (fig. 14-3) is simply a big, flat object that resists movement perpendicular to its plane. If driven into consolidated snow at a slight angle, like a tent stake, it becomes very good anchor. The angle should be such that increased pull on the deadman only serves to drive it deeper into the snow, anchoring it more firmly.

SLEEPING EQUIPMENT

Sleeping equipment for winter mountaineering should be maximized for warmth. It may be worth 5° to 15° of extra warmth if an optional vapor-barrier or flannel liner is used. An obvious and easy way to increase insulation, if really needed, is to wear some or all of your insulating layers of clothing inside your bag—assuming there's enough room inside the sleeping bag.

A weight-conscious backpacker who happily takes a lightweight, three-quarter-length sleeping pad for the other three seasons should not skimp on a pad for winter use. Much of a sleeping person's body heat escapes downward into snow if there isn't a sufficient insulating barrier.

Many people like to connect two sleeping bags together to share intimate sleeping quarters. This arrangement provides extra warmth and space for the pair. During cold-weather campouts, however, this arrangement may be less practical for restless sleepers, since warm air easily escapes and cold air rushes in. Attaching sleeping bags together in the winter should be used for emergencies involving hypothermia, where it may be necessary to help warm a victim by body-to-body contact. It's a good idea for a group of winter wilderness travelers to have at least one pair of mating sleeping bags.

SPECIAL ITEMS

Certain items not normally needed on most three-season trips may be of special use on winter trips. A lightweight snow shovel can help speed up tasks such as digging trenches or snow caves for shelter. An aluminum snow saw is indispensable for cutting blocks used for igloos.

Altimeters can be of critical importance if it's necessary to navigate in white-out or poor-visibility conditions. As discussed in Chapter 8, The Weather, *Grace Under Pressure*, they can also be used to keep track of barometric pressure and thus changes in the weather.

Weather radios can be a good tool, but remember that batteries must be in top condition to perform at reduced temperatures. In remote areas, the signal strength of the nearest station may not be adequate for good reception.

Most normal sunglasses are not adequate for snow travel in the bright sunlight. In addition to a pair of normal sunglasses for use in shady conditions or on overcast days, one should have glacier glasses. They feature extra-dark lenses and opaque panels on the sides to keep out glare.

If you're including equipment to cover an expedition's special needs, add repair items to keep that equipment in working order. Consider taking extra fasteners and lightweight tools for equipment such as snowshoes, rope to lash things together and for making splints, and possibly hose clamps, duct tape, and wire for general repair of a variety of equipment.

171

WINTER TRAVEL TECHNIQUES

OVER SNOW AND ICE

When traveling on a hard crust of snow or ice, an ice axe and (in more extreme cases) crampons become necessary tools.

When carrying an ice axe that isn't needed for emergency use, tie it to your pack, or carry it in either of two ways (fig. 14-4): Grasp the shaft at the balance point with the tip forward and the pick to the rear and down. Or use the ice axe as a hiking stick with your palm resting on the head of the axe directly over the shaft with the pick forward (see fig. 14-1 for ice-axe terminology).

In the ready position (fig. 14-5), the ice axe is ready for emergency action. Hold it so that the pick is to the rear. Then lift the axe until it is diagonal across your chest and grasp the lower part of the shaft with the opposite hand. Normally the axe head is in the uphill hand. In the ready position, the wrist strap is always used to retrieve a lost axe if necessary. The ready position allows you to immediately go into a self-arrest maneuver (fig. 14-6) that will minimize sliding after a fall.

During a slide or fall on snow or ice, the pick must be driven hard and quickly into the surface to stop the slide. This must be done while simultaneously keeping the point off of the surface. If the point snags, it has a tendency to pull out the pick. If wearing crampons, it is important that they don't become snagged either.

During most falls, speed builds up rapidly, so quick reflexes are mandatory. Personal instruction and considerable practice is necessary for learning the various ways of self-arrest for the various types of falls. An ice-axe does little good, and may even do harm, to a person unskilled in its use.

Fig. 14-4. Carrying an ice axe, left *to* right: *carrying at balance point with pick down; using as cane; tied to pack.*

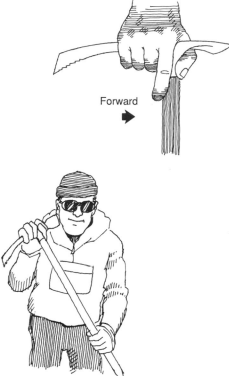

On steeper slopes with snow that is consolidated but not too icy, use your ice axe as a kind of anchor during ascent, planting its point in a new spot ahead of yourself after every step or two. If you're wearing boots, kick-step by driving the toe of the boot far enough into the snow to form a level platform you can step up on.

On steep, hard-packed snow or ice, either resort to wearing crampons or chop-stepping. Chop-stepping utilizes the adze of the ice axe to cut a small platform for weight transfer. In either case, rope together with others or be belayed (protected by rope). Detailed information on these techniques can be found in *Mountaineering: The Freedom of the Hills*, published by The Mountaineers.

When descending a steep slope, all of the same conditions for ascending must be considered, with some additions. Descending has the nice feature of being less exhausting. Unfortunately, the tradeoff is that it can be much harder to locate secure

Fig. 14-5. Top, *the ready grip;* Bottom, *the ready position*

Fig. 14-6. Self-arrest

Fig. 14-7. Plunge step

Fig. 14-8. Sitting glissade

footings.

If the slope is not too steep, you can use a plunge-step technique (fig. 14-7) to walk downhill, or "glissade" down. A glissade (fig. 14-8) is nothing more than sliding on one's feet or backside to the bottom of a slope, but using an ice axe (in a ready position with point dragging) as a kind of brake and rudder. In the plunge step, compaction of snow does the braking. The descent becomes a bouncy and somewhat animated jaunt down the slope with the ice axe ever ready to handle a fall.

Glaciers present problems not encountered in most other hiking, not the least of which are the crevasses (cracks) that develop when a glacier flows over a convex surface. Some crevasses are visible, while others may lie under a thin veneer of snow, ready to swallow the incautious traveler. Even when "on the level," all members of a climbing party must be tied into a rope so that if one drops into a crevasse, the others can use their ice axes to arrest the fall. The rescue of that climber is an advanced but necessary technique that must be mastered by prospective glacier travelers.

CROSS-COUNTRY SKIING

Cross-country skiing, also known as Nordic skiing, is a means of gaining access to the wilderness in the winter that is gaining in popularity. It may require one to traverse both flat and mountainous areas during a wilderness trek, sometimes on groomed tracks and other times on virgin snow. The latter conditions particularly attract those who cherish the solitude and unblemished natural beauty of winter scenery as well as a good physical workout.

There are many ways for the cross-country skier to move around the backcountry. The diagonal stride technique is a good way to get around on the flats or on gently rolling terrain. This is the technique that most resembles walking, except that the feet slide instead of being lifted. At the same time, extra propulsion is gained by planting one pole at a time in the snow and pushing back and down on it.

Proper position is important to avoid fatigue and falls. Keep the knees a little bent and the body's center of gravity above the ski bindings. The bent knees serve as a shock absorber that cushions the effects of moving over uneven snow.

On level or near-level terrain, the step turn is the basic technique for changing direction. The step turn is carried out just as though one were walking and turning at the same time, using poles for balance. However, each step can provide only a small amount of turn because one cannot cross skis without risking a fall. Another basic technique for changing direction is the kick turn. The kick turn is accomplished by first lifting one ski and thrusting it forward and upward, finally placing it in a vertical position with the heel of the ski resting on the snow at a point approximately even with the shovel of the other ski. Now lower and pivot that ski so that it ends up on the snow parallel to the first ski but facing in the opposite direction. Use your poles to maintain balance while lifting and swinging the second ski into place beside the first ski, both now facing in the same direction. The kick turn is an excellent means to make quick reversals of direction or turns in tight spaces.

When going downhill, it is frequently necessary to change direction while on the move. Such turns can be accomplished by a simple snowplow (wedge) technique or by the more sophisticated telemark technique. Such turning techniques also allow you to control your speed on the slope. To make a snowplow turn, push outward from your heels to force the backs of the skis apart and bring the shovels (tips) of the skis together. This action produces the "V" pattern of the snowplow. By pinching the knees together, the skis are rolled onto their inside edges, increasing the friction of the skis against the snow. To turn with the snowplow, simply shift your weight

onto the ski that is opposite the direction you want to go. Thus, a right turn is accomplished by shifting your weight onto the left ski and holding it there until the turn is accomplished. To stop completely, hold the snowplow wedge through the turn until you are heading slightly uphill. Gravity and friction will combine to bring you to a stop.

The telemark turn is an advanced technique requiring considerable athletic ability and practice. The telemark technique is well described in Chapter 6 of *Cross Country Skiing* by Gillette and Dostal. It is used in conditions that do not let you use the snowplow (wedge) or kick turn.

Wedge or snowplow techniques can help control speed or turn while going downhill. You put your feet apart at greater-than-shoulder width and turn your ankles in so that the inside edges of the skis form an arrow pointing forward. By applying more pressure with one leg or the other, it's possible to veer right or left.

When skiing downhill, don't bend forward from the hips. This puts your head in a vulnerable position during a fall. Instead, bend your knees deeper, especially when going faster. The bent position lowers your center of gravity and makes it easier to recover from being off balance. If a fall is inevitable, then try to do so to either side, with both legs together and bent. Don't try (which is instinctive) to catch the fall and land on a hand or elbow. This response invites injury!

Another instinctive problem for beginning skiers is "fear of the fall line". This fear is triggered when a turn is initiated and as the skis turn toward the downhill direction, you sense that you are leaning downhill. Instinctively, you recoil from danger, lean back on the skis, and the skis zoom downward, now out of control. What the beginner skier must remember is to keep composure and maintain center of gravity over the turning ski, even when pointed downhill. By keeping the knees bent, center of gravity slightly forward, and weight on the turn ski, the skis will turn smoothly. And best of all, you won't lose control!

If you do fall, recover by getting the skis below you and perpendicular to the slope. Roll your body forward so that your knees are over the front of the skis. By pushing off your poles, you should be able to resume standing on your skis with some effort. This technique also requires practice to become natural.

When choosing a route on skis, look for areas where the snow has been softened slightly by the sun. Try to stay away from shaded spots where an ice crust can occur. Avoid embedded rocks and trees— holes may lie next to them. Also try to pick routes away from windblown or icy patches (these often have a sheen), and always be aware of avalanche hazards. With experience, you'll be able to "read" the snow, and pick the most efficient and safe routes.

A host of advanced techniques (best left to personal instruction or references such as those at the end of this chapter) can be used for both ascending and descending on skis.

SHELTER

Shelters in the winter wilderness can range from easily moveable "four-season" tents to semipermanent igloos to emergency snow caves. Any shelter—even a cozy cabin—may require frequent attention if snow is falling thick and fast. It may be necessary to go outside often and dig out entrances or doors, clear ventilation holes, or brush off accumulated snow from tent walls.

TENTS

Four-season tents are generally heavier to carry, but their safety and comfort in the winter environment are well worth the extra weight. Compared to ordinary tents, they usually have:

- a weather-resistant tunnel for entering and exiting the tent (more than one entrance is desirable)
- a vestibule for cooking and storage of gear
- a structural design that withstands severe winds and resists collapse when weighted by an accumulation of snow
- a design that maintains an adequate separation between the tent's inner walls and its outer, waterproof shell, or "fly"; this improves ventilation, reduces condensation on the inner walls, and improves the tent's insulating ability
- enhanced water resistance

Regarding the last point, some tents designed for use in the snow lack a sewn-in floor. This allows ski poles to be used as tent poles, and it also reduces the likelihood of a fire in the tent due to a cooking mishap. The lower edges of this type of tent should buried in the snow to eliminate drafts.

The flimsy tent stakes normally used for summer camping are practically useless in the snow. Needed are wide, strong, lightweight aluminum stakes, or improvise in the field and make your own "deadman" tent stakes: Tie a 2-foot section of $1/8$-inch or thicker rope to each staking grommet on the tent, and tie 6-inch or longer pieces of rigid material (thick tree or shrub branches will do) to the other ends of the ropes. Dig a shallow pit in the snow for each deadman and bury it with rope attached. By compacting the snow above and around each deadman with your boot, you can create anchors almost as rigid as blocks of ice. If the snow is powdery and compaction is inadequate, try pouring water into the snow above the deadmen to freeze them in. Very secure deadman anchors can be difficult to remove; either use an ice axe or snow shovel, or chip away at the snow by kicking them with a boot.

When choosing a tent site, avoid spots

View of an igloo from the inside out. (Photo by Jerry Schad)

beneath trees that have (or potentially could collect) large amounts of snow. High winds or a rising temperature could dump that snow on the tent. Never pitch a tent with an entrance facing the prevailing wind, otherwise falling or drifting snow will pile up there.

Once the tent is pitched, set up some kind of comfortable quarters outside for cooking and eating—if the weather is good. Use a snow shovel (or improvise using pots and pans) to scoop out a two-tier trench to be used as a kind of picnic table. In a larger group, it's fun to construct a circular trench with an island in the middle.

IGLOOS

There's no doubt igloos are the most luxurious accommodations a traveler can fashion in the winter wilderness. A well-built igloo with warm bodies inside can maintain a temperature well above freez-

ing, regardless of the weather outside. Igloos are amazing absorbers of sound as well. Very little outside noise can penetrate the walls.

An igloo can make a wonderful base camp for longer trips, but it should not be the shelter of choice when time, energy, or daylight are in short supply. A group may require two or three hours to build one, assuming at least one experienced person directs the operation.

First, a flat site with a thick base of consolidated snow is selected as a "quarry." Then, members of the party stomp on the quarry site to compress the snow as much as possible. It may be helpful to wait an hour or two to let the snow consolidate further after compaction.

Blocks of snow are cut from the quarry using a snow saw, carried to the igloo site, and placed in an ascending spiral pattern. The first level, or "race," should be about 6 to 8 feet in inside diameter—or larger if

177

the builders are experienced. The blocks must lean inward, slightly on the first race, and more severely on successive races. The curve in the walls must begin almost immediately or else the top will become too high to install the final wedge-shaped ceiling blocks. Gaps between the blocks must be "chinked" with loose snow. With a little foresight, blocks can be cut from the quarry so as to sculpt outside dining quarters.

When the igloo dome is completed, a short tunnel must be dug under the wall of the igloo (not on the side of the prevailing wind), with its exterior end below the floor level of the igloo. That will help prevent warm air from escaping. A hole is then punched in the top of the roof for ventilation. A single candle can provide all the light needed, even on the darkest nights. If you must do any cooking inside, make absolutely certain there's plenty of ventilation.

EMERGENCY SHELTERS

If caught unexpectedly in the winter wilderness without a tent, you can fairly quickly create an emergency shelter. In a real pinch, a large trash bag can be used as a kind of emergency bivvy sack. Compact emergency bags made of "space-age" material can be purchased and carried with your first aid kit for such possibilities.

Other solutions may exist in the form of caves or crevices in rocks for short-term shelter. While bivouacking, it's helpful to assume a fetal position to minimize the body's surface area that comes in contact with the cold environment. Snow trenches can be quite easy and quick to construct, especially if you have a shovel or items that will scoop snow. A snow trench is little more than a rectangular pit dug into compacted snow. Dig to a sufficient depth and length to accommodate your body and whatever gear you want to be inside, but don't make the trench so wide that it can't be covered easily. Snow blocks can be cut to form an inverted "V"

for the roof. Gaps should be chinked and a ventilation hole must be installed if the whole thing is sealed. Ideally, you would dig a tunnel with an entrance lower than the sleeping enclosure to keep out cold-air drafts. If that isn't possible, a horizontal entry with a wind block can be fashioned.

Snow caves can be described as igloos built from the inside out. Select a place where a thick blanket of consolidated snow lies against a slope—except where an avalanche might occur. Start by digging straight in and then up, where a sleeping platform can be hollowed out. When finished, poke a hole in the roof for ventilation. Snow caves are easier to construct than an igloo and are used in normal situations in the Northwest as well as for emergencies.

Several of the references at the end of this chapter describe in detail the various kinds of emergency shelters.

COOKING

There are some significant differences between cooking and nutrition during summer camping and during winter camping. If the weather forces you to cook inside a tent, you must make sure there is enough ventilation, especially if a blanket of snow surrounds you. You must also be aware that all tent materials will burn. Be extremely careful to control the size of the flame, and keep the stove in a location near the doorway or inside the vestibule, if your tent has one. If your stove becomes warm or hot underneath, don't place it on the tent floor, as it will melt the snow underneath and possibly tip over. Instead you can place it on a small insulating pad, a piece of wood, or another stable platform.

Besides adding more fat to your diet for calories and warmth, heated foods and hot drinks should be an integral part of every meal. As mentioned in Chapter 6, Foods and Cooking, *Nutrition Basics*, alcohol is a depressant that can actually make a person lose body heat faster under cold conditions, so its excessive use must be avoided.

Refueling liquid-fuel stoves can be dangerous under subfreezing temperatures, because stove fuel remains in a liquid state down to about −40° F. Also, fuel evaporates very rapidly, causing a pronounced chilling effect even at room temperature. Fuel can cause instant frostbite if spilled on bare skin at very cold temperatures. Always wear nonporous gloves when pouring fuel under these conditions.

In the winter, it may be impossible to locate a source of flowing water. Thus you will often be forced to collect and melt snow. Because snow occupies so much more volume than water, this is a tedious process. On clear days, water may be obtained by exposing snow-filled water bottles (dark-colored bottles work best) to sunlight, but this is slow. Melting snow with a stove is much faster, but uses considerable fuel. When planning fuel needs, consider both the extra demands of cooking in the winter environment and the need to melt snow for water.

On subfreezing nights, water bottles left outside, and often inside, a tent will freeze up. If possible, put those bottles inside the sleeping bag and use body heat to keep them warm. A second choice would be to bury those bottles in the snow outside, where ambient temperatures often stay close to the freezing point, which is probably much warmer than the winter air. Make sure the bottles can be located in the morning.

HAZARDS AND INJURY AVOIDANCE

During winter travel, always be concerned about special hazards and the possibility of injury. Below are several.

HYPOTHERMIA

Hypothermia (once called "exposure") is the decrease of core body temperature to a level at which normal muscular and cerebral functions are impaired. Hypothermia occurs most rapidly in cold and windy environments, especially if wetness is a factor. In the winter environment, hypothermia is brought on by immersion in cold water, thin clothing, physical activity or struggle to the point of exhaustion, slim body mass, or a combination of these. Particularly when clothing gets wet, it no longer insulates effectively, thereby promoting a rapid loss of body heat to the environment. Again, this is why it is important to have an extra set of dry clothing with you.

Mere temperature readings are not always a reliable indicator of the severity of the cold environment. The wind-chill index (tabulated in fig. 14-9) provides a better guide for cold, windy conditions. When wetness is a factor, the effective temperatures are even lower.

It's important to recognize the signs of hypothermia, both in oneself and in companions, so that remedial actions may be taken immediately. The symptoms and treatment for hypothermia are discussed in Chapter 15, Wilderness First Aid, *Environmental Hazards in the Wilderness*.

FROSTBITE

Unlike hypothermia, frostbite is a local effect, readily affecting extremities such as fingers and toes, or the tips of the nose and the ears. When exposed to cold temperatures (or wind-chills), blood vessels in these areas tend to shrink, reducing or cutting off circulation. That lowers the skin temperature in those areas. With continued cooling, the tissue freezes and the frozen area enlarges and extends deeper. The tissue is injured by ice crystals in the frozen area, by dehydration, and by disruption of osmotic and chemical balances in the cells.

WIND CHILL TABLE								
Wind Speed (in mph)	**Actual Temperature in °F**							
Calm	40	30	20	10	0	−10	−20	−30
	Equivalent Wind Chill Temperature in °F							
5	35	25	15	5	−5	−15	−25	−35
10	30	15	5	−10	−20	−35	−45	−60
15	25	10	−5	−20	−30	−45	−60	−70
20	20	5	−10	−25	−35	−50	-65	−80
25	15	0	−15	−30	−45	−60	−75	−90
30	10	0	−20	−30	−50	−65	−80	−95
35	10	−5	−20	−35	−50	−65	−80	−100
40	10	−5	−20	−35	−55	−70	−85	−100

Fig. 14.9. Wind-chill table

Frostbite can occur in any cold, winter environment but it is usually associated with inadequate clothing, reduced food consumption, exhaustion, injury, or a combination of these factors. A good preventative measure is vigorous physical activity (if that's possible). When the body tries to cool itself, blood flows to the extremities where it circulates and sheds its heat. For more about frostbite signs and treatment, see Chapter 15, Wilderness First Aid, *Environmental Hazards in the Wilderness.*

DEHYDRATION

Though it may seem unlikely, one can easily become dehydrated during winter conditions, particularly at higher altitudes. This is because both cold air and thin air contain little water vapor. Every time you inhale and warm the air inside your lungs, moisture is taken up by that dry air. With each exhalation, that moisture is lost to the outside environment—which in fact, can be seen.

Since the sensation of thirst may not be strong in a winter environment, a conscious effort must be made to consume enough fluid during winter travels. Hot liquids, of course, are best, but cold water is fine as well. Don't eat snow unless you become overheated from exertion. In that case, only small quantities are of any use, as it requires a great deal of energy (body heat) to transform snow into water.

If you are consuming enough fluid, then the need to urinate at least every few hours (preferably more often) should be felt. If not properly hydrated, then symptoms of dehydration may come on, including fatigue, dizziness, and a feeling of faintness.

SUNBURN

The winter environment presents some unique challenges pertaining to excessive ultraviolet radiation. Clean, dry, thin air allows ultraviolet energy to pass more easily than thick, warm, humid air does. Snow and ice act like a mirror that directs the UV upward to such uncovered areas as the cheeks, ears, nose, lips, and chin. Even the inside of the nostrils can burn. Keep this in mind when applying sun block.

AVALANCHE

Avalanches can consist of simply snow, or snow mixed with rock, mud, or earth, depending on the season and location. They represent probably the most serious hazard for the winter wilderness traveler.

Cross-country skiers survey a potential avalanche slope. (Photo by Marge and Ted Mueller)

They can occur almost without warning, carry a hapless victim down a steep slope at high velocity, and bury him or her beneath tons of icy material.

An avalanche can only occur where snow has collected on an inclined surface, and where the snow cover, built up in layers, lacks the necessary cohesion to stick together. Cohesion depends on:

- the steepness of the slope
- the crystalline nature of the snow of adjoining layers
- the temperature change over time
- the depth of the snow mass

As temperatures rise and fall, and as new snow is added or snow is melted, the snow cover can become either more stable or less stable. When unstable conditions exist, the slightest mechanical force—even the sound pressure of a sonic boom, thunder, or gunfire—can set off an avalanche. A traveler walking or skiing across such an unstable slope can easily trigger them also.

There are basically two types of avalanches: loose-snow (sluff) avalanches and slab avalanches. Loose-snow avalanches (fig. 14-10) occur when snow accumulates on a slope that is steeper than the maximum "angle of repose." This loose snow may be made unstable by light, fluffy snowfall falling onto the slope, any loss of cohesion between new snow and old, and lubrication between layers produced by percolating meltwater, popcorn snow, or rain. These conditions cause a chain

Fig. 14-10. Loose-snow avalanche

reaction, starting with a small amount of moving snow that snowballs into a much larger, ominous mass of sliding snow and debris. In spring and summer, loose-snow avalanches are often caused by wet snow falling on top of cold, dry snow. The wet snow, which fails to stick to the layer underneath, can be destructive, even at low velocity, because it is heavy. In fall and winter, loose-snow avalanches consist of powdery snow that packs less punch because of its lighter weight.

Slab avalanches (fig. 14-11) are the most destructive of all. They consist of a layer or layers of snow that break off and slide as one large block, pushing other snow in front. The slab breaks loose suddenly, often accompanied by a loud crack like that of a gunshot. Tons of icy debris then accel-erate downslope. The larger slab avalanches are capable of flattening forests and buildings.

Avalanches of both kinds tend to recur periodically in the same steep gullies or chutes, called avalanche paths. Each path has three segments: a "release zone" at the top where the avalanche begins and the snow accelerates; a middle section, or "track," where the snow maintains a steady velocity; and a "run-out zone," where the snow decelerates. The top two zones are the most hazardous.

Large avalanches originate in release zones with slopes between 30 degrees and 55 degrees, although small avalanches, or sluffs, will start tumbling from slopes as steep as 80 degrees. Open, smooth slopes are more dangerous than those covered

Fig. 14-11. Slab avalanche

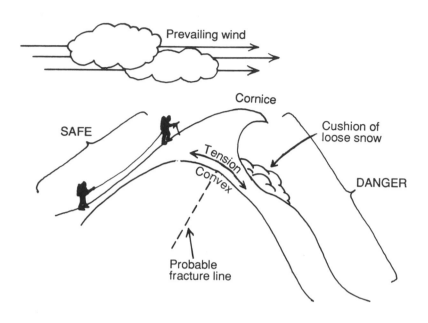

Fig. 14-12. Approaching the windward side of a cornice

with rocks, trees, or brush, because there's little in them to anchor the snow cover.

In avalanche-prone terrain, try to stick to ridgelines wherever possible. Especially avoid a mountainside with a broad release zone and a funnel-like chute underneath that would concentrate the sliding snow. Always be on the lookout for evidence of past avalanche activity, like icy debris or smashed trees at the foot of a steep slope.

Avalanches can start on both concave and convex slopes, although more avalanches originate on convex slopes where the slow creeping of icy snow produces tension. On or near a ridgeline, always avoid the lee side of a cornice (a wavelike feature in the snow caused by prevailing winds—see fig. 14-12). Stay on the windward side of a cornice to avoid dislodging it and starting an avalanche.

When crossing a slope, cracks radiating from your tracks or a "whoomping" sound indicates an unstable slope. Either turn back or head quickly to a safer position.

More than 80 percent of avalanches occur during or immediately after a major snowstorm. If a recent storm has brought 3 to 6 feet of new snow in a short time, then a strong possibility of avalanche exists. Aside from that, rapid changes in temperature (particularly warming) will destabilize layers in the snow cover and increase the chances for an avalanche.

If you are forced to travel across the paths of potential avalanches, try to observe as much of the following as possible.

- Space the group so that each person can be seen by as many people as possible.
- Loosen belts and straps that could encumber any attempt to dig out of an avalanche.
- Cross hazardous areas one at a time.

- Walk across hazardous areas (rather than ski) if the snow is not too soft. Ski tracks tend to release slab avalanches.
- Wear warm clothing and carry emergency items in accessible pockets.
- Carry shovels and ski poles that can be used as snow probes.
- Use avalanche cords, securely tied to all members of the party, and carry avalanche beacons or "electronic rescue transceivers."

If you do get involved in an avalanche, use the tips below.

- If on skis, try to steer out of the avalanche area. If this is not possible, then jettison poles, skis, and pack.
- If you are caught up in sliding snow, try to "swim" to stay on the surface.

Some experts believe the backstroke is the best technique (see fig. 14-13).
- When the sliding snow begins to slow, lunge forward. Reach up with one hand and also keep legs spread. An arm or leg sticking out of the snow will be visible to rescuers and speed the rescue. Use the other hand to create an air pocket in front of the face for breathing.
- Once halted, the snow will settle and harden, restricting movement or voice communication. Relax to conserve oxygen, and await rescue.

Self-rescue from an avalanche. Avalanches often occur in very remote, sparsely populated areas. When winter travelers are caught by an avalanche in a remote spot, they must handle their own rescue effort until a trained "search-and-

Fig. 14-3. "Swimming" to stay on the surface when caught in an avalanche

rescue" (SAR) team can take over. Rescue for victims of avalanches must be fast and efficient, because the probability of survival drops below 50 percent after 30 minutes. Survivors must act promptly to save any victims.

If an avalanche occurs, fight the instinct to panic. Rather, take a few seconds and formulate a strategy that encompasses the whole group and the whole situation. The leader should send a member of the party (with good navigation skills) to summon a trained SAR team and lead them to the site. Next, someone should be assigned to help the injured get to a safe position. Then, a search party can be organized. If the avalanche area is not overly hazardous, establish a systematic search pattern and assign members to search specific areas. Searchers should use ski poles or other rods to probe several feet down into the debris. During the search, look for clues (such as clothing, skis, or limbs protruding from the snow) of the victim's whereabouts. When a victim is found, dig rapidly to uncover him or her. Assess for life signs, and look for indications of frostbite, hypothermia, or injury. Treat as necessary, but *do not* reheat victims too quickly.

Continue the SAR effort until all victims have been accounted for or until rescue becomes futile. In at least one case, a victim survived encased in avalanche debris for 29 hours, so don't give up prematurely.

Avalanche transceivers/beacons. Each member of a group traveling in avalanche country should carry a strong, lightweight snow shovel. Additionally, there is one piece of equipment that can be of even greater use in avalanche country: a radio beacon or avalanche transceiver.

The transceiver is really nothing more than a low-power, low-frequency transmitter and receiver. The three-position switch can easily be switched to off, transmit, or receive. Essentially, all avalanche transceivers operate on one of two frequencies,

designated by kilohertz (kHz). The frequencies are 2.275 kHz and 457 kHz. All parties traveling together must use the same frequency. Some transceivers are capable of both frequencies. The group must decide which frequency they will use before entering avalanche country.

Both frequencies offer advantages and disadvantages. Proponents of the 2.275-kHz signal cite its good sensitivity, stability, and freedom from radio interference. But the 2.275-kHz units require more space, use more power, and have a shorter range (less than 100 feet). The 2.275-kHz units are widely used in the United States.

The 457-kHz transceiver acts more like a conventional radio transmitter, with lower power consumption, smaller components, and a good range (greater than 200 feet). Stability in the 457-kHz device requires more costly electronics.

When purchasing an avalanche beacon or transceiver, look for reliability, an impact-resistant case, ease of use with gloves, controls that are unlikely to be adjusted accidentally, and a built-in battery test capability. Use long-life alkaline batteries with your unit, not rechargeable or inexpensive carbon-zinc batteries. Carry spare batteries and test them regularly.

A rescue party entering an avalanche area should switch all units to RECEIVE, set them to the same frequency, and test each member's transmit capability. When all transceivers are verified, turn all units to TRANSMIT and traverse the dangerous area. When the avalanche area is successfully traversed, units should be turned off to conserve batteries.

In case of an avalanche, all parties should switch their transceivers to RECEIVE. The area where the victim was last seen should be traversed systematically until the strongest signal is located. The area of strongest signal should rapidly narrow to a small area where digging should begin immediately. Victims rarely survive longer than one hour, so rescuers must act quickly. Some avalanches become a solid block so that digging with one's hands is futile. Shovels are the answer. The value of "one shovel per party member" will never become more obvious than now. If trained, well-equipped help is very close and if someone can be spared, send for help immediately.

Lives can be saved only if transceivers are worn and used properly. A transceiver in the pack or on the belt may be ripped from the victim by the force of the avalanche. Another transceiver will find the buried transceiver whether or not it's with a victim. The transceiver should be kept on a small chain under clothing. Ownership of a transceiver neither lessens the danger nor certifies that its bearer is competent in its use. Like many things, there is no substitute for training and experience. It cannot be emphasized enough that these techniques must be practiced long before they are needed.

RECOMMENDED READING

Beck, Dave. *Ski Touring in California.* Wilderness Press, 1980. (Contains instructional material as well as a collection of Sierra Nevada ski tours for beginning through advanced skiers.)

Curtis, Sam. *Harsh Weather Camping.* Menasha Ridge Press, 1987. (If you are a fair-weather camper, this book will either convert you or kill you. Curtis has experienced all the joys and hardships of winter camping.)

Graydon, Don, ed. *Mountaineering: The Freedom of the Hills.* The Mountaineers, 1992. (Includes extensive coverage of snow and glacier travel. A classic in its field.)

La Chapelle, Edward R. *The ABC of Avalanche Safety.* The Mountaineers, 1985. (A

detailed look at all the things that can go wrong in avalanche country, and how to avoid them.)

Prater, Gene. *Snowshoeing.* The Mountaineers, 1988. (Includes a well-illustrated section on snow camping.)

Randall, Glenn. *Cold Comfort.* Nick Lyons Books, 1987. (No other book addresses the issue of avoiding cold so succinctly and completely.)

ADDITIONAL READING

Bein, Vic. *Mountain Skiing.* The Mountaineers, 1982.

Brady, Michael. *Cross Country Ski Gear.* The Mountaineers, 1987.

Daffern, Tony. *Avalanche Safety for Skiers and Climbers.* Rocky Mountain Books, 1983.

Fredson and Fessler. *Snow Sense.* Alaska Department of Natural Resources, 1984.

Gillette, Ned and John Dostal. *Cross Country Skiing.* The Mountaineers, 1988.

Hall, B. *Cross Country Skiing Right.* Harper and Row, 1985.

Parker, P. *Free-Heel Skiing.* Chelsea Green Publishing Co., 1988.

Tejada-Flores, Lito. *Backcountry Skiing.* Sierra Club Books, 1981.

U.S. Department of Agriculture. *Avalanche Handbook.* USDA Publication #489, 1978.

Watters, R. *Ski Camping.* The Great Rift Press, 1989.

Wilkerson, James. *Hypothermia, Frostbite and Other Cold Injuries.* The Mountaineers, 1986.

Wilderness First Aid

CAROL P. MURDOCK AND CARL W. TRYGSTAD

Once you step past the threshold of the wilderness, you trade the conveniences of swift medical attention for the uncertainties of adventure. It is essential, then, to be familiar with the elements of basic first aid, as well as the particular problems and medical complications that may occur in outdoor situations. We strongly urge that anyone venturing into the wilderness take an American Red Cross Standard First Aid course, along with either the American Red Cross or American Heart Association Cardiopulmonary Resuscitation (CPR) course. On trips to remote areas, at least one person in the group should have advanced training in first aid.

This chapter briefly addresses a wide variety of medical concerns pertinent to those who travel in the wilderness environment. More complete sources of wilderness first aid information are listed at the end of this chapter.

BEFORE YOU GO

The one advance procedure that most benefits the wilderness traveler is the tetanus immunization. Tetanus spores are found everywhere and can be introduced into the body through even minor wounds. With prior immunization, tetanus is quite preventable. Adults should have a tetanus booster every 10 years. If you sustain a puncture wound, cut, or burn in the wilderness and are not sure of your immunization status, you should seek medical advice as soon as you return home. A variety of other immunizations are recommended for trips to foreign countries, but these are not normally needed for wilderness travel in North America.

In general, you should be aware of your state of health and any pre-existing conditions, and anticipate any particular problems that you might experience in the wilderness. Add any necessary items to your basic medical or first aid kit. If you are on any medication, plan to take it on your regular basis, unless advised otherwise by your physician.

WHAT TO TAKE

First aid kits can range from sophisticated to very simple, but what you need depends upon the length of your trip and how far you'll be from medical help. A skimpy kit—suitable for certain day hikes or short overnight trips—could include only band-aids, gauze wrap, some 1-inch cloth tape, a needle for removing slivers and thorns, moleskin, aspirin tablets, and a pencil and notepad. After gaining some experience, you will become aware of additional items, appropriate for your type of trip, that you should be adding to those above.

If you purchase a packaged first aid kit, you'll probably want to eliminate some items and add others to suit your needs, and also repackage the items to save weight. Any lightweight, sealed container, such as a plastic carton or container, will do. The list shown in fig. 15-1, containing items for a rather complete kit, is appropriate for extended trips into remote areas—up to 2

RECOMMENDED ITEMS	QUANTITY	USE
Adhesive bandages, 1/2" or 3/4"	20-30	For cuts and abrasions
Cloth tape, 1" roll	1	To secure splints
Gauze wrap, 2" roll and 4" roll	1 each	To secure dressings
Gauze pads, 4" size	6-10	To cover abrasions
Moleskin or molefoam, 6" square	1	To prevent and treat blisters
Triangular bandage, 36"	1	Multiple uses
Elastic wrap, 4"	1	To support sprains and secure dressings
Aspirin, 5 gr (325 mg) tablets	30-50	For pain and fever
Antibiotic ointment, 15 mg tube	1	To prevent skin infections
Antihistamine, 8 mg chlorpheniramine or 25 mg Benadryl tablets	6-10	To counter allergic reactions
Decongestant with antihistamine tablets	6-10	For nasal congestion
Ibuprofen 200 mg or Tylenol with codeine 1/2 gr (32 mg)	6-10	To treat pain
Iodine solution, 2% tincture or 10% Betadyne	1 oz	For wound disinfection
Thermometer	1	To measure body temperature
Lip balm with sunscreen	1 tube	To prevent sun damage
Insect repellent	1 oz tube	To discourage insect bites
Wire-mesh splint	1	For a cervical collar or splints
Sawyer Extractor	1	Removal of venom from insect/snake bites

In addition, the following are suggested medicines taken from a recent medical journal article [Vol. 78, No. 2, August 1985 Post Graduate Medicine. *Travel Medicine.] Each of the first three items requires a prescription.*

SUGGESTED ITEMS	QUANTITY	USE
Cavit (obtain from a dentist)	7 gm tube	For tooth fillings
Acetazolamide (Diamox), 250 mg tablets	14	For acute mountain sickness
Phenergan (Promethazine), 25 mg suppos.	4	For nausea and vomiting
Imodium, 2 mg tablets	12/person/week	For diarrhea
Neo-Synephrine	15 gm tube	Nasal congestion, sinusitis, nasal bleeding
Bacitracin-polymixin ointment	30 gm tube	For burns, abrasions, blisters
Sudafed tablets	12-24	For nasal congestion
Corticosteroid cream	15 gm tube	For rashes, swelling and itching from plant contact or insect bites

Fig. 15-1. Top: *First aid kit. What you need depends on the length of your trip, how far you'll be from medical help, and the climate in which you'll be traveling.* Bottom: *These additional medications will give you a more complete kit.*

weeks. Supplies are adequate for a group of four people. These supplies, of course, would not be adequate for the long-term treatment of victims with serious injuries or illnesses. After first aid is rendered to such victims, evacuation from the wilderness and treatment at a hospital is the appropriate course of action.

In addition, the medications list gives suggested medicines taken from a recent medical journal article ("Travel Medicine," *Post Graduate Medicine*, August 1985, Vol. 78, No. 2). Each of the first three items requires a prescription.

Women may want to add certain supplies to their medical kit such as vaginal suppositories for yeast infections and antibiotics for urinary-tract infections. Vaginal suppositories need to be kept cool, so pack them where they will be least exposed to heat.

FIRST AID IN THE FIELD

Despite the best planning, injuries and unexpected illnesses can occur on trips. Although it is hoped that these difficulties can be quickly remedied and the trip continued, sometimes a trip has to be aborted. The participants may need to devote all their efforts to returning to the trailhead (or other exit point) quickly and safely. A careful plan to assess the extent and nature of the illness or injury is needed in order to determine whether or not the trip can continue, and what future course of action to take.

ASSESSMENT OF AN INJURED PERSON

If the stricken person is conscious but does not know you, the first thing to do is to identify yourself as someone who is able to help. A simple statement such as, "I'm Mary. I'm trained in first aid and I want to help you," will decrease the anxiety of any victim of serious injury or illness. If the victim is movable, but not in a safe position, he or she should be moved to a safer environment.

Next, the history of events leading to the accident or ill health of the victim should be obtained if possible. Questions such as, "Where do you hurt?," "Are you having difficulty breathing?," and "What happened?" or "What do you think is wrong?" can bring out useful information not only about what happened, but also about the current state of the victim. If you obtain satisfactory answers to these questions, then you can plan what to do next.

If there is no response by a stricken person, then immediately invoke the "ABC" procedure of basic life support:

A—Airway. The airway must be open and free of debris. Often, proper positioning is all that is needed. Keep the neck of an unconscious victim supported and straight with in-line traction. Remember, however, that the victim of a fall may have a neck fracture, so any manipulation of the head must be done carefully.
B—Breathing. If the victim does not breathe spontaneously, then start rescue breathing.
C—Cardiopulmonary Resuscitation. If there is no carotid pulse, begin CPR.

The ABC procedure described above is documented in the CPR-course workbook.

For a conscious victim, a complete survey should be undertaken to determine the extent of injury or the severity of illness. This is the "secondary survey" described in the American Red Cross First Aid workbook. Where appropriate, this should include checking the pupil size and response to light, feeling the neck for tenderness, and observing the chest motion as the victim takes a deep breath. All tender areas should be examined for fractures or bleeding. Communicate with and try to calm the victim. Movement, pulse, and sensation in all extremities should be investigated.

All information, especially breathing rate, pulse rate, and responsiveness, should be written down. It is more important to note changes than it is to be preoccupied with detail. Keep the victim warm, stop any bleeding with direct pressure, and splint all fractures to prevent any further motion.

In general, evacuation is necessary for any victim who is unconscious, or has bone fractures, difficulty breathing, a serious eye injury, or pain that does not respond to simple measures such as taking aspirin or ibuprofen.

The following list summarizes the proper sequence of action in the event of a serious accident or illness suffered by a member or members of your party:

1. Approach the victim safely without jeopardizing your own safety.
2. Restore and/or maintain breathing and heartbeat.
3. Control any heavy bleeding.
4. Examine the victim carefully (secondary survey) after the above problems are controlled.
5. Decide where and how you (or others in your group) will obtain help.
6. Write down the following information before going (or sending some one) for help: the name of the person or group reporting the acci dent (if a sponsored trip, include the phone number of the parent or ganization); the name, address, and home phone number of the vic tim(s); the date and time of the accident and the nature of the acci dent; the condition of the victim; first aid treatment rendered; and the exact location of the victim (it may be best to mark this location on a map). All written information, along with any map, is carried with you when you go for help.
7. When you reach help (by telephone, radio, or in person), find out to whom you are talking.

8. Convey all the pertinent information listed in Number 6 above, taking special care to give explicit map directions to the site of the victim, including any information about where rescuers could get lost.
9. Give an estimate of how many rescuers you think may be required and the expected difficulty of the rescue.
10. If you have notified any other agencies, reveal that information.
11. Have the person to whom you gave the information repeat that informauon to ensure it was understood. And finally, if you're on the phone, let the other party end the conversation. Never hang up first.

While waiting for help at the site of the accident, the person(s) remaining with the victim should:

- continually monitor the victim's condition
- protect the victim from the environment and from further injury
- supply any necessary liquids, foods, or further first aid treatments, as applicable
- provide emotional support in a tactful way
- maintain a written log of any changes in the victim's condition and of any treatment given

In any emergency situation, one person should take charge. This person can be the leader of the group or the person with the most medical knowledge or experience in first aid. This person can designate responsibilities and assign tasks. Everyone should stick to his or her plan. Only changes in the victim's condition or the weather should alter that plan.

SHOCK—A COMMON COMPLICATION

Shock occurs when the circulatory system fails to provide enough blood and oxygen to vital parts of the body. It can occur as a result of trauma, bleeding, burns, heart attack, breathing difficulties, spinal cord damage, infection, diabetes, and extreme allergic reactions. In the wilderness, early recognition of shock is essential because shock can progress rapidly, and treatment is limited. An early sign of shock may include a feeling of anxiety. Other symptoms may include a rapid, weak pulse; altered consciousness; lethargy; stupor; and slurred speech.

The best treatment for shock is the correction of the cause, if that's possible. Stabilize suspected neck fractures; perform rescue breathing and administer CPR if necessary; control bleeding; splint fractures; and treat allergic reactions.

Whether the cause is treatable or not, you can provide first aid for shock by keeping the victim warm and comfortable. A victim in shock may lose body heat even in weather conditions that seem warm to you. Victims should be kept flat, except those with heart and breathing problems, who should be allowed to sit up. Reassure and comfort the victim. Avoid any rough handling, and monitor the victim's condition by frequent physical evaluations. Give fluids to the victim unless medical assis-

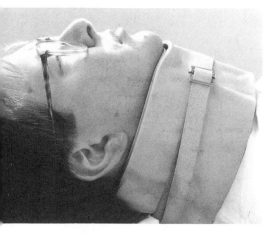

Improvised cervical collar (Photo by Carol Murdock)

tance will arrive shortly, and as long as the victim is not unconscious, having convulsions, vomiting, or clearly has an injury requiring surgery.

A severe allergic reaction known as anaphylactic shock can occur from insect bites, medications, or foods. The symptoms are itching or burning skin (especially on the face and chest), flushed skin, hives, swelling of the face and tongue, blue lips, a tight feeling or pain in the chest, and breathing difficulties. There may be a weak pulse, dizziness, faintness, or even coma. The treatment is to maintain an open airway. If available, give an antihistamine, such as diphenhydramine (Benadryl) orally while the victim is still able to swallow. Those known to be allergic to specific substances should carry either an Epipen or Anakit injection kit available by prescription.

MEDICAL PROBLEMS IN THE WILDERNESS

ABDOMINAL PAIN

Abdominal pain is frequently encountered in the wilderness. Most of the time it will resolve itself spontaneously. The objective in assessment is to decide which types will go away, and identify those for which the victim should be evacuated. Constant pain is usually more significant than intermittent pain. Pain around the umbilicus, or a pain that shifts from one place to another, is generally less significant than pain located at one of the corners of the abdomen.

Vomiting is usually an attempt by the body to rid itself of toxins. Small amounts of fluid, and Phenergan (see the first aid kit list in fig. 15-1) will help. Persistent vomiting, and vomiting associated with a head injury, requires evacuation. If several people on an outing start to vomit at the same time, think of food poisoning (which will usually resolve itself) or altitude sickness. Diarrhea may occur in the wilderness, especially if the water supply is impure, or the food is spoiled or contaminated. Most diarrhea can be treated with modification of diet, fluid intake, and possibly Imodium. If there is fever or if blood is present in the stool, the condition is more serious and an attempt to evacuate the victim should be made. Diarrhea causes dehydration, so large amounts of fluid may be needed to restore the fluids lost in watery stools.

Appendicitis is always a feared cause of abdominal pain. There is usually a history of vague discomfort or pain around the umbilicus which then moves to the lower-right part of the abdomen. A low-grade fever, constipation, loss of appetite, and nausea are common. These victims should be evacuated as soon as possible.

STROKE

Stroke is a name applied to a group of disorders that disrupt the blood supply to a part of the brain. It can be caused by either a ruptured or a blocked blood vessel in the brain. Signs and symptoms occur suddenly. The specific symptoms depend on which part of the brain is involved. A victim's face may be flushed and warm, with perhaps a grayish pallor. The pupils of the victim may be unequal in size; often one eyelid droops. There may be weakness or paralysis on one side of the body. The victim may lose speech. Breathing can be slow and of a "snoring" type. The victim may be unconscious and lose control of bowels and bladder.

Treatment is of a protective kind. Keep the airway open and anticipate the need for CPR. Handle the victim gently and don't move him or her more than necessary. Keep the victim warm and, if unconscious, position the victim on his or her affected side with an arm supporting the head, so secretions drain from the side of the mouth.

HEART ATTACK

Heart attack (or myocardial infarction) is the death of a section of the heart muscle from lack of blood and oxygen. There are other conditions that can cause chest pain, but this condition is the most life-threatening. Signs and symptoms may include chest pain, which may be denied by some victims. Other victims may describe this pain as an ache, a feeling of being squeezed or crushed, or a heaviness in the

Proper positioning of an unconcious person (Photo by James Glenn Pearson)

193

center of the chest behind the breastbone. The pain may spread to one or both arms, shoulders, neck, jaw, or back. It lasts longer than two minutes and is not relieved by rest. Other symptoms may include sweating, nausea, or shortness of breath.

Treat by having the victim stop what he or she is doing and rest quietly. Rescue personnel must be notified as soon as possible. CPR may be required suddenly and for long periods of time. CPR should be started at the scene on all cardiac arrest victims and be continued until resuscitation is successful, the rescuers are exhausted, the rescuers are placed in danger, there is failure to respond to prolonged efforts, or definitive care is provided. CPR should also be started in other cases of cardiac arrest besides heart attack; i.e, from hypothermia, suffocation in an avalanche, lightning strike, and smoke inhalation.

DIABETES

Diabetes is a chronic disease resulting from a lack of insulin. Two major problems can happen with diabetics. One is diabetic coma (too much sugar) and the other is insulin shock (too much insulin or too little sugar).

Signs and symptoms of diabetic coma happen slowly. The victim may complain of a dry mouth and thirst, or experience excessive urination, abdominal pain, and/ or vomiting. The skin is dry, red, and warm. Pulse may be weak and rapid. The victim's breath smells very "fruity" or sickeningly sweet. If left untreated, confusion and then coma result. Treatment consists of keeping the victim warm and evacuating him or her to a medical facility.

Insulin shock occurs rapidly, usually when a diabetic on insulin skips meals or overexercises. Signs and symptoms include dizziness and headache; aggressive behavior abnormal for the victim (similar to alcohol intoxication); complaints of intense hunger; pale, cold, and clammy skin; and profuse perspiration. Symptoms can progress and lead to fainting, convulsions,

and, finally, coma.

Insulin shock must be treated immediately. If the victim is conscious, give two pieces of hard candy, half a candy bar, or six or seven Lifesavers. You can also give a 4-ounce glass of orange juice, apple juice, or milk. The symptoms should improve in about 20 or 30 minutes. If they do not, give another dose of sugar. If the victim becomes unconscious, you can sprinkle sugar under the tongue or use one of the commercially prepared gels made for this purpose. If in doubt that the condition is either diabetic coma or insulin shock, give sugar. It will help for insulin shock and won't aggravate the symptoms of diabetic coma much.

WOMEN'S HEALTH CONCERNS

An intrauterine device (IUD) should never be inserted just prior to going into the wilderness. The cramping and/or bleeding following insertion may last days. One out of every four or five women will spontaneously expel or need to have the device removed for intolerable side effects. If you use an IUD, allow plenty of time to adjust to it before venturing far from medical help.

Menopause can bring on a different set of considerations for the outdoorswoman. Until the menstrual cycle has been absent for a full year, there's always the possibility of having an unexpected episode. Estrogen therapy can result in a return of menstrual-like cycles. In either situation, it's important to pack in the usual supply of sanitary products, and pain medications, if necessary, until the change is complete.

If you're troubled by "hot flashes" during menopause, getting overheated only makes the problem worse. Avoid hiking in hot weather if you can, make use of shade during rest breaks, and stay well hydrated by drinking plenty of liquids. On group trips, inform the leader of your needs.

Bone thinning (osteoporosis) is actually a health problem for all aging people. For women, a high rate of bone loss seems to be associated with menopause. Thinner bones are more likely to break, possibly in rugged areas that might be far from medical facilities. If you know you are at risk for osteoporosis, you can adapt by keeping your pack weight to a minimum and perhaps foregoing trips to remote areas. If carrying a backpack causes low back or hip pain, you can still continue to enjoy the wilderness by day hiking.

ENVIRONMENTAL HAZARDS IN THE WILDERNESS

Attacks by crawling, flying, biting and/or stinging creatures can range from being a nuisance to life-threatening. Exposure to allergens in certain plants or overexposure to the sun can be incapacitating or at least misery-inducing. These and other environmental hazards can usually be avoided by being aware of the potential dangers. Here, we'll focus on treatment for some of the more important problems.

BITES

Poisonous snakes. Relatively few snake-bite victims in the United States actually die from the effects of the venom, primarily because most are able to reach help relatively quickly. The seriousness of a poisonous snake bite depends on the amount of venom injected (some bites are actually "dry"); the species of the snake; the condition of the victim; and other factors.

Where venom has been injected, there is immediate swelling, warmth, and pain. Later, tingling or numbness around the victim's mouth may develop and nausea and vomiting may occur. The victim may become weak, feel faint, sweat, and have a weak, rapid pulse. Breathing difficulties, muscle twitching, and paralysis can follow in time. The use of a suction device (such as a Sawyer Extractor) to remove some of the venom can be somewhat effective if performed immediately. Five or more minutes after the injection of venom, it does little good. The only lasting treatment is that given by a hospital.

While being evacuated, or awaiting rescue or professional medical help, a snake-bite victim should be kept at rest so as not to speed up the movement of venom through the body. Some physicians advise the use of a constriction band 2 to 4 inches above the bite to prevent the spread of venom. A constriction band is not a tourniquet—it is tied loosely enough so that one's fingers can fit underneath it. An extremity can be splinted and kept at heart level for comfort. Do not use ice or pressure dressings, or make incisions around the bite. Any rings or jewelry the victim is wearing near the site of the bite should be removed, since a great deal of swelling can occur.

Ticks. Ticks are common in wooded areas and attach themselves to a victim's skin, usually under the clothing, in order to draw blood. They can transmit diseases such as Rocky Mountain spotted fever, Colorado tick fever, and Lyme disease. The best method of removal is to grasp the tick close to the skin with a pair of tweezers and pull gently. Avoid crushing or puncturing the tick and do not grasp it with your bare hands. After removal, disinfect the site and wash your hands. If parts of the tick break off in the skin or symptoms of any of the above diseases appear (fever, headache, red-spotted rash), seek advice from your physician.

Poisonous spiders. A *black widow spider* bite produces pain similar to a pin prick, slight burning, and redness at the site. Local tissue reactions vary, with some victims exhibiting an immediate 1- or 2-inch area of blanching around puncture wounds surrounded by redness. Other victims have no significant reaction at all. If a large amount of venom has been injected, the victim develops painful muscle cramps that rapidly spread to the entire body. The victim may be anxious and restless, and may complain of weakness and sweating. Most people recover without help over the course of one or two days. However, children and the elderly are most likely to have serious reactions. Treatment consists of applying ice to the bite and immediately transporting any victim with symptoms to the hospital.

Initially, *brown recluse spider* bites cause very little pain. They often develop a characteristic red blister within one to five hours, surrounded by a "bull's-eye" of whitish-blue discoloration. Generalized reactions include itching, a rash, chills, fever, nausea, vomiting, and headache. The damage from these bites is caused by tissue destruction, which can take place weeks or months after the bite. These victims should be seen by a physician, who will either give drugs or remove the tissue surgically.

Bees, wasps, and hornets. These cause injury by attacking the victim, and bees leave a stinger with a venom sac attached

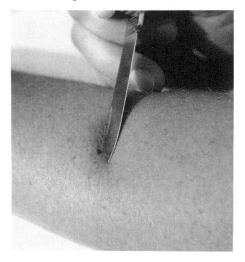

When removing a stinger by scraping with a knife, be sure not to squeeze the poison sac. (Photo by Carol Murdock)

to it. The immediate reactions are pain, swelling, redness, warmth at the site, and itching. Some victims may experience a severe allergic reaction called anaphylactic shock. A stinger can be removed by scraping it from the skin with a knife edge or other keen edge, taking care not to squeeze out more venom from the sac. Chilling the sting site brings relief.

Other insects. Several kinds of flies, mosquitoes, and fleas can cause irritating bites with local skin reactions. Treatments called Afterbite or Campho-phenique, or a cold application are helpful in relieving the discomfort. In situations of heavy insect populations, try to keep all skin covered with thick clothing or netting. Chemical repellents containing a 40 percent to 60 percent concentration of diethyl metatoluamide (DEET) applied sparingly to skin and liberally on clothing work best. Some adults may experience skin irritation and/or rare severe side effects. Do not use a stronger than 15 percent concentration of DEET on children under age 6. In those cases, protective clothing and netting may be the only defenses.

Scorpions. Scorpions have a thin tail with a stinger on the end that can inflict a painful sting. Most in North America are nonlethal and produce a reaction similar to a wasp or a hornet. These bites can be treated by applying an ice pack or chilling the bite area in some way. One species lethal to humans is found in northern Mexico and less commonly in parts of the Southwest American desert. The sting from a lethal species may initially go unnoticed. In 5 to 60 minutes, pain develops and may be severe. Tapping the area lightly produces a tingling or prickly feeling, and the affected area becomes quite sensitive to touch. Children, who are most susceptible to the reaction, experience elevated blood pressure. Any victim experiencing these symptoms should be transported to a hospital as quickly as possible.

Rodents. Rodents such as mice, squirrels, chipmunks, raccoons, and marmots occasionally carry rabies, and also fleas that can spread other diseases to humans. Avoid any wild animal that appears tame or friendly. If you are bitten, clean the wound with soap and water and seek medical care. Don't attempt to befriend or feed animals in the wild.

RASHES

Poison oak is a three-leafed bush, and poison ivy and poison sumac are three-leafed vines, found throughout North America whose sap contains a resin producing an irritating allergic reaction on the skin of susceptible individuals. The onset of a rash may appear anywhere from one hour to two or three days after exposure. Many "favorite" treatments abound, but all serve only to relieve the irritation. Lotions such as calamine are soothing and help dry the rash and control itching. Antihistamines control itching but can cause drowsiness. Severe involvement may require the use of oral medication prescribed by a physician.

Susceptibility to poison oak/ivy/sumac rash varies widely among individuals. Those who are particularly allergic should become familiar with and avoid contact with the plant. After contact, the resin must be removed from the skin within about 10 minutes, or the reaction may occur. If possible, wash the skin with plain soap and water or with a specially formulated soap, and remove any contaminated clothing. If the resin stays on the skin, scratching can spread the rash from one area of the body to another. It helps to cover the exposed area with a light gauze wrap, to keep from spreading the resin. The rash can last up to six weeks.

OVEREXPOSURE TO ULTRAVIOLET RADIATION

Sunburn. Sunburn is caused by overexposure to the ultraviolet radiation of the sun. Overexposure can occur quite rapidly whenever the sun is high in the sky and at high altitudes, where the atmosphere is thinner. UV can penetrate thin clouds easily, and it readily reflects off of rock, soil, water, and especially snow. In most wilderness situations, virtually all persons (children especially) need protection from the sun in the form of sun-screening clothing or sunscreen lotions.

Sunburned skin becomes red and sensitive to touch, and the victim may experience chills after the sun sets. Besides the immediate damage, repeated overexposure to the sun produces degenerative changes in the skin that can eventually lead to skin cancer.

Treatment consists of relieving the discomfort and avoiding any further sun exposure. Apply cold, wet dressings to the affected areas if the skin is unbroken. Hydrocortisone preparations are also effective if applied early, but sparingly. Aspirin may prevent some of the inflammation if taken early.

Snow blindness. This is a sunburn of the cornea, typically brought on at high altitudes where intense ultraviolet light reflects from snow and strikes the surface of the eye. Symptoms include excessive tearing, swelling, and redness in the eyes. About 8 to 12 hours after exposure, the victim may complain that the eyes feel irritated and gritty. There is also headache and a decrease in vision.

Do not let the victim rub his or her eyes. Cover the eyes with cold compresses and keep them closed. Recheck the eyes in 24 hours. If they are infected, leave them uncovered and have the victim wear sunglasses. Early and frequent application of ophthalmic ointment or drops helps relieve pain.

BURNS

Burns are damage to the skin caused by heat, chemicals, or radiation. The signs and symptoms depend on the degree of burn sustained. With a first-degree burn, the skin appears red, as in a sunburn. A second-degree burn is red with blisters and may be swollen for several days. A third-degree burn involves several layers of skin and is white or charred in appearance with broken blisters and evidence of damage to underlying structures. In a third-degree burn, there may be no pain if nerve endings in the skin have been destroyed.

The severity of burns can also be described in terms of the percentage of the body affected. To estimate the percentage of body surface involved, use the palm of your hand—it represents about 1 percent of your body's surface area.

First-degree burns are treated with cold-water applications. A cool, wet T-shirt or clean cloth can be applied to a burn that does not have a broken skin surface. Second- and third-degree burns have broken skin. Do not use ointment, spray, or any home remedy on these burns.

With a third-degree burn, do not remove adhered particles of clothing. Instead, bandage over the burns and cover with any clean dressings (sterile if available). Elevate hands, feet, or legs if involved. When the face is involved, maintain an open airway with the victim sitting up. You may apply cold packs to burn areas, but not directly on the burn. If the victim is con-

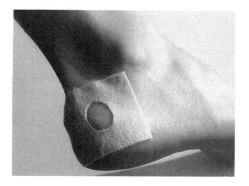

Cut a hole in the moleskin patch to relieve pressure on the blister site. (Photo by Carol Murdock)

scious and not vomiting, you can give one of the commercially prepared electrolyte fluid replacements (Gookinaid, Gatorade, et cetera) slowly in small amounts. If burns cover a joint, are near the eyes or genitals, or are deep, or if the victim is over age 50 or under age 5, evacuate to medical help. Burn victims have a high risk of going into shock from fluid loss.

LIGHTNING

Lightning injuries can occur from direct strikes, secondarily after another object has been hit, or from ground current. Many people can be struck at once, causing multiple victims.

The first assessment should be to check for breathing and heartbeat. The victim may need prolonged CPR before you can check for further injuries. Other common problems include spiderlike burns, fractures, and temporary paralysis. These should be treated accordingly.

BLISTERS

Blisters are caused by friction, which results in an accumulation of fluid under the skin. The most common place is on the feet, from poorly fitted boots or shoes.

The first sign of a blister is a "hot spot" which appears red and is tender to touch. If untreated, fluid forms and the skin covering the fluid may break and leave a very sensitive, irritated, open, bleeding area.

Treat blisters early in their formation by covering with tape or moleskin. Products called Newskin or Second Skin can be used to coat the friction area and protect it against further rubbing. Do not open a blister unless there is a danger of it rupturing or if it interferes with walking. Before opening a blister, wash your hands and clean the skin with soap and water or disinfectant. Sterilize a pin over a flame, holding the end of the pin with a cloth. Puncture the edge of the blister, not the top, and drain. Cut a hole in a piece of moleskin and apply it to the skin around the blister.

For further protection from friction, you

may want to put a piece of molefoam over the blister itself.

OVERHEATING

Heat cramps. Heat cramps are caused by the loss of electrolytes (sodium, potassium, magnesium, and chloride) from the body during heavy exertion. They often occur in warm weather or after prolonged strenuous physical activity. They are usually characterized by severe, spasmodic contractions in one or more of the large muscles of the legs.

Treat heat cramps with rest, gentle massage, and stretching, and by drinking lots of fluids containing electrolytes. For a cramp in a calf muscle, straighten out and support the affected leg, grasp the foot at the toes, and pull slowly and gently. Never pound or twist a cramped or sore muscle.

Heat exhaustion. This is caused by the inability of the body to dissipate heat and the loss of electrolytes during strenuous exercise in a hot, humid environment. Heat exhaustion and heat stroke are thought to be the same phenomenon but of different severity.

Signs and symptoms of heat exhaustion include fatigue, faintness, dizziness, and nausea which may lead to vomiting. The victim's skin becomes pale and moist. The heart rate and temperature are normal, however. Immediate treatment for the victim includes rest. Give the victim electrolyte fluid replacement, or water if that is all that is available. Apply wet cloths to the victim and fan vigorously. When the victim is rested and feels improved, activity can be resumed.

Heat stroke. This is a very serious condition, caused by dehydration and the loss of the body's ability to dissipate enough heat in a hot environment. The onset of heat-stroke symptoms can be rapid. The victim becomes confused, loses coordination, and may become unconscious. The skin becomes hot and dry, and the body temperature rises to 102° F. or higher. There may be shortness of breath, diarrhea, and seizures.

Treatment must begin at once. Stop all activity and protect the victim from the source of heat. To provide shade, you may have to place the victim under some vegetation, or make your own shade by holding a tarp or ground cover above him or her. Remove the victim's clothing, wet him or her down, and fan vigorously if there is no wind. If water is limited, sponge the victim, especially under the armpits, behind the neck, and in the groin. Give liquids only if the victim is conscious and able to swallow. Recheck the victim's temperature every 30 minutes and continue cooling until his or her temperature is down to normal. Do not give aspirin products or stimulants. After the victim's condition has stabilized, medical help should be sought.

CHILLING

Frostbite. Frostbite is an injury produced by severe cold in which flesh freezes. It is caused by exposure of a body part to cold air, wind, and/or snow. The extent of injury is categorized as either simple, superficial, or deep frostbite, depending on the symptoms and on the depth of tissue damage. The method of treatment depends on the depth of the frozen tissue.

Simple frostbite (or frostnip) commonly affects the hands, feet, face, or ears. The earliest signs are a sensation of cold or pain with redness of the affected skin. As freezing progresses, the tissues become whiter and all sensation is lost. The victim may not be aware of the problem until someone indicates that there is something unusual about his or her skin color.

Simple frostbite is treated by slowly warming the affected area, either with your own bare hands, blowing warm air on the site, or, if fingers are involved, holding them in your armpits. Complaints of tingling or a burning sensation during recovery is normal. Never rub snow on frostbitten areas—this promotes further chilling. Never expose frostbitten flesh to a source of extreme heat, such as directly above a campfire!

Superficial frostbite affects deeper tissues and the skin appears white and waxy. The area will feel frozen on the surface but will still have its normal pliant texture when you press on it. Begin rapid rewarming of the area only if there is no chance of refreezing. The entire body should be kept warm during and after the treatment. Rapid rewarming procedures are described in *Medicine for Mountaineering* (see Recommended Reading). Protect the superficial frostbitten area by covering it and handling the affected part gently. As soon as possible, transport the victim to a medical facility with the affected limb slightly elevated.

Deep frostbite or frozen limbs have the feel of a frozen piece of meat and have no resilience when touched. The skin turns mottled or blotchy and is white, then grayish yellow, and finally grayish blue.

Deep or severe frostbite should not be treated under field conditions. Walking out on frozen feet does less damage than inadequate rewarming and subsequent refreezing. If the victim is unable to walk, the victim will have to be carried.

Hypothermia. Hypothermia is a generalized cooling of the body's core temperature to a point where the body can no longer generate its own heat. It can happen within a matter of minutes in the case of immersion in cold water, or over a period of hours following the onset of cold, wet weather conditions. Even in temperatures well above freezing, hypothermia can come on as a result of inadequate clothing and shelter. Physical exhaustion and wet clothing accelerate the process. Children and the elderly are particularly predisposed to hypothermia.

To avoid the later, serious stages of hypothermia, be alert for early signs and symptoms, such as undue fatigue, weakness, slowness, apathy, forgetfulness, and confusion. These symptoms may be observable by others, but the victim may not be aware of them.

Hypothermia is classified as either mild or profound. The victim of mild hypothermia usually experiences little or no change in mental ability, with either normal or slightly impaired coordination for activities such as walking. The victim may be shivering and typically has difficulty manipulating buttons, zippers, and bootlaces. The victim may also be somewhat lethargic, and his or her speech may be vague, slow, and slurred.

It is important to recognize these signs and to begin treatment immediately. Get the victim out of the wind, rain, or cold environment, and remove any wet clothing. Protect the victim from further heat loss, especially from the head and neck. Give the victim warm liquids (but no alcohol). Complications from mild hypothermia are minimal, and those stricken by it can resume their activities when warmed up.

A victim who advances to profound hypothermia experiences a definite change in mental status. The victim may be apathetic and uncooperative; shivering is replaced by muscle rigidity. All movements become erratic and jerky. As the victim's core temperature falls further, he or she becomes irrational, loses contact with his or her surroundings, and falls into a stupor. If untreated, the victim eventually lapses into unconsciousness and then dies from cardiac arrest or other complications.

In addition to the treatments given for mild hypothermia, handle the victim gently when removing clothing and giving care. Do not rub the extremities to stimulate circulation. Instead, place wrapped warm rocks or hot-water-filled bottles around the victim to accelerate the warming process. If possible, place the victim in a sleeping bag in contact with two other people who are non-hypothermic. Continue warming the victim until evacuation to a medical facility is possible.

In practice, such treatments in the field can be problematic, since other members of a party may be afflicted by varying degrees of hypothermia as well. In bad weather it is essential that all members of a party stick together, so that each member can look after the others' welfare.

ALTITUDE ILLNESSES

High-altitude illnesses have been recognized for many years, but they've become more common as more people experience rapid ascents into the mountains. These illnesses range from mild conditions of headache, nausea, and fatigue to the truly life-threatening conditions of high-altitude pulmonary edema (HAPE) and high-altitude cerebral edema (HACE). As with most conditions, prevention is much better than any of the current treatments.

The development of acute mountain sickness (AMS) is related to a person's physical activity, past acclimatization, rate of ascent, and altitude reached. It is uncommon below 8,000 feet, but occurs in 30 percent of persons abruptly exposed to 10,000 feet, and 70 percent of persons exposed abruptly to 14,800 feet. The most effective preventive measure is to remain at 8,000 to 10,000 feet for a few days and then gradually ascend to the planned altitude. If ascent is less than 1,000 feet per day above 10,000 feet, the condition is not likely to occur. Another preventive measure is to avoid alcohol and sleeping pills.

The symptoms of AMS vary in severity in different individuals, but tend to be constant for a given person with each re-exposure to altitude. Symptoms usually begin from 12 to 24 hours after ascent. A throbbing, generalized headache, decreased appetite, nausea and vomiting, and general fatigue characterize this relatively mild illness. The symptoms have been compared to that of a hangover from an alcohol binge. They tend to gradually decrease as long as further ascent is postponed. A high-carbohydrate diet begun a few days before ascent may help to prevent or decrease these symptoms.

While most persons with AMS do well and can remain at 8,000 to 10,000 feet, some persons will have more severe symptoms, or symptoms that begin at higher altitudes. These may include cough, shortness of breath, intermittent breathing, and difficulty with coordination. (To check for coordination, you can have the person try to walk a straight line putting the heel of the forward foot to the toe of the back foot.) Individuals with these symptoms should descend at least 1,000 feet to prevent further complications. Conditions that may mimic AMS include dehydration, hypothermia, carbon monoxide poisoning, and severe infections.

HAPE is less common than AMS, but much more serious and potentially fatal. It strikes 1 or 2 percent of climbers above 12,000 feet and is most common on the second night at these altitudes. It, too, is related to rate of ascent, exertion, use of alcohol or sleeping pills, and cold. Early symptoms may include a dry cough, an increased pulse rate, and decreased exercise performance. Shortness of breath, bluish skin color, and a phlegm-producing cough occur as the condition progresses. In some cases, a victim of HAPE can lapse into coma or suddenly die without any warning signs at all. Although several forms of medication, including diuretics and oxygen have been used, descent is the only uniformly successful form of treatment.

HACE represents a markedly more severe form of high-altitude illness. There is a progression of symptoms such as lack of coordination, changes in consciousness, severe headache, bizarre behavior, and coma. Descent is the only successful treatment.

Although slow ascent is the best prevention for high-altitude illnesses of all types, there are medications that can help when this is not possible. Acetazolamide (Diamox) in doses of 250 mg twice a day beginning 24 hours before ascent and continuing 24 to 48 hours at altitude will decrease the likelihood of AMS. (Acetazolamide is a sulfonamide; persons who have reacted in the past to sulfa drugs should not take it. Side effects include tingling of the lips and fingers and an altered sense of taste. Because it is a diuretic, water consumption should be increased after taking this medication.)

Dexamethasone (Decadron), a cortisone-type drug, can also be used at a dosage of 4 mg taken every six hours starting 24 hours before ascent and continuing for several days. Because there may be some serious side effects to this drug, it should not be taken unless under the direction of a medical professional in the group.

High-altitude illness is a preventable condition. Mild forms are inconvenient, but the more severe forms can be fatal. Slow ascent, especially above 10,000 feet with sleep at a lower altitude, use of Diamox, and avoidance of alcohol and sleeping pills will help to make your trip pleasant and safe.

TRAUMA

BLEEDING

Bleeding is the loss of blood from the body's circulation and can be either external or internal. Uncontrolled bleeding can quickly lead to shock.

The first step in controlling bleeding is the application of direct pressure to the bleeding site. A clean or sterile dressing is preferred but, if not available, your hand can be used. If bleeding has been difficult to stop, do not remove the dressing, but add more dressings on top of the first ones. If you do not suspect a fracture, you can elevate an extremity above the heart. Pressure points (places where an artery crosses a bone) can also be used to control bleed-

ing but are not usually effective when used alone. Tourniquets should only be used when the loss of limb is necessary to save a life. The presence of the tourniquet should be clearly indicated on the victim.

A bruised, swollen, tender, or rigid abdomen is a sign of internal bleeding. Penetrating chest or abdominal wounds, fracture of the pelvis, and bleeding from the rectum or vagina are also likely to indicate internal bleeding. These victims should be evacuated as soon as possible.

Small bruises can be treated with cold compresses or cold-water immersion for the first 48 hours along with a mild compression dressing.

Wounds such as lacerations should be cleaned with soap and water or a disinfectant. Grossly contaminated wounds can be irrigated with cooled boiled water or water disinfected using iodine or chlorine. Closing wounds with sutures should be avoided, but adhesive tape or sterile cloth strips may be used. Highly contaminated wounds should be observed for signs of infection (swelling, redness, warmth around the wound, and foul-smelling drainage). These wounds should be treated at a medical facility.

FRACTURE

Fractures are classified as either closed (no broken skin) or open (bone protrudes through the skin). Signs and symptoms are pain, swelling, deformity, bruising, tenderness over the area, and inability to move the injured part. The victim may also say the sound of "snapping" was heard at the time of injury.

Treat fractures with splints to prevent movement. If it is a compound fracture, you may also have to place a dressing and bandage over the open area. Splints should be carefully padded and improvised from whatever is available. Practice splinting on an uninjured individual first before applying the splint to a victim. You can splint one extremity against an uninjured one if necessary. Use such items as Ensolite and

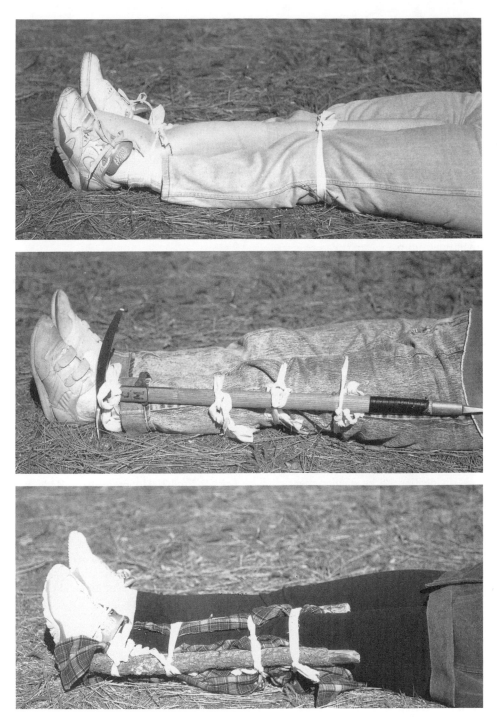

Splinting with available materials. (Photo by Carol Brody)

pack waist bands (as cervical collars), wire splints, ice axes, camera tripods, and parts of pack frames.

SPRAINS, STRAINS, AND DISLOCATIONS

Sprains are stretched or torn tendons, ligaments, and blood vessels around joints. The ankle is the most common site of a sprain. Signs and symptoms are pain at the joint, tenderness, discoloration, and swelling.

A mild or moderate sprain may be treated by wrapping the joint with an elastic bandage in a figure-eight pattern and applying cold (snow or stream water). A more severe sprain (blue-purple discoloration below the ankle bone after 12 to 24 hours) should be elevated, wrapped with an elastic bandage, and not used to bear weight. The boot may be kept on as long as it does not interfere with circulation from swelling.

Strains are stretched or torn muscles, often occurring in the back. They are caused by lifting a heavy object improperly. Signs and symptoms include sharp pain, stiffness, and swelling. Treatment consists of applying cold over the area for 24 hours, rest, and use of pain-control medicines.

A dislocation is the displacement of a bone end from its socket. A common type involves the shoulder joint. Signs and symptoms include a pointed rather than rounded appearance to the joint and pain when at rest. This normally requires medical help, so if none is available in the field, then immobilize the affected joint, and remove the victim to a source of out-side help.

If there is doubt about an injury being a sprain, strain, or dislocation, treat it as a fracture.

CONCLUSION

Although this chapter covers many first-aid issues, it is far from all-inclusive. Anyone who spends time in remote areas should continue learning more about the problems specific to the wilderness. Our recommended reading list contains several books that will give you more help in preparing for emergency situations.

RECOMMENDED READING

Auerbach, Paul S. *Medicine for the Outdoors*. Little, Brown and Company, 1986 (Comprehensive and easily understood by the layman. However, procedures for CPR and choking are outdated.)

Bezruchka, Stephen. *The Pocket Doctor,* 2d Edition. The Mountaineers, 1992. (Concise, compact, and written for those headed for foreign lands.)

Darvill, Fred T. *Mountaineering Medicine*. Wilderness Press, 1985. (Concise and easily understood. This should be carried in every backpacker's first aid kit.)

Wilkerson, James A., ed. *Medicine for Mountaineering*, 4th Edition. The Mountaineers, 1992. (Good for the avid outdoor enthusiast, but too technical for many.)

Search and Rescue

DON STOUDER

If everyone who ventured into the wilderness followed the Scout's motto, there would be little need for a chapter like this. But for many a circumstance—sometimes avoidable and sometimes unavoidable—people do get lost or injured in the outdoors. Thoughtful planning can often prevent these occurrences from ever happening.

People accustomed to living in remote places for several days at a stretch are usually well prepared to deal with adverse circumstances. Those who run into difficulty in the wilderness are more often casual users—day hikers, anglers, hunters—who really don't travel very far from the nearest road or civilized place. With too little equipment and too little know-how, they risk getting into situations they can't handle.

Thoughtful planning—even for day trips—greatly reduces the risk of being stranded without help.

First, leave a detailed itinerary with someone you trust. Agree on a time of return (allowing plenty of room for changes in your schedule) and then do your best to meet the intended itinerary. Instruct your contact person to call for help if you do not return. Don't expect the Army to come charging after you on a moment's notice if you get stuck, but at least someone will be aware of your predicament and help will come eventually.

Second, never go into an unfamiliar area without the basic tools of navigation—map and compass—and the competence to use both effectively.

Third, carry the essential safety and survival items appropriate for your trip. For frequent, shorter trips, it's handy to put together a small "survival kit" (see Chapter 5, Outfitting: The Basic Equipment, Essentials) or purchase a commercially available kit. No matter how well prepared you are, there's always the possibility of getting injured or lost.

BEING LOST, AND DEALING WITH IT

The old warning on railroad crossings told you to "stop, look, and listen." That's not a bad idea, either, for the disoriented hiker. If you've gotten separated from a group and become disoriented, stop and try listening for them. They may be signalling you. Call to them or, better yet, use a whistle. You can make some tentative movements toward where you think they went, or climb to a nearby high point for a better view. But don't wander about without a coherent plan.

If you aren't successful, then remember the cardinal rule: don't panic! If you've absorbed all the information contained in this book and are reasonably well equipped, then you know that everything you need to survive, perhaps rather comfortably, is at your disposal. The most important thing you need now is the patience to sit down and think clearly and calmly about your choices.

Should you sit still, make yourself comfortable, and wait to be found? Or should you attempt to find your way out? The alternative you choose would, of course, depend on many factors. Will the weather hold up? How long until sunset? How prepared are you for a bivouac? Do you have the proper navigational tools, and if so, can you locate yourself on the map and navigate to a position of safety? What obstacles lie along the way? How long will it be before someone reports you as missing?

You may decide to stay put and let the searchers find you. If so, make yourself as conspicuous as possible. If the sun is up, build a smoky fire (but think very carefully about how you'll do this safely in wildfire-prone areas). To catch the attention of aerial searchers, lay out bright-colored clothing or camping gear on a hilltop or in a clearing. Rearrange the natural features of the landscape into some unnatural geometric form—if that doesn't take too much energy. Remember, three of anything (whistle blasts, gunshots) is the universal signal for distress. Use a signal mirror if you have one. Conserve your food, water, and strength; protect yourself as best you can from heat, cold, and excess sunlight. At night, build a fire both to keep warm and to attract attention. Above all, know that when you are missed, you'll be looked for. Relax.

If you're certain you can reach help by your own muscles and know-how, then be reasonable about it. Don't stumble through unknown terrain in the dark. Don't hurry across the desert in the midday heat if you need to conserve your water supply.

If you reach civilization before rescuers can find you, then your first order of business is to make sure that fact is communicated to anyone who may be out looking for you.

THE CASE OF THE MISSING HIKER

Discovering that a friend, relative, or member of your party is missing is a ter-

ribly unnerving experience. But again, there's never any excuse to panic. You must weigh the urge to do something immediately against the possibility that launching a search or going for help too soon may put the searchers, or the messenger, at risk. Take into consideration who is missing, and that person's experience, age, and medical condition, whether or not the person has the proper equipment, and how long he or she has been unaccounted for. The appropriate time to initiate a search may depend on current or anticipated weather conditions, and the time of day.

First try to establish where the person was last seen (Point Last Seen, or PLS, in rescuer's parlance). It's very important that the area near the PLS remain undisturbed so that future searchers can examine it carefully for clues such as tracks and scents. Shouting or other noises should be tried first to see if the lost person responds. This should be followed by a brief search of the trails or other possible places a person could have gone in the area around the PLS. Those who are searching should stay in pairs and keep communicating with others as much as possible. Each searcher should be on the lookout for clues such as footprints or personal belongings. If there's no indication of success after about 2 hours, then it's time to "call in the cavalry."

Fortunately for outdoor enthusiasts in the West, most areas are served by volunteer rescue teams. Some are part of the local sheriff's or parks department, while others are independent groups. As a rule, the individual rescuers are required to participate in extensive training and qualifying sessions. Most teams are linked together in an organization called the Mountain Rescue Association, which sets standards for training and facilitates mutual assistance when needed. To summon the help of a rescue team (not only to help find a lost person, but also to evacuate an injured person), you must notify the local law-enforcement authority, be it the county sheriff, park ranger, or other authority. (Where applicable, the emergency telephone number 911 is the fastest way to reach the right agency.)

If the distance to the nearest source of help is long, send at least two well-equipped persons. They must carry detailed information about a lost hiker's identity, PLS, equipment, and condition, if known. (For a detailed list of information messengers should carry about injured persons, see Chapter 15, Wilderness First Aid, First Aid in the Field.) Since the authorities may have questions about a lost person's personality, attitude, and other psychological factors, it is best to send a messenger who knows the lost person well.

When the search and rescue team arrives, let them take over. Allay your considerable anxiety with the knowledge that they know their business better than anyone else.

Studies of lost persons and search missions have revealed some very interesting statistics. The following information is from a study done by William G. Syrotuck published as "Analysis of Lost Person Behavior." It is shared here to help guide those who may be faced with searching for a lost individual.

Generally there are three broad categories of circumstances in which people become lost, as shown in the subsections below.

PREDETERMINED OR KNOWN LOCATION

The missing person, when lost, was at a known or semifamiliar location such as a campground, picnic area, popular fishing area, home, automobile, et cetera. This category usually involves children and the elderly. Kids tend to be inquisitive and wander off, while the elderly may wander off, become confused, and simply not remember the way back. Senile persons may attempt to "return" to some fondly remembered place from their past. Of those in

this category:

- 34 percent followed a road, pathway, or trail
- 33 percent went cross-country
- 25 percent went down a drainage ditch or a path of least resistance
- 8 percent were found stuck in hazardous terrain

EN ROUTE

The lost person was traveling in the company of one or more persons along a road, trail, stream, or other known route of travel, and at some point became separated from the group. Often, separations are caused by confusion about directions, or by the fatigue of a person who has to struggle to keep up with the group. Examination of these cases showed that:

- 22 percent stayed on a path or trail
- 61 percent left the main trail
- 11 percent got stuck in a hazardous area
- 5 percent had a medical problem

WILDERNESS

The victim had intentionally entered a wilderness area for recreation of some kind. Subjects in this category were mainly hunters seeking prey in off-the-beaten-path locales. But these statistics also apply to birdwatchers, flower pickers, and photographers. Preoccupied with their own interests, these individuals often fail to pay proper attention to changing terrain, weather conditions, or the time of day. The data shows that, of those in this category:

- 62 percent found and stayed on trails
- 23 percent remained in heavy brush or timber
- 8 percent headed for the sights or sounds of people
- 4 percent were victims of hazardous terrain

CONCLUSION

Although no one relishes the prospect of being in an emergency situation, Murphy's Law dictates that if you visit the wilderness often enough, something will go wrong sometime. With a little foresight and planning, you can reduce the risk of someone in your group getting lost or injured, and you'll be better prepared to act intelligently, either as a victim or a rescuer.

RECOMMENDED READING

Setnicka, Tim J. *Wilderness Search and Rescue. AMC Books, 1980.* (The bible of search and rescue techniques.)

(Photo by Jerry Schad)

Appendix

WILDERNESS BASICS
AUTHORS

A retired engineering manager, **Scott Anderson** was raised in a family that spent much vacation time camping in the western United States. He was introduced to backpacking as a Boy Scout, and later did some backpacking while his son was a Scout member. His interest in wilderness travel was renewed when he took the Sierra Club's Basic Mountaineering (now Wilderness Basics) Course in 1983. He's been involved in the program ever since, presently as the snow camp coordinator.

Priscilla Anderson has had fourteen years' experience as a teacher in the public school system, and six years' experience as a designer of training programs in the business world. She has enjoyed camping both as a child and as a parent, and she became an avid backpacker once her children had grown. She participates in the Sierra Club San Diego Chapter's Wilderness Basics Course and enjoys helping others appreciate the wilderness experience.

Hal Brody has been exploring the Southwestern deserts since 1980. Since becoming a Sierra Club trip leader in 1981, he has served as a Wilderness Basics Course leader, specializing in desert outings. For more than seven years, he has carefully prepared and led qualified adventurers on summer desert trips. He shares his love and knowledge of the desert with his trip members in order to help them gain a deep appreciation of the desert, and to create environmentalists whose votes and political actions may help safeguard the remaining desert wilderness.

A geologist by training, **Nelson Copp** is pursuing a career in computer graphics. His many interests include bicycling, hiking, backpacking, and cross-country skiing. His leadership role in the Sierra Club San Diego Chapter has included the Wilderness Basics map-and-compass coordinator, the Bicycle Section outings, and membership chair. Currently he's serving as the Chapter's outings leader coordinator and Leadership Training coordinator.

Jan Craven's fascination with nature began with childhood explorations on the grounds of the Philbrook Art Museum in Tulsa, Oklahoma. Aside from catching tadpoles in the ponds of the Italian garden, she fantasized about the life of the Plains Indians whose finely crafted artifacts in the museum's basement generated more excitement than the Renaissance art displayed upstairs. Family vacations in southern Colorado added hiking, fishing, pack trips, stargazing, and snipe hunts to the essentials of life. After a period when the demands of homemaking and career took precedence, her interest in the outdoors was rekindled by taking the Basic Mountaineering (now Wilderness Basics) Course. This, along with Sierra Club San Diego Chapter Outing Leader training, provided her with the tools to handle the challenges and intrigues of the Southwestern deserts, mountains, and canyons. Hiking and backpacking continue to bring her great satisfaction, as well as lending physical, mental, and social balance to her high-tech marketing career.

Mary Engles, R.P.T., has been a physical therapist in San Diego for eighteen years. She has a masters degree in orthopedic physical therapy, and has been an avid cyclist, hiker, and backpacker for twenty years in spite of her own orthopedic problems.

Robert L. (Bob) Feuge has lived in the Southwest for all of his forty-eight years, the last twenty-two in California. A psychologist, he has been an avid hiker, backpacker, skier, and canoeist since childhood. Another of his avocations is Southwestern anthropology. Bob has been a member of the Sierra Club since 1986, and has been involved in various environmental issues dealing with land use in the San Diego area since 1973.

Bob Frost has lived in San Diego County since 1952, and his appreciation for the outdoors was fostered by a family of naturalists. His grandfather, Marvin H. Frost, Sr., was a staff photographer for the Arizona Sonora Desert Museum and his father Charlic was an avid Baja traveler and skin diver. Bob continues to share outdoor experiences with his two (grown) kids, Cindi and Justin. Bob's timely participation in the 1990 Wilderness Basics Course provided him an opportunity to illustrate this book. Bob currently designs, fabricates, and installs stained-, beveled-, and etched-glass windows from his studio in La Mesa and is happiest with a daypack and fishing pole and any kind of body of water to hike around.

Mike Fry has been hiking and backpacking since his early experiences with the Boy Scouts in the late 1950s. He discovered lightweight equipment and the Sierra Club in 1968, took the Basic Mountaineering (now Wilderness Basics) Course in 1970, and has been an outings leader and environmental activist ever since. He continues to experiment with clothing, equipment, and nutrition to ensure safe and enjoyable outings. Aside from his work as an electronics engineer, Mike spends about sixty days a year on backpacking and cross-country skiing trips, mostly in his native San Diego County, in southern Utah, and in the Sierra Nevada.

Keith Gordon is a former mountaineering store manager and a former instructor at the Aspen School of Mountaineering. In 1974 he unstrapped his rucksack and strapped into the cockpit, where most of his ascents are now made as a captain on corporate jets.

David Moser is a physicist by education and an avid hiker, photographer, and amateur astronomer. He has been involved with the Sierra Club since 1983 and has held the positions of outings editor, outings coordinator, outings chairman, and chairman of the Wilderness Basics Course for the San Diego Chapter. His latest endeavor has been as project manager for this book. He has traveled to many points on the globe and has plans for many more.

Carol P. Murdock is a registered nurse, a Red Cross Standard First Aid instructor of long standing, and a member of the Wilderness Medical Society. She has been a Sierra Club outings leader since 1975 and has led many day hikes, backpacks, mule trips, and bicycle rides. For more than thirteen years, she has organized an annual weekend Wilderness First Aid seminar for the San Diego Chapter. She is also responsible for coordinating and teaching a first aid program for San Diego Chapter outings leaders and trainees.

While car-camping as a child, **Marianne Ringhoff** learned well the elements of outdoor living. From her mother she learned how to improvise with very little. From her father she acquired the wisdom of common sense and the love of traveling and exploring new areas. Her brothers unwittingly taught her the life of rough and tumble, and that a little dirt can be fun. Her children, now teenagers, have been camping and enjoying the outdoors since they were infants. Marianne, an Intermediate Care Unit nurse, has been active in the Sierra Club San Diego Chapter's Focus on Youth section, and has assumed a leadership role in the Wilderness Basics Course. She also participates in a Wilderness Survival for Children program.

Jerry Schad introduces his students at San Diego Mesa College to the wonders of the natural world by way of courses in the physical sciences. He also guides hikers and bicyclists along thousands of miles of California roads and trails by way of his several guidebooks and columns written for various publications. A Sierra Club outings leader since the late 1970s, Jerry enjoys trips to the celebrated parks and wilderness areas around the West, as well as to the "vest-pocket wildernesses" that lie very near some of California's most populated areas.

Donald B. Stouder is a health and safety educator and an emergency medical technician. A native of New Jersey, Don has been a hiker and camper most of his life, and has been involved in rescue organizations for thirteen years. He wishes to dedicate the contributions he has made to this book to his father.

Emily B. Troxell has taught a variety of subjects to audiences ranging from handicapped middle school students to college students. She is currently an adjunct faculty member at Palomar College, but also works as an interpretive ranger at Cabrillo National Monument. At Cabrillo, she often relates the story of the gray whale, but her most enjoyable task is wading into the tidepools to tell of the lifestyles of the creatures found there. She believes that programs such as outdoor education for grade-schoolers and courses in wilderness appreciation for adults will help people better use and appreciate the world's natural places.

Eugene A. Troxell is an associate professor of philosophy at San Diego State University. He has taught there continuously since receiving his Ph.D. in philosophy in 1966 from the University of Chicago. He is co-author of *Making Sense of Things,* published in 1976 by St. Martin's Press. His academic specialties include the philosophy of Wittgenstein, and ethics—particularly environmental ethics. He has served as president of the San Diego Ecology Centre, is an aikido instructor, and counts among his avocations hiking, camping, and backpacking.

Carl W. Trygstad, M.D., is a senior consultant in urgent care and emergency medicine and Scripps Clinic and Research Foundation, La Jolla. He is a long-time member of the Sierra Club, and has spent many vacations backpacking in the Sierra Nevada and in other mountainous areas of the world.

David Ussell came to California by way of Canada and England, where he was born in 1949. His initial experiences with backpacking as a Boy Scout in Canada helped prepare him for a stint in the U.S. Army starting in 1971. Dave earned a bachelors in physics from San Diego State University, and furthered his interest in the outdoors by becoming involved with the Sierra Club San Diego Chapter's outings program and Wilderness Basics Course. He has held a variety of Sierra Club offices in recent years. Winter mountaineering is his favorite outdoor activity. His other interests include music, photography, science, computers, dance, drama, and people—especially children.

Olive Wenzel has loved the wilderness since she experienced its healing quietude as a small child. She's written many articles about nature's beauty, and is proud to have helped establish the Forest Fire Laboratory in Riverside, California.

Carolyn Wood, has lived and traveled throughout the world. Introduced to backpacking through the Basic Mountaineering Course in 1983, she has also developed an interest in outdoor photography, especially the macrophotography of wildflowers. She regularly gives a presentation entitled "Tips for Beginners" for the San Diego Chapter's Wilderness Basics Course.

A native southern Californian, **Ted Young** has long enjoyed visiting California's deserts in winter and the mountains in summer. His favorite kind of summer vacation is backpacking to a base camp above timberline in the Sierra Nevada and then spending the days hiking cross-country—ideal circumstances for refining map and compass skills.

INDEX

Other titles you may enjoy from the Mountaineers:

Mountaineering: The Freedom of the Hills, 5th Ed., Graydon, editor.
The newest edition of the classic text on climbing and mountaineering. Includes new material on winter and expedition climbing as well as extensive updates to sections on equipment and belaying. All new illustrations and a new format.

Medicine for Mountaineering & Other Wilderness Activities, 4th Ed., Wilkerson, M.D., editor.
Written by climber-physicians for travelers more than 24 hours away from medical aid, and for climbing expeditions.

Mountaineering First Aid, 3rd Ed., Lentz, Carline & Macdonald.
Basic outdoor first aid for wilderness travelers. Conforms to latest mountaineering-oriented first aid classes.

Hypothermia, Frostbite & Other Cold Injuries: Prevention, Recognition, Prehospital Treatment, Wilkerson, M.D., editor.
Experts describe symptoms, solutions, and prevention. Includes information on immersion-related accidents.

Glacier Travel and Crevasse Rescue, Selters.
Comprehensive how-to covers knowledge of glaciers, crevasses, and how to cross them in every climate.

The ABC of Avalanche Safety, 2nd Ed., LaChapelle.
Classic guide to the basics—determining potential traveling safety in avalanche terrain; what to do if caught in one; search and rescue.

The Pocket Doctor, 2nd Ed.: Your Ticket to Good Health While Traveling, Bezruchka, M.D.
Completely updated. Covers water, food, hygiene, health in different environments, jet lag, treatments for common illnesses and bites, sprains, infections, life-threatening emergencies.

Emergency Survival Handbook, American Outdoor Safety League.
Indexed information for fast response to medical emergencies anywhere.

Gorp, Glop & Glue Stew: Favorite Foods from 165 Outdoor Experts, Prater & Mendenhall.
Well-known outdoor folks share favorite recipes. Humorous and practical.

Snowshoeing, 3rd Ed., Prater.
The latest information about equipment and techniques for varying terrain and snow conditions.

Cross-Country Skiing, 3rd Ed., Gillette & Dostal.
Loaded with sequenced photos and examples, this informative book covers everything from track to backcountry.

Available from your local book store or outdoor store, or from The Mountaineers Books, 1011 SW Klickitat Way, Suite 107, Seattle, WA 98134. Or call for a catalog of over 200 outdoor books: 1-800-553-4453.

The MOUNTAINEERS, founded in 1906, is a non-profit outdoor activity and conservation club, whose mission is "to explore, study, preserve and enjoy the natural beauty of the outdoors . . ." Based in Seattle, Washington, the club is now the third largest such organization in the United States, with 12,000 members and four branches throughout Washington State.

The Mountaineers sponsors both classes and year-round outdoor activities in the Pacific Northwest, which include hiking, mountain climbing, ski-touring, snowshoeing, bicycling, camping, kayaking and canoeing, nature study, sailing, and adventure travel. The club's conservation division supports environmental causes through educational activities, sponsoring legislation, and presenting informational programs. All club activities are led by skilled, experienced volunteers, who are dedicated to promoting safe and responsible enjoyment and preservation of the outdoors.

The Mountaineers Books, an active, non-profit publishing program of the club, produces guidebooks, instructional texts, historical works, natural history guides, and works on environmental conservation. All books produced by The Mountaineers are aimed at fulfilling the club's mission.

If you would like to participate in these organized outdoor activities or the club's programs, consider a membership in The Mountaineers. For information and an application, write or call The Mountaineers, Club Headquarters, 300 Third Avenue West, Seattle, Washington 98119; (206) 284-6310.